The Stone Vessels

Danish Archaeological Investigations on Failaka, Kuwait

FAILAKA | DILMUN
THE SECOND MILLENNIUM SETTLEMENTS

volume 4

The Stone Vessels

by Anna Hilton

Jutland Archaeological Society

Moesgård Museum, Denmark
National Council for Culture, Arts and Letters, Kuwait

Failaka | Dilmun
The Second Millennium Settlements
volume 4
The Stone Vessels

Anna Hilton © 2014

ISBN 978-87-88415-80-3
ISSN 0107-2854

Jutland Archaeological Society Publications vol. 17:4

Edition: Flemming Højlund
English revision: Anne Bloch and David Earle Robinson
Design: Narayana Press
Drawings: Anna Hilton, Rune Soria
Photos: Anna Hilton, Rune Soria
Printed by Narayana Press

Published by
Jutland Archaeological Society in cooperation with Moesgård Museum
and the National Council for Culture, Arts and Letters, Kuwait

Distributed by Aarhus University Press
Langelandsgade 177
DK-8200 Århus N
www.unipress.dk

Contents

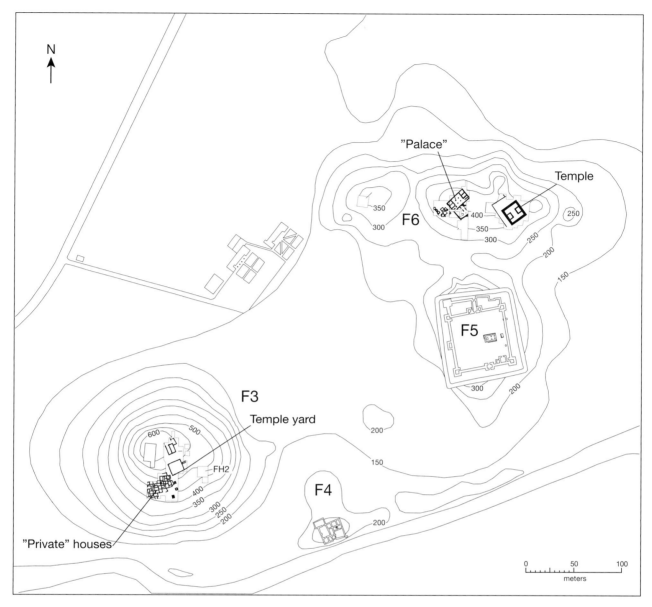

Fig. 1. Map of the archaeological area on the SW corner of Failaka with Tells F3, F4, F5 and F6 (joint plan of the Johns Hopkins University Expedition, the French Archaeological Mission and the Danish Expedition).

1. Introduction

The assemblage of stone vessels presented here was recovered by the Danish Archaeological Expedition during excavations carried out from 1958 to 1963 at three tells, F3, F5 and F6, on the south-western shore of the island of Failaka in Kuwait (fig. 1). Tell F3 contained mostly small private houses from the 2nd millennium BC, whereas in Tell F6 a 400 m² large contemporary production and storage installation named the "Palace" was uncovered; and tell F5 covered a fortified Hellenistic settlement. Detailed information on these architectural remains and their dating has been published elsewhere (Højlund 1987. Kjærum & Højlund 2013. Jeppesen 1989) (fig. 2).

The stone vessel corpus dates to the 3rd and 2nd millennium BC and consists of 1465 pieces; these include a few complete vessels, but most are fragments. From these, 387 diagnostic pieces have been selected for special study and are presented here. They comprise all decorated rim and base sherds and a selection of undecorated rim and base sherds, in addition to all figuratively decorated side sherds and a few undecorated or geometrically decorated side sherds. The 387 diagnostic sherds are listed in the Appendix.

The Failaka stone vessels have been briefly mentioned previously in the literature. In the 1980s Ciarla studied how stone vessel sherds from Failaka were reused and reworked into other types of objects (1985: 396-406, 1990: 475-491). In 1989 Howard-Carter briefly discussed some decorated stone fragments from her own excavations on Failaka in 1973-74, as well as some from the Danish excavations. Furthermore, a few figuratively carved stone vessels from the Danish excavations have been published in exhibition catalogues (Aruz 2003: 319-320, no. 219; Calvet 2005: 57. See also Failaka 1964: figs. 32, 49-53).

In the 1980s a French team continued excavations at Tell F6 and found a temple dating to the 2nd millennium BC just 15 m southeast of the "Palace" and from here 29 stone vessel fragments have been published (Calvet & Pic 1986: 62-65; David 1990: 141-147). Most of the stone vessel sherds with cuneiform inscriptions found in the Danish and French excavations were studied in this context (Glassner 1984: 31-50, nos. 29-39, 2008: 171-205, nos. 31-44).

In 2008-2012 new excavations were carried out at Tell F6 in collaboration between the Kuwait National Museum and Moesgård Museum, Denmark. The stone vessel fragments found during these excavations will be published elsewhere (Hilton in prep.), although a few are also mentioned here.

The Failaka stone vessel assemblage from the 1958-1963 excavations is kept at the Kuwait National Museum, Kuwait, and at Moesgård Museum, Denmark. The portion of the assemblage stored at the Kuwait National Museum comprises 775 pieces and was examined and recorded by the author during several stays on Failaka as a member of the *Kuwaiti-Danish Archaeological Mission to Failaka* directed by Dr Flemming Højlund. In November 2008 all the material was examined with respect to shape, decoration, colour, type of stone, general condition, and traces of manufacturing, use and reuse, and the information was entered into a database. In February 2009 the entire collection was photographed and c. 550 vessel sherds were drawn in pencil on natural tracing paper (62g/m²) at a scale of 1:1. Rune Soria assisted the author in this work. Subsequent analyses were carried out by the author between 1st April and 3rd October 2011 as part of an MA thesis at the University of Copenhagen. Additional studies were made on Failaka in October-November 2011, again as a member of the Kuwaiti-Danish mission, and in 2012 the portion of the assemblage kept at Moesgård Museum, comprising 690 pieces (mostly small side sherds), was analysed and the most important pieces were drawn and photographed. Final preparation of this manuscript took place in 2013.

The stone vessels have been recorded using three different systems. During excavation the objects were furnished with a field number (e.g. F3.aj, F6.1055 and F5.1962AQY). They were then given a Moesgård Museum accession number (e.g. 881.VC and 1129.ARJ) (cf. Højlund 1987: 8-9). Later a Kuwait National Museum registration number was added (e.g. KM3015 and KM367). A KM registration number can encompass between one and 42 fragments, derived from different contexts; consequently these were sub-numbered for this study (e.g. KM6042/01, 6042/02 etc.). Needless to say, the use of different recording systems, combined with the long period of time between excavation and analysis, has introduced a fair amount of numbering errors.

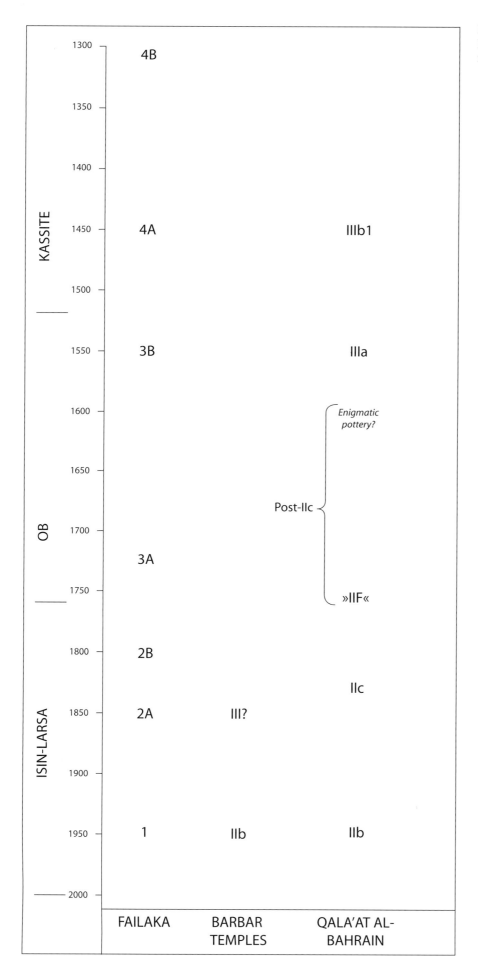

Fig. 2. Chronological chart for Failaka and Bahrain in the 2nd millennium BC.

The Failaka Tells F3, F5 and F6 have been exposed to extensive stone plundering both in antiquity and in more recent times. Numerous pits have been cut into them in search of stone building material, causing a general disturbance of the layers, architecture and finds. Since these disturbances were rarely recognised during excavation, it has not been possible to produce a reliable chronology for the stone vessels based on stratigraphic context information and the material has therefore been classified on the basis of typological and stylistic considerations.

In the following chapters a typology of stone types (chapter 2.1), vessel shapes (chapter 2.2) and decoration (chapter 2.3) is presented, leading to the definition of eight stone vessel styles with some comments on their primary (chapter 3) and secondary use (chapter 4). The distribution of these styles through the different settlement phases, primarily at Tell F3, is then finally investigated in order to elucidate the various functions and the wider significance of the Failaka stone vessel assemblage (chapter 5).

Unless otherwise stated, drawings are reproduced in half size (1:2) and photos in full size (1:1).

Acknowledgements

The present publication could not have been produced without the help and support of a large number of people and institutions. I sincerely wish to thank the Secretary General of the *National Council for Culture, Arts and Letters* in Kuwait, Mr Ali Hussain Al-Youha, the Assistant Secretary General of the *National Council for Culture, Arts and Letters* in Kuwait, Mr Shehab A.H. Shehab, and the staff of the *Kuwait National Museum* for permission to study this stone vessel assemblage and for their kind help and hospitality during my stays in Kuwait.

I appreciate all the assistance and encouragement I have been given by Dr Flemming Højlund and by Dr Steffen Terp Laursen of the Oriental Department at *Moesgård Museum*, Denmark. Furthermore, I wish to thank Ms Hélène David-Cuny, Dr Holly Pittman, Dr Daniel T. Potts, Dr St John Simpson and Dr Christian Velde for enlightening and stimulating comments.

Additionally, many thanks to Ms Aiysha Abu-Laban MA and Ms Ann Andersson MA for support and numerous inspiring talks about Dilmun archaeology.

Publication of this volume was supported by the Carlsberg Foundation.

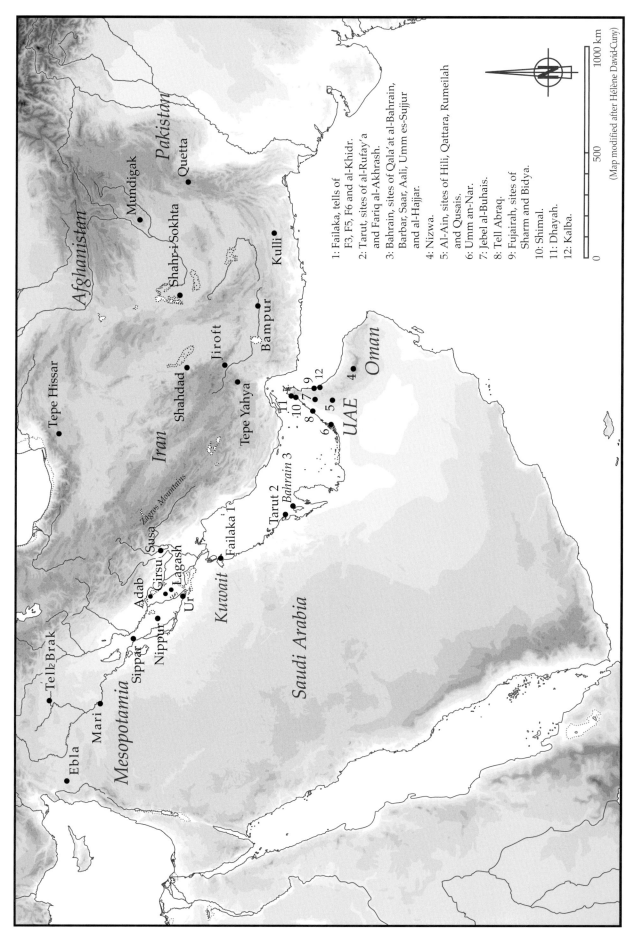

1: Failaka, tells of
   F3, F5, F6 and al-Khidr.
2: Tarut, sites of al-Rufay'a
   and Fariq al-Akhrash.
3: Bahrain, sites of Qala'at al-Bahrain,
   Barbar, Saar, Aali, Umm es-Sujjur
   and al-Hajjar.
4: Nizwa.
5: Al-Ain, sites of Hili, Qattara, Rumeilah
   and Qusais.
6: Umm an-Nar.
7: Jebel al-Buhais.
8: Tell Abraq.
9: Fujairah, sites of
   Sharm and Bidya.
10: Shimal.
11: Dhayah.
12: Kalba.

(Map modified after Hélène David-Cuny)

Fig. 3. Map of the Middle East with sites mentioned in the text.

2. Typology

Relatively little has been published on stone vessel classification (Ciarla 1981: 49), in contrast to the comprehensive publications available on the classification of ceramics (e.g. Shepard 1976; Rice 1987). With respect to the initial studies on stone vessels there is significant variation in the features scholars have chosen to focus on in their classifications. For instance, in their studies of 3rd millennium soft stone vessels in *Série Ancienne/Intercultural Style* from Mesopotamia, Iran and Tarut Miroschedji (1973), Kohl (1975) and Zarins (1978) focused primarily on decorative patterns and, to a lesser degree, on variations in vessel form and stone type (fig. 3).

Häser (1990, 1991) and Velde (2003) analysed soft stone vessels from the Oman Peninsula and the United Arab Emirates belonging to the 2nd millennium *Série Tardive/Wadi Suq* and *Late Bronze Age Styles* and focused on shape and decoration, but refrained from discussing variations in stone fabric.

Specific studies on stone types have been conducted (Kohl *et al.* 1979: 131-159), but these were not integrated into the typological framework of the *Série Ancienne/Intercultural Style*. Variation in stone types within the soft stone vessel traditions of the Oman Peninsula began to be studied on the basis of visual characterization in the early 1990s (David *et al.* 1990: 951-958; David 1991: 175-177).

It is argued here that a greater insight into the stone vessels of the Middle East could be gained if studies were to include stone typology, as well as morphology and decoration, leading to a more comprehensive classification; this approach will be attempted in the following.

2.1. Stone

The need for a stone fabric typology was recognised during the recording process. It was realised that categorising stone types by colour is problematic and potentially misleading, as sherds of different colours sometimes prove to derive from the same vessel. The colour of some stones may be affected by conditions during the vessel's lifetime, for example exposure to heat or moisture, or by post-depositional conditions.

Previous studies on stone types applied scientific methods (cf. Kohl *et al.* 1979). These analyses provided information on the stone's unique geological fingerprint but did not give any detailed description of its colour and composition which could be used as a basis for visual comparison by other archaeologists working in the field.

In producing a stone typology for the Failaka assemblage the author has drawn on David's general considerations with respect to her five soft stone types applied to material dating from the 3rd and early 2nd millennium, i.e. Figurative Style, Umm an-Nar and Wadi Suq Styles (David 2002, 2011: 198-199). A total of eleven stone types were defined for the Failaka assemblage. The author had the opportunity to discuss this stone classification with Hélène David-Cuny on Failaka in 2009. The Failaka material was examined with the naked eye and a magnifying glass under natural or strong electric light.

The methodological approach to differentiating between the stone types was based on the colour, composition and structure of the stone matrix. Three representative samples of each stone type were used as a reference key when identifying the bulk of stone vessel fragments. The determination of each diagnostic sherd is given in the Appendix.

Calculations of relative percentages of the eleven stone types are based on the 775 vessel fragments kept at the Kuwait National Museum. Of this assemblage 82.8 % (N: 642) was determined with respect to stone type. Of the 387 diagnostic pieces 89.6 % were identified (N: 347). The rest could not be identified with certainty, either because the fractured edges were secondarily worked or because the vessel was complete, in all cases hiding the natural mineralogical matrix. When in doubt, a sherd was not classified.

With respect to hardness, stone can be roughly classified into three categories on the Mohs scale: soft stone (1-3 Mohs), medium-hard stone (3-6 Mohs) and hard stone (6-10 Mohs). Of the eleven stone types described below, stone types 1 to 7 belong to the soft stones formed in metamorphic rocks, including steatite, chlorite and talc. Types 8, 10 and 11 comprise medium-hard to hard stones, termed igneous rocks, which include basalt and dolerite. Type 9, calcite, was generated under different conditions, i.e. in calcareous springs, resulting in its distinct banded appearance.

Soft stones

Type 1

Dark blue-greenish, fine-grained, very dense and homogeneous (fig. 4). A foliated structure (i.e. schistosity) becomes visible when the stone breaks. A variation of this type has black inclusions (porphyroblasts) of varying grain size. Type 1's dense and homogeneous fabric makes it suitable for complex decorations. Type 1 corresponds to David's type 1 (2011: 198) and, according to Kohl's analysis (1992), at least six sherds of this stone type have been identified as chlorite (fig. 17). Chlorite is a soft stone with a hardness of 2-2.5 on the Mohs scale. Type 1 constitutes 7.4 % (N: 57) of the total assemblage of identified pieces (775) and 12.7 % (N: 49) of the diagnostic fragments (387).

Type 2

Dark blue-greenish to greyish, less fine-grained than type 1, with a non-foliated, coarse inhomogeneous matrix and crystal inclusions (fig. 5). Type 2 is softer than type 1, and corresponds to David's type 2 (2011: 198); two sherds of this stone type were identified by Kohl as chlorite (fig. 17). Type 2 constitutes 18.9 % (N: 147) of the total assemblage and 17.3 % (N: 67) of the diagnostic fragments.

Type 3

Dark grey to light beige-greyish, less compact matrix than types 1 and 2, but of the same hardness as type 2 (fig. 6). Type 3 has a foliated structure with larger grains and crystal inclusions of varying colours which give a vitreous sheen to the stone. Stone type 3 corresponds to David's type 4 (2011: 198), and two sherds of this stone type were identified by Kohl as chlorite (fig. 17). Type 3 constitutes 23.3 % (N: 180) of the total assemblage and 14.4 % (N: 56) of the diagnostic fragments.

Type 4

Light beige to darker greyish-green with a sandy matrix displaying grains of multiple colours and translucent mica (fig. 7). Type 4 is non-foliated and its composition varies from fine to coarser grained. It has a finer and denser composition than type 3, but is coarser than type 1. Five sherds of this stone type were identified by Kohl as chlorite (fig. 17). Type 4 constitutes 28.9 % (N: 224) of the total assemblage and 37.9 % (N: 147) of the diagnostic fragments.

Type 5

Light grey to light greenish-grey, very dense and with a foliated matrix as in types 1 and 3 (fig. 8). The grains are very fine and the stone has numerous flat, translucent inclusions and occasionally a few reddish inclusions of varying size. Type 5 has a pearly sheen, a greasy feel and a very low hard-ness value. These characteristics are common for the mineral talc, which has a hardness of 1 on the Mohs scale. This stone corresponds to David's type 3 (2011: 198). Type 5 constitutes 0.9 % (N: 7) of the total assemblage and 1.6 % (N: 6) of the diagnostic fragments.

Type 6

Reddish, spotted with numerous black inclusions, rough with medium-sized to large grains and relatively hard for a soft stone; does not have a foliated structure (fig. 9). Type 6 constitutes 0.3 % (N: 2) of the total assemblage and 0.3 % (N: 1) of the diagnostic fragments.

Type 7

Light brown-greenish, very compact and with a hard sandy-grained matrix with numerous small black inclusions; the sand grains are larger than in types 1 and 4 (fig. 10). The surface is matt and dusty and does not become shiny when polished. Type 7 constitutes 0.5 % (N: 4) of the total assemblage and 0.5 % (N: 2) of the diagnostic fragments.

Harder stones

Type 8

Light grey, rather hard and significantly lighter in weight than the other stone types (fig. 11). It has very small, fine grains that generally comprise a dense matrix; however, the stone has an inhomogeneous composition as it contains large brownish inclusions and occasional holes. The surface of vessels made from this stone is rough even when worked. Based on these characteristics the stone is identified as volcanic basalt, which has a hardness of 4-6 on the Mohs scale. Type 8 constitutes 0.3 % (N: 2) of the total assemblage and 0.5 % (N: 2) of the diagnostic fragments.

Type 9

White-beige with layered, banded veins ranging from white through orange to brown, generally hard and compact and breaks in parallel aggregates (fig. 12). This stone is a calcite which has a hardness of 3-6 on the Mohs scale. Type 9 constitutes 1.6 % (N: 13) of the total assemblage and 3.1 % (N: 12) of the diagnostic fragments.

Type 10

Black with large white spots, extremely hard and compact with an exceptionally fine-grained sandy matrix (fig. 13). The stone was identified as Grey limestone containing whitish fossil corals (*Waageno-phyllum*) (pers. comm. M. Vidale 2012). Type 10 constitutes 0.3 % (N: 2) of the total assemblage and 0.5 % (N: 2) of the diagnostic fragments.

Type 11

Dark grey-greenish, coarse, inhomogeneous with crystal inclusions (the mineral pyroxene) (fig. 14). Type 11 has a non-layered structure that resembles type 2, but is much harder. Probably dolerite, a fine-grained version of gabbro which scores 5-6.5 on the Mohs scale. Type 11 constitutes 0.5 % (N: 4) of the total assemblage and 0.8 % (N: 3) of the diagnostic fragments.

The great majority of the stone vessel assemblage was made from only four of these eleven stone types (fig. 15), and the same is true of the diagnostic types, with type 4 being the most frequent (37.9 %), followed by types 2 (17.3 %), 3 (14.4 %) and 1 (12.7 %) (fig. 16). The remaining types constitute only small proportions, sometimes being represented by only a few fragments.

None of these stone types, soft or hard, has been attested on Failaka Island or mainland Kuwait. Soft stone sources are distributed to the north-east, east, south and west of Failaka. Basalt and chlorite can be obtained on both sides of the Gulf, in Iran, the Oman Peninsula, Saudi Arabia and Yemen (Kohl 1975: 30; Reade & Searight 2001; David 2002b: 317-318; Ziolkowski & Al-Sharqi 2006: 155; Magee *et al.* 2005: 129). As for calcite, it is attested on the Iranian side of the Gulf, namely in the Hilman and Kerman provinces, close to the ancient sites of Shahr i-Sokhta and Shahdad. Sources in Afghanistan in the region of Kuh-I Khan Nashin and in the area of Nok Kundi in Pakistan have also been confirmed (Ciarla 1979: 321-324). The black and white spotted limestone (type 10) can apparently be found at several loca-

tions along the Zagros Mountains, but deposits have also been found in Oman (pers. comm. M. Vidale 2012).

In a major study Kohl analysed 375 samples of soft stone vessels, 21 of which came from Failaka. The Failaka sherds all proved to be chlorite, with one exception (KM1515) which was made of talc (fig. 17). The chlorite was classified into four different groups, Sumerian, Arabian Peninsula A, Arabian Peninsula B and Tepe Yayha; however, none of these samples could be linked to specific localised natural occurrences (Kohl 1975: 20-21, 1978: 464, 2001: 220; Kohl *et al.* 1979: 131-159).

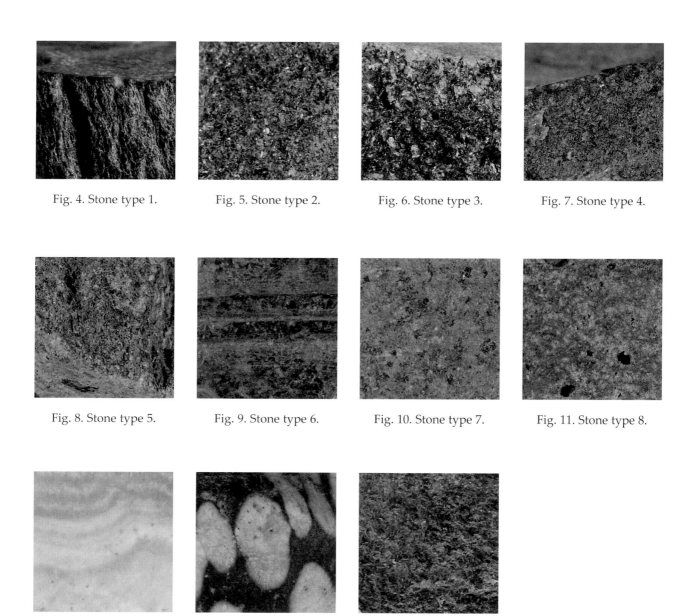

Fig. 4. Stone type 1.   Fig. 5. Stone type 2.   Fig. 6. Stone type 3.   Fig. 7. Stone type 4.

Fig. 8. Stone type 5.   Fig. 9. Stone type 6.   Fig. 10. Stone type 7.   Fig. 11. Stone type 8.

Fig. 12. Stone type 9.   Fig. 13. Stone type 10.   Fig. 14. Stone type 11.

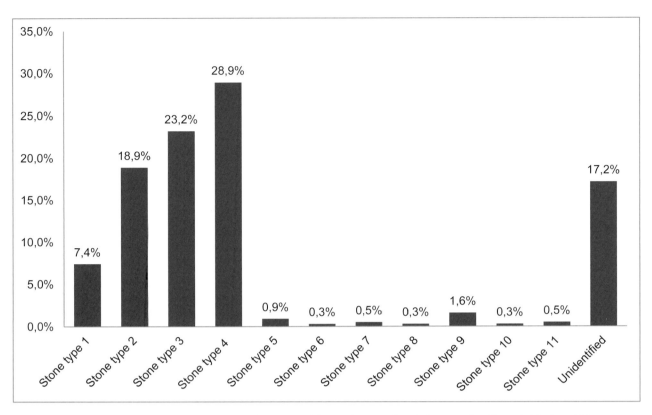

Fig. 15. Frequency of stone types in the complete assemblage of stone sherds kept at the Kuwait National Museum (Σ 775).

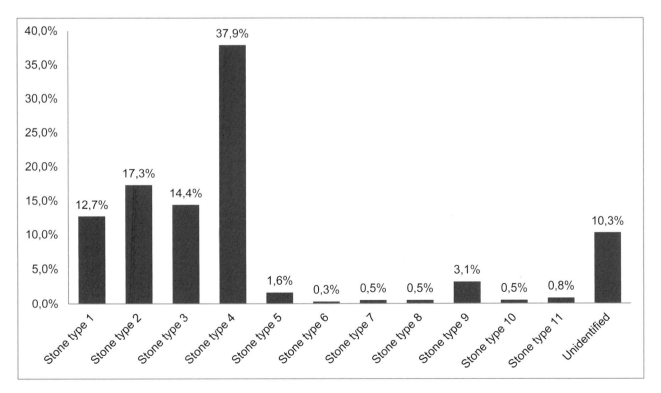

Fig. 16. Frequency of stone types in the diagnostic assemblage (Σ 387).

KM number	Moesgård number	Kohl's number	Kohl's identification	Stone type
KM3119	881.AIP	245/CF01	Chlorite	1
KM3112	881.YX	256/FA08	Chlorite	1
KM3043	881.AIC	257/FA09	Chlorite	1
KM3074	881.AXM	251/CF04	Chlorite	1
KM3067	881.ATZ	249/FA02	Chlorite	1
	881.ACJ	264/FA15	Chlorite	1
KM1514	881.AQL	246/FA01	Chlorite	2
KM3185_09	881.AGR	261/FA12	Chlorite	2
KM6108_06	881.BSB	260/FA11	Chlorite	3
KM6107_03	881.AFP	262/FA13	Chlorite	3
KM3101	881.AKT	252/FA04	Chlorite	4
KM3008_02	881.BBC	250/FA03	Chlorite	4
KM3008_03	881.APY	248/CF03	Chlorite	4
KM3008_01	881.BDK	258/FA10	Chlorite	4
KM3197_05	881.BNE	263/FA14	Chlorite	4
KM1515	881.BAR	253/FA05	Talc or Steatite	–
KM3109	881.AEJ	259/CF05	Chlorite	–
KM3051	881.BQK	254/FA06	Chlorite	–
KM3015	881.VC	255/FA07	Chlorite	–

Fig. 17. Correlation between Kohl's samples from Failaka and the stone typology used in the current study (Kohl *et al.* 1979: 154-155; Kohl 1992).

2.2. Morphology

The morphological analysis was inspired by Shepard's geometric vessel shape terminology, e.g. spherical, ellipsoid, ovaloid or cylindrical forms, and by Rice's approach to use-oriented classification into plates, bowls, jars and vases (Shepard 1976: 224-236; Rice 1987: 215-217, fig. 7.4).

The 387 diagnostic stone vessel fragments were sorted into groups of rims, bases, body sherds, spouts, handles and lids (fig. 18).

Type	N
Rims	219
Bases	99
Body sherds	75
Spouts	15
Handles	15
Lids	10

Fig. 18. Frequency of sherd types within diagnostic assemblage.

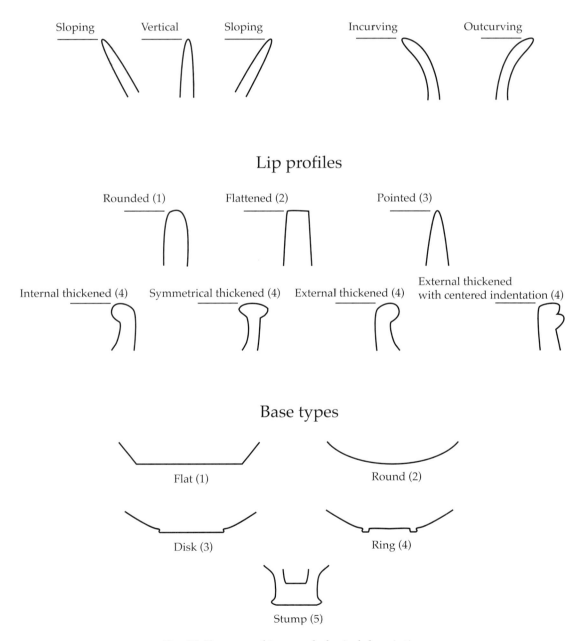

Rim orientation

Sloping Vertical Sloping Incurving Outcurving

Lip profiles

Rounded (1) Flattened (2) Pointed (3)

Internal thickened (4) Symmetrical thickened (4) External thickened (4) External thickened with centered indentation (4)

Base types

Flat (1) Round (2)

Disk (3) Ring (4)

Stump (5)

Fig. 19. Terms used in morphological description.

Rims were then divided into open and closed forms and thereafter classified according to similarities in rim and lip profiles (fig. 19) and given a *form code* which is further explained in the Appendix. A rim type could then be subdivided into variants using characteristics such as undecorated/decorated, size, stone type etc.

Bases were assigned to the types: flat, round, disc, ring and stump, each of which was given a form code. These were similarly further subdivided according to individual characteristics.

Body sherds were not classified on the basis of their form, but on stone fabric, decoration or other features.

Spouts, handles and lids were each grouped as a single type, further sub-divided into variants.

A total of 69 morphological types have been defined, encompassing 178 variants. The assemblage is presented below in the following order: open rims (types 1-19), closed rims (types 20-40), bases (types 41-58), spouts (type 60), handles (type 61), lids (type 62) and body sherds (types 63-71).[1] In the recording

of the types presented below, a vessel can have several form codes, for example one for its rim shape, another for its handles and a third for its base shape. More detailed information on the individual stone fragments is given in the Appendix.

The diameters of rims, bases and side sherds are given under the heading *Size*.

Under the heading *Manufacture* notes are given on chisel and punch marks, traces of polishing, and possible traces of the use of a lathe.

Under the heading *Use*, information is given on wear marks, residue traces, exposure to heat, traces of soot, repair holes (some times with *in situ* copper wire) and intentional cutting and/or breakage of the vessels into pieces to be used for other purposes (secondary cut marks). A few vessels and a lid have small parallel thin incised lines on their external surface, "scarification marks", also seen occasionally on stone vessels dating from the Umm an-Nar and Wadi Suq periods found in funerary contexts on the Oman Peninsula (pers.comm. Hélène David-Cuny 2009 and Christian Velde 2012).

---

[1]   Type numbers 14 and 59 were not used.

Open rims (types 1-19)

The 219 rim sherds comprise 50.6 % of the diagnostic fragments. Of these, 123 rims (28.4 %) are open and could be divided into 19 types with variants. The majority of the open rims originate from open bowls of various shapes: spherical, ellipsoid, cylindrical, ovaloid, conical and carinated. Some bowls have spouts and handles. The bowls vary with respect to rim, size, fabric and decoration. A number of plates were also identified.

Type 1A (fig. 414-415): Open plain spherical bowl, straight vertical rim with externally thickened lip.
Form code: RO4, a
Size: 230-240 mm
Stone type: 2
Decoration: Plain
Manufacture: Polished on surfaces.
Use: Internal and external surfaces worn. One vessel has a repair hole and another vessel shows secondary cut marks.
Quantity: 2
Comparanda: -
Style: Miscellaneous

Type 1B (figs. 286-288): Open geometrically decorated spherical bowl, straight sloping or vertical rim with externally thickened lip. Type 1B is associated with a disk base of type 48B.
Form code: RO4, a
Size: 130-200 mm
Stone type: 2

Decoration: Dot in single circle, dot in double circle, horizontal lines and zigzags.
Manufacture: External surface polished prior to incised decoration.
Use: Surfaces worn. Soot and discolouration on the external surface indicates exposure to fire. One vessel has repair holes with copper wire *in situ*.
Quantity: 3
Comparanda: Al-Hajjar, chamber 1, Bahrain (c. 1550 BC) (Denton 1994: 139, fig. 36e).
Style: Geometric Failaka Style.

Type 1C (figs. 324-331): Open plain ellipsoidal bowl, straight sloping or vertical rim with externally thickened lip.
Form code: RO4, a
Size: 200-380 mm
Stone type: 3 and 4
Decoration: Plain
Manufacture: Polished on external and internal surfaces.
Use: Internal and external surfaces worn. Four of the bowls had been exposed to heat/fire, as evident from traces on their external surfaces.
Quantity: 8
Comparanda: -
Style: Plain Failaka Style.

Type 1D (figs. 334-335): Open plain ellipsoidal bowl with spout, straight vertical rim with externally thickened lip.

The open square spout projects horizontally from the rim, cf. type 60A.
Form code: RO4, a, S1
Size: 160-190 mm
Stone type: 3 and 4
Decoration: Plain
Manufacture: Finished with fine polishing of internal and external surfaces.
Use: Internal and external surfaces worn.
Quantity: 2
Comparanda: No exact parallels in stone, but a metal vessel with square spout from a Jebel al-Buhais tomb dating to Late Bronze Age-Iron Age shows some similarity (exhibited in Sharjah National Museum).
Style: Plain Failaka Style.

Type 1E (figs. 289-294): Open geometrically decorated spherical to ovaloid bowl, vertical rim with externally thickened lip.
Form code: RO4, a
Size: 90-250 mm
Stone type: 4
Decoration: Horizontal and oblique lines.
Manufacture: External surface polished prior to incised decoration.
Use: Internal and external surfaces worn.
Quantity: 6
Comparanda: Tell F6, Temple, Failaka (level III) (Calvet & Pic 1986: 64-65, no. 104).
Style: Geometric Failaka Style.

Type 1F (fig. 255): Open figuratively and geometrically decorated spherical bowl, straight vertical rim with an externally thickened lip. Type 1F is associated with base type 51E.
Form code: RO4, a
Size: 140 mm
Stone type: 6
Decoration: Combination of carved figurative branch and incised geometric dot in single circle.
Manufacture: Decorated in both carved raised relief and by incision.
Use: Internal and external surfaces worn.
Quantity: 1
Comparanda: -
Style: Figurative/Geometric Failaka Style.

Type 1G (fig. 198): Open geometrically decorated ellipsoidal bowl, everted straight sloping rim with externally thickened lip. Probably associated with base type 56.
Form code: RO4, b
Size: 200 mm
Stone type: -
Decoration: Dot in double circle, vertical lines and ladder.
Manufacture: External surface polished prior to incised decoration.
Use: Internal and external surfaces worn.
Quantity: 1
Comparanda: Shimal, UAE. The type is unique to Shimal (David 1996: 40, fig. 6.12; Franke-Vogt 1991: 187-204, fig. 5.8).
Style: Late Bronze Age Style.

Type 2A (figs. 410-411): Open plain spherical bowl, everted sloping rim with externally thickened lip.
Form code: RO4, b
Size: 190-220 mm
Stone type: 2 and 4
Decoration: Plain
Manufacture: Finely polished on internal and external surfaces.
Use: Internal and external surfaces worn. One vessel shows secondary cut marks.
Quantity: 2
Comparanda: -
Style: Miscellaneous

Type 2B (figs. 412-413, 447): Open plain ridged-walled spherical bowl, everted sloping rim with externally thickened lip.
Form code: RO4, b
Size: 150-190 mm
Stone type: 4
Decoration: Plain
Manufacture: Possibly finished on a lathe and finely polished.
Use: Internal and external surfaces worn. One sherd has a secondary Greek graffito.
Quantity: 2
Comparanda: -
Style: Miscellaneous

Type 3 (figs. 96-97): Open plain ovaloid carinated bowl, straight vertical rim with externally thickened lip. One sherd has a complete vessel profile (cf. base type 55).
Form code: RO4, a
Size: 60-90 mm
Stone type: 10
Decoration: Plain
Manufacture: External surface highly polished.
Use: No significant wear marks.
Quantity: 2
Comparanda: Shahdad, Cemetery A, Iran (Hakemi 1997: 608, figs. Ff.2, Ff.7, Ff.8); Girsu, Mesopotamia (Potts 1994: 239-241, tab. 6.5.5.); Tarut, KSA (Burkholder 1984: 23-24, 192, pl. 21a).
Style: Undecorated 3rd Millennium Style.

Type 4A (figs. 336-339): Open plain ellipsoid bowl, everted sloping rim with externally thickened lip with centred indentation.
Form code: RO4, c
Size: 210-260 mm
Stone type: 4
Decoration: Plain
Manufacture: Some chisel and punch marks visible on internal surface, roughly polished.
Use: Internal and external surfaces worn. Two bowls had been exposed to heat and show traces of soot on external surface. One vessel has traces of a dark residue on its internal surface. Three bowls have repair holes with copper wire *in situ*.
Quantity: 4
Comparanda: -
Style: Plain Failaka Style.

Type 4B (fig. 304): Open geometrically decorated ellipsoid bowl, everted sloping rim with externally thickened lip with centred indentation.
Form code: RO4, c
Size: 210 mm
Stone type: 4
Decoration: Dot in double circle, horizontal and oblique lines.
Manufacture: Some chisel marks visible on internal surface. External surface roughly polished prior to incised decoration.
Use: External surface worn and has been exposed to heat. Sherd shows secondary cut marks.
Quantity: 1
Comparanda: -
Style: Geometric Failaka Style.

Type 4C (figs. 340-343): Open plain ellipsoid bowl, vertical rim with externally thickened lip with centred indentation.
Form code: RO4, d
Size: 170-260 mm
Stone type: 4
Decoration: Plain
Manufacture: Some chisel marks on internal surface, roughly polished on internal and external surfaces.
Use: Internal and external surfaces worn. Two bowls have repair holes and traces of soot on external surface showing exposure to heat.
Quantity: 4
Comparanda: -
Style: Plain Failaka Style.

Type 4D (figs. 305-308): Open geometrically decorated ellipsoid bowl, vertical rim with externally thickened lip with centred indentation.
Form code: RO4, d
Size: 180-280 mm
Stone type: 4
Decoration: Dot in single circle, dot in double circle, horizontal lines, oblique lines and herringbone.
Manufacture: Roughly polished prior to incised decoration.
Use: Internal and external surfaces worn. One sherd has a repair hole. Another shows secondary cut marks followed by intentional breakage.
Quantity: 4
Comparanda: -
Style: Geometric Failaka Style.

Type 5A (figs. 69-77): Open plain spherical bowl, everted sloping rim with out-curved rounded lip and occasional indentation below the rim. Type 5A can be described as a bell-shaped bowl.
Form code: RO1, a
Size: 60-300 mm
Stone type: 1
Decoration: Plain
Manufacture: Finely polished on internal and external surfaces. One bowl has chisels marks preserved on internal surface.
Use: Internal and external surfaces worn. Two bowls have repair holes and one shows signs of reworking.
Quantity: 9

Comparanda: Shahdad, Cemetery A, Iran (Hakemi 1997: 605, Fa.1); Tepe Yahya, Iran (IVB) (Lamberg-Karlovsky 1970: fig. 23, E, H, O; Kohl 1979, fig. 18); Jiroft, Iran (*DA 2003*: 140, figs. 148c, 149c-e); Ur, Royal tombs, Mesopotamia (ED III) (Woolley 1934: 235, no. 51); Tarut, Rufay'a, KSA (Zarins 1978: pl. 64:33, pl. 64:43, pl. 65:587); Hili North Tomb A (David 2011: DLA/m90: figs. 231, 232).
Style: Undecorated 3rd Millennium Style.

Type 5B (fig. 211): Open decorated spherical bowl, everted sloping rim with out-curved rounded lip.
Form code: RO1, a
Size: 160 mm
Stone type: 4
Decoration: Hatched band.
Manufacture: Finely polished prior to relief decoration.
Use: Wear marks in particular on the external surface. Edges smoothed subsequent to breakage.
Quantity: 1
Comparanda: Qala'at al-Bahrain, Excavation 519, Bahrain (period IIIb1). Similar hatched band below rim, but vessel shape is different (Højlund & Andersen 1997: 83, fig. 327).
Style: Figurative Failaka Style.

Type 6A (figs. 300-301): Open geometrically decorated spherical bowl, everted sloping rim with indentation below the rounded lip.
Form code: RO1, b
Size: 150-160 mm
Stone type: 4
Decoration: Dot in single circle, dot in double circle, horizontal and oblique lines.
Manufacture: -
Use: Internal and external surfaces worn.
Quantity: 2
Comparanda: -
Style: Geometric Failaka Style.

Type 6B (fig. 302): Open geometrically decorated spherical bowl, everted sloping rim with indentation below rounded lip.
Form code: RO1, b
Size: 250 mm
Stone type: 11
Decoration: Oblique lines and cuneiform inscription.
Manufacture: -
Use: Internal and external surfaces worn.
Quantity: 1
Comparanda: -
Style: Geometric Failaka Style.

Type 7A (figs. 212-214): Open figuratively decorated spherical bowl, vertical rim with indentation below rounded lip.
Form code: RO1, c
Size: 200-240 mm
Stone type: 2 and 4
Decoration: Hatched band, bovine/caprid, humans, sun/star/moon and branch.
Manufacture: External surface finely polished.
Use: Internal and external surfaces worn. One sherd shows secondary cut marks.
Quantity: 3

Comparanda: -
Style: Figurative Failaka Style.

Type 7B (fig. 215): Open decorated spherical/ellipsoid bowl with spout, everted sloping rim with indentation below rounded lip. The round open spout projects horizontally from the rim, cf. type 60E.
Form code: RO1, b, S5
Size: 140 mm
Stone type: -
Decoration: Hatched band and cuneiform inscription.
Manufacture: External surface polished prior to carving decoration and inscribing cuneiform script.
Use: Internal and external surfaces worn.
Quantity: 1
Comparanda: -
Style: Figurative Failaka Style.

Type 8A (figs. 416-417): Open plain spherical bowl, everted sloping rim with flattened lip.
Form code: RO2, a
Size: 160-170 mm
Stone type: 4
Decoration: Plain
Manufacture: -
Use: Internal and external surfaces worn. One bowl shows several repair holes and secondary cut marks. These cut edges were subsequently smoothed.
Quantity: 2
Comparanda: Qala'at al-Bahrain, Excavation 520, Bahrain (period IIc) (Højlund & Andersen 1994: fig. 1917).
Style: Miscellaneous

Type 8B (fig. 197): Open geometrically decorated spherical bowl, everted sloping rim with a flattened lip.
Form code: RO2, a
Size: 140 mm
Stone type: 4
Decoration: Dot in double circle, triangles with horizontal lines and ladder.
Manufacture: External surface polished prior to incised decoration.
Use: Internal and external surfaces worn. The bowl has a repair hole with a copper wire *in situ.*
Quantity: 1
Comparanda: Shimal, surface, UAE (Vogt & Franke-Vogt 1987: fig. 47.5).
Style: Late Bronze Age Style.

Type 9A (figs. 98-99): Open plain spherical bowl, vertical rim with rounded lip.
Form code: RO1, d
Size: 200-220 mm
Stone type: 3
Decoration: Plain
Manufacture: -
Use: Internal and external surfaces worn. One bowl has blackish residue on its external surface.
Quantity: 2
Comparanda: Susa, Iran (Miroschedji 1973: 55, fig. 7.1); Ur, Mesopotamia (Reade & Searight 2001: 156-161, fig. 6).
Style: Umm an-Nar Style.

Type 9B (figs. 127-133): Open geometrically decorated spherical bowl, vertical rim with rounded lip, occasional hatched lines on top of rim.
Form code: RO1, d
Size: 120-230 mm
Stone type: 2, 3 and 4
Decoration: Dot in single circle, dot in double circle, horizontal lines and oblique lines.
Manufacture: One vessel has chisel marks on its internal surface. External surfaces finely polished prior to incised decoration.
Use: Internal and external surfaces worn. Two bowls show traces of exposure to heat on external surface and residue traces on internal surface. Two bowls show secondary cuts.
Quantity: 7
Comparanda: Shimal, s.t. 6, Ras al-Khaimah UAE (De Cardi 1988: 67, fig. 12:2-3); Shimal, Ras al-Khaimah, UAE (David 1996: 40, fig. 6.1); Failaka, temple at Tell F6 (level Vb), Kuwait (Calvet & Pic 1986: 64, fig. 26: 100).
Style: Wadi Suq Style.

Type 9C (fig. 148): Open decorated spherical bowl with rounded spout (cf. type 60E), vertical rim with rounded lip.
Form code: RO1, d, S5
Size: 130 mm
Stone type: -
Decoration: Dot in single circle, horizontal lines.
Manufacture: Chisel marks preserved on the internal surface. External surface finely polished prior to incised decoration.
Use: Internal and external surfaces worn. External surface exposed to heat.
Quantity: 1
Comparanda: Shimal cemetery, tomb SH 95 (Mus.No. RAK – SH0095CL15) and tomb SH 102 (Mus.No. RAK 2452 – SH0102CL03) (unpublished, stored in the Museum of Ras al-Khaimah).
Style: Wadi Suq Style.

Type 10A (figs. 102-105): Open geometrically decorated ellipsoid bowl, everted sloping rim with rounded lip. Type 10A is associated with base type 41A-B.
Form code: RO1, e and RO1, d
Size: 110-215 mm
Stone type: 2 and 3
Decoration: Dot in single circle, dot in double circle and horizontal lines.
Manufacture: -
Use: Internal and external surfaces worn. One bowl has been exposed to fire and heat and has traces of a blackish residue on its internal surface.
Quantity: 4
Comparanda: Al-Rufay'a, Tarut, KSA (Zarins 1978: pl. 71, nos. 104, 565, 586); Saar, Bahrain (Killick & Moon 2005: 207, fig. 5.24.a-d).
Style: Umm an-Nar Style.

Type 10B (fig. 107): Open decorated ellipsoid bowl with spout, everted sloping rim with rounded lip. The rounded spout is open and undecorated, cf. type 60E.
Form code: RO1, e, S5

Size: 220 mm
Stone type: 3
Decoration: Dot in single circle, horizontal lines.
Manufacture: External surface polished prior to incised decoration.
Use: Internal and external surfaces worn.
Quantity: 1
Comparanda: -
Style: Umm an-Nar Style?

Type 10C (figs. 124-126): Open geometrically decorated ellipsoid bowl, everted sloping rim with rounded lip.
Form code: RO1, e
Size: 280-320 mm
Stone type: 2 and 3
Decoration: Dot in single circle, horizontal lines and oblique lines.
Manufacture: Chisel marks on internal surface. External surface polished prior to incised decoration.
Use: Internal and external surfaces worn. One vessel had been exposed to heat and has a blackish residue on its internal surface. Two vessels have secondary cutmarks with the edges subsequently smoothed. One vessel has a star-shaped graffito.
Quantity: 3
Comparanda: Ur, Mesopotamia (unstratified context) (Reade & Searight 2001: 161-163, fig. 8); Qala'at al-Bahrain, Excavation 520, Bahrain (period Ib/IIa) (Højlund & Andersen 1994: 386, fig. 1899).
Style: Wadi Suq Style.

Type 11A (fig. 344): Open plain ovaloid bowl, everted sloping rim with rounded lip, two incised indentations on external surface close to rim.
Form code: RO1, e
Size: 220 mm
Stone type: 4
Decoration: Plain
Manufacture: Surfaces polished.
Use: Internal and external surfaces worn.
Quantity: 1
Comparanda: -
Style: Plain Failaka Style.

Type 11B (figs. 309-312): Open geometrically decorated ovaloid to ellipsoid bowl, everted sloping rim with rounded or pointed lip, two to three incised indentations on external surface close to rim.
Form code: RO1, e and RO3, a
Size: 180-190 mm
Stone type: 2 and 4
Decoration: Dot in double circle and horizontal lines.
Manufacture: External surface polished before decorations incised.
Use: Internal and external surfaces worn. Two of the vessels have repair holes and one shows secondary cut marks.
Quantity: 4
Comparanda: Ur, Mesopotamia (British Museum, BM 124426) (Reade & Searight 2001: 161-162, no. 7).
Style: Geometric Failaka Style.

Type 11C (fig. 52): Open figuratively decorated ovaloid bowl, everted sloping rim with a rounded lip.

Form code: RO1, e
Size: 340 mm
Stone type: 4
Decoration: Date palm.
Manufacture: External surface polished prior to engraved decoration.
Use: Internal and external surfaces worn, blackish residue on internal surface.
Quantity: 1
Comparanda: Al-Rufay'a, Tarut, KSA. Decoration comparable, but not vessel shape and size (Zarins 1978: 71, pl. 69: 51 and 581; Burkholder 1971: 309, pl. IV no. 9).
Style: 3rd Millennium Figurative Style.

Type 12A (figs. 141-143): Open geometrically decorated ovaloid bowl, vertical rim with flattened lip.
Form code: RO2, b
Size: 180-270 mm
Stone type: 2 and 3
Decoration: Dot in single circle, horizontal lines.
Manufacture: Surfaces polished prior to incised decoration.
Use: Internal and external surfaces worn. One bowl had been exposed to heat and fire, another was cut secondarily and then intentionally broken.
Quantity: 3
Comparanda: -
Style: Wadi Suq Style.

Type 12B (fig. 152): Open geometrically decorated ovaloid bowl with spout, vertical rim with flattened lip. The open squarish spout is positioned horizontally at the rim, cf. type 60C.
Form code: RO2, b, S3
Size: 200 mm
Stone type: 3
Decoration: Dot in double circle, horizontal lines, vertical lines.
Manufacture: -
Use: Internal and external surfaces worn.
Quantity: 1
Comparanda: Dhayah, tomb 2, UAE (Häser 1991: 227, fig. 3a).
Style: Wadi Suq Style.

Type 12C (fig. 154): Open geometrically decorated ovaloid bowl with solid handles. The rim is vertical with a flattened lip. The solid square handle is positioned horizontally at the rim, cf. type 61D.
Form code: RO2, b, H4
Size: 220 mm
Stone type: 3
Decoration: Dot in single circle, horizontal lines, vertical lines.
Manufacture: External surface polished prior to incised decoration.
Use: Internal and external surfaces worn. The bowl has been exposed to heat and has traces of soot. Broken edges smoothed.
Quantity: 1
Comparanda: -
Style: Wadi Suq Style.

Type 13A (fig. 134): Open geometrically decorated spherical bowl, vertical rim with pointed lip.
Form code: RO3, a
Size: 230 mm
Stone type: 3
Decoration: Dot in single circle, horizontal lines.
Manufacture: External surface polished prior to incised decoration.
Use: Internal and external surfaces worn. The bowl has been exposed to heat and has soot traces. It has repair holes with copper wire *in situ* in one of the holes and secondary cut marks indicate reutilisation.
Quantity: 1
Comparanda: -
Style: Wadi Suq Style.

Type 13B (figs. 149-150): Open geometrically decorated spherical bowl with spout, vertical rim with pointed lip. An open spout is positioned at the rim, cf. types 60C and 60E.
Form code: RO3, a, S3, S5
Size: 150-200 mm
Stone type: 4
Decoration: Dot in single circle, dot in double circle, horizontal lines, oblique lines, vertical lines.
Manufacture: One bowl has chisel and punch marks on its internal surface. External surface polished prior to incised decoration.
Use: Internal and external surfaces worn. One bowl has two repair holes. Edges of both bowls secondarily smoothed and reworked.
Quantity: 2
Comparanda: Dhayah, tomb 2, UAE (Häser 1991: 227, fig. 3a).
Style: Wadi Suq Style.

Type 13C (fig. 135-136): Open geometrically decorated spherical to ellipsoidal bowl, straight vertical rim with pointed lip.
Form code: RO3, a
Size: 360-420 mm
Stone type: 2
Decoration: Dot in single circle, horizontal lines, vertical lines.
Manufacture: Chisel marks on internal surfaces. External surfaces polished prior to incised decoration.
Use: Internal and external surfaces worn. One bowl has been exposed to heat and fire and has several repair holes. The other was recut and its edges smoothed.
Quantity: 2
Comparanda: -
Style: Wadi Suq Style?

Type 15 (fig. 316): Open decorated ellipsoid bowl, oval in shape, with vertical loop handles on top of rim, cf. type 61E, everted sloping rim with a rounded lip.
Form code: RO1, e, H5
Size: 210 mm
Stone type: 4
Decoration: Horizontal lines, oblique lines and triangles with horizontal lines.
Manufacture: Chisel marks on internal surface. External surface polished prior to incised decoration.

Use: The bowl has been exposed to heat and has traces of soot on its external surface and a blackish residue on its internal surface.
Quantity: 1
Comparanda: No stone vessel parallels, but the shape resembles contemporary bronze and ceramic vessels: Ceramic (type B53) from Qala'at al-Bahrain (period II and period IIIc) (Højlund & Andersen 1994: 91, 476, fig. 187), unpublished ceramic sherd from Tell F3, Failaka (period 4A), and a metal version from Bidya 1 in Fujairah (Yasin al-Tikriti 1989 pls. 71A-B and 96B).
Style: Geometric Failaka Style.

Type 16 (fig. 51): Open figuratively decorated cylindrical bowl, straight vertical rim with flattened lip. Type 16 has a complete wall profile with a flat base, cf. type 47.
Form code: RO2, b
Size: 300 mm
Stone type: 4
Decoration: Scorpions
Manufacture: -
Use: External surface in particular shows wear marks.
Quantity: 1
Comparanda: Tarut, al-Rufay'a, KSA. Comparable vessel shapes, size and panels for decoration; however, decoration elements differ (Zarins 1978: pl. 68 nos. 542, 545).
Style: 3rd Millennium Figurative Style.

Type 17A (figs. 27-29): Open figuratively decorated cylindrical bowl, straight vertical rim with externally thickened lip. Two complete profiles suggest that a flat base, cf. type 46, is associated with type 17A.
Form code: RO4, a
Size: 90-110 mm
Stone type: 1
Decoration: Basketry
Manufacture: One has chisel marks on its internal surface.
Use: Wear marks on external surface, especially on base. Only one rim shows wear marks on internal surface. One was secondarily cut and then intentionally broken.
Quantity: 3
Comparanda: Susa, Iran (Miroschedji 1973: 53, fig. 5.9); Jiroft, Iran (Pittman 2003: 85); Bampur, Burial F, (IV/V) (De Cardi 1968: 149, pl. IVb).
Style: 3rd Millennium Figurative Style.

Type 17B (figs. 31-37): Open figuratively decorated cylindrical bowl, straight vertical rim with rounded or pointed lip. One type 17B rim (KM3040) is associated with a flat base cf. type 44.
Form code: RO3, a and RO1, d
Size: 70-140 mm
Stone type: 1
Decoration: Scorpion, inlay, date palm, textile, bovine/caprid, feline, bird and snake.
Manufacture: -
Use: Internal and external surfaces worn, but some examples mainly worn on external surface. Three sherds cut secondarily and then intentionally broken.
Quantity: 7
Comparanda: Mesopotamia (Aruz 2003: 336, no. 233); Jiroft, Iran (Madjidzadeh 2003: 44-46, figs. 78, 82, 80, p. 54, fig.

114); Tarut, KSA (Burkholder 1971: pl. VII no. 18); Tarut, al-Rufay'a, KSA (Zarins 1978: pl. 69 nos. 51, 122, 581).
Style: 3rd Millennium Figurative Style.

Type 18Aa (figs. 399-401): Open plate with straight side and internally thickened lip. Complete profiles suggest that a flat thick base (cf. type 52A) is associated with rim type 18A.
Form code: RO4, e
Size: 140-250 mm
Stone type: 3 and 4
Decoration: Plain
Manufacture: -
Use: Internal and external surfaces worn. External base of one plate discoloured by exposure to heat and fire.
Quantity: 3
Comparanda: Ur, Mesopotamia (British Museum: BM 118555).
Style: Plain Failaka Style.

Type 18Ab (fig. 402): Open plate with straight side and internally thickened lip.
Form code: RO4, e
Size: 360 mm
Stone type: 11
Decoration: Inscribed with cuneiform script.
Manufacture: Internal and external surfaces highly polished.
Use: Internal and external surfaces worn.
Quantity: 1
Comparanda: Ur, Mesopotamia (British Museum: BM 118555).
Style: Plain Failaka Style.

Type 18B (figs. 403-405): Open plate with concave side and internally thickened lip. Type 18B is in several cases combined with flat thick bases and concave walls, cf. type 52B.
Form code: RO4, e
Size: 185-210 mm
Stone type: 2
Decoration: Plain
Manufacture: One plate shows chisel marks. External and internal surfaces finished with a fine polish.
Use: Internal and external surfaces worn. One plate shows discolouration from exposure to fire.
Quantity: 3
Comparanda: Ur, Mesopotamia (British Museum: BM 118555).
Style: Plain Failaka Style.

Type 18C (fig. 406): Open plate with everted sloping walls, everted sloping rim with flattened lip.
Form code: RO2, a
Size: 420 mm
Stone type: 4
Decoration: Rim inscribed with cuneiform script.
Manufacture: -
Use: Internal and external surfaces worn. Sherd smoothed on broken edges.
Quantity: 1
Comparanda: No stone vessel parallels, but a resemblance to a ceramic plate/bowl from the Barbar Temples, a vari-

ety of plate type B30 (Andersen & Højlund 2003 fig. 480 (Temple IIb), figs. 569-570 (Temple III?).
Style: Plain Failaka Style.

Type 19A (figs. 100-101): Open plain spherical to ellipsoidal small bowl, everted sloping rim with pointed lip.
Form code: RO3, b
Size: 110-130 mm
Stone type: 2 and 4
Decoration: Plain
Manufacture: External and internal surfaces finished with a fine polish.
Use: Internal and external surfaces worn.
Quantity: 2
Comparanda: Hili North Tomb A, UAE (David 1996: 36, fig. 5.1); Qala'at al-Bahrain, Excavation 520, Bahrain (period IIc) (Højlund & Andersen 1994: 388, fig. 1916); Tarut, Rufay'a, KSA (Zarins 1978: pl. 64, nos. 77, 90).
Style: Umm an-Nar Style.

Type 19B (figs. 378-380): Open plain ellipsoidal bowl of small diameter, with round or externally thickened lip and indentation below.
Form code: RO1, c and RO4, a
Size: 90-100 mm
Stone type: 2 and 4
Decoration: Plain
Manufacture: External and internal surfaces finished with a fine polish.
Use: Internal and external surfaces worn.
Quantity: 3
Comparanda: -
Style: Plain Failaka Style.

Type 19C (fig. 195-196): Open small conical plain bowl, vertical to everted sloping rim with rounded lip. In one case connected with a flat base with rounded base edge, cf. type 57.
Form code: RO1, d and RO1, e
Size: 70-100 mm
Stone type: 3 and 4
Decoration: Plain
Manufacture: External and internal surfaces finished with a fine polish.
Use: Internal and external surfaces worn.
Quantity: 2
Comparanda: Tell Abraq, UAE (Potts 1991: 71, fig. 93); Tell Abraq, UAE (Iron Age) (Potts 1991: 95, fig. 134).
Style: Late Bronze Age-Iron Age Style?

Closed rims (types 20-40)

A total of 96 rim sherds (or 22.2%) were closed; these were classified into 20 types with further sub-division into variants. The 20 types include spherical, ellipsoid, ovaloid, conical and cylindrical bowls of various sizes. Further to these a large number of conical, ovaloid and cylindrical jars and vases of various sizes, fabrics and decoration were identified, along with a number of squarish boxes.

Type 20A (figs. 356-360): Closed plain ellipsoidal bowl, incurved rim with externally thickened lip. Type 20A is associated with base types 50A and 51A and a number of body sherds, cf. type 68A.
Form code: RC4, f
Size: 95-160 mm
Stone type: 4
Decoration: Plain, one vessel was inscribed with cuneiform script.
Manufacture: Two vessels show fine horizontal striations all over their internal surfaces, suggesting possible finishing on a lathe. All vessels were finely polished.
Use: Internal and external surfaces worn. One sherd had been exposed to heat, one has repair holes and one was cut secondarily.
Quantity: 5
Comparanda: -
Style: Plain Failaka Style.

Type 20B (fig. 216): Closed figuratively decorated ellipsoidal bowl, incurved rim with indentation below the externally thickened lip.
Form code: RC4, f
Size: 280 mm
Stone type: 4
Decoration: Branch and cuneiform inscription on top of rim.
Manufacture: Finely polished prior to decoration and cuneiform inscription.
Use: Internal and external surfaces worn. Broken edges smoothed.
Quantity: 1
Comparanda: -
Style: Figurative Failaka Style.

Type 20C (figs. 297-299): Closed geometrically decorated ellipsoidal bowl, incurved rim with indentation below the externally thickened lip. One full profile shows type 20C associated with disk base type 48A.
Form code: RC4, f
Size: 140-230 mm
Stone type: 4
Decoration: Dot in single circle and horizontal lines.
Manufacture: One sherd possibly finished on a lathe.
Use: Internal and external surfaces worn. Two of the vessels have been exposed to fire, as evident from soot traces. One vessel has "scarification marks".
Quantity: 3
Comparanda: -
Style: Geometric Failaka Style.

Type 21A (figs. 137-138): Closed plain spherical bowl, incurved rim with rounded lip.
Form code: RC1, f
Size: 120-200 mm
Stone type: 3 and 4
Decoration: Plain
Manufacture: -
Use: Internal and external surfaces worn and one sherd has a repair hole.
Quantity: 2
Comparanda: -
Style: Wadi Suq Style?

Type 21B (figs. 139-140): Closed decorated spherical bowl, incurved rim with rounded lip.
Form code: RC1, f
Size: 140-200 mm
Stone type: 3
Decoration: Dot in single circle, horizontal lines, oblique lines.
Manufacture: -
Use: Internal and external surfaces worn. One vessel has been exposed to heat and fire, evident from discolouration. Two sherds have repair holes.
Quantity: 2
Comparanda: -
Style: Wadi Suq Style.

Type 21C (fig. 151): Closed plain spherical bowl with spout and flat base with rounded base edge (cf. type 41E), incurved rim with rounded lip. The open spout is rounded and protrudes from rim, cf. type 60E.
Form code: RC1, f, S5
Size: 160 mm
Stone type: 3
Decoration: Plain
Manufacture: -
Use: Internal and external surfaces worn and broken edges smoothed.
Quantity: 1
Comparanda: Ur, site A.H grave 182, Mesopotamia (Reade & Searight 2001: 163-164, fig. 10).
Style: Wadi Suq Style?

Type 22A (fig. 106): Closed geometrically decorated ovaloid bowl, rim sloping slightly inwards rim with rounded lip.
Form code: RC1, k
Size: 160 mm
Stone type: 4
Decoration: Dot in double circle, horizontal lines.
Manufacture: External surfaces polished prior to incised decoration.
Use: Internal and external surfaces worn.
Quantity: 1
Comparanda: Al-Rufay'a, Tarut, KSA (Zarins 1978: pl. 71, no. 252).
Style: Umm an-Nar Style.

Type 22B (figs. 144-147): Closed decorated ovaloid bowl, rim sloping slightly inwards with rounded lip.
Form code: RC1, k
Size: 95-230 mm

Stone type: 2 and 3
Decoration: Dot in single circle, dot in double circle, horizontal lines.
Manufacture: External surfaces polished prior to incised decoration.
Use: Internal and external surfaces worn. Two bowls had been exposed to heat and fire. One bowl cut secondarily.
Quantity: 4
Comparanda: -
Style: Wadi Suq Style.

Type 22C (fig. 153): Closed decorated ovaloid bowl, rim sloping slightly inwards with rounded lip. At the rim a protruding squarish spout, cf. type 60C.
Form code: RC1, k, S3
Size: 150 mm
Stone type: 3
Decoration: Dot in single circle, dot in double circle, horizontal lines.
Manufacture: External surfaces polished prior to incised decoration.
Use: Internal and external surfaces worn and exterior has been exposed to heat.
Quantity: 1
Comparanda: -
Style: Wadi Suq Style.

Type 23A (figs. 345-348): Closed plain ovaloid bowl, with rim sloping slightly inwards with rounded lip. Two to three incised indentations on the external surface close to rim.
Form code: RC1, k
Size: 140-180 mm
Stone type: 2 and 3
Decoration: Plain
Manufacture: -
Use: Internal and external surfaces worn. Two vessels had been exposed to heat and fire; one of these has three repair holes. One vessel cut secondarily and one had its broken edges smoothed.
Quantity: 4
Comparanda: -
Style: Plain Failaka Style.

Type 23B (fig. 349): Closed plain ellipsoidal bowl, incurved rim with pointed lip. Four incised indentations on the external surface close to the rim.
Form code: RC3, c
Size: 125 mm
Stone type: -
Decoration: Plain
Manufacture: -
Use: Internal and external surfaces worn.
Quantity: 1
Comparanda: No stone vessel parallels, but similarities can be seen in a multiple grooved ceramic type: Type 67C, Failaka, Kuwait (period 3B) (Højlund 1987: 79, figs. 301-304, 689), from Excavation 519, Qala'at al-Bahrain (period IIIa) (Højlund & Andersen 1997 fig. 131) and Excavation 520, Qala'at al-Bahrain (period IIIa) (Højlund & Andersen 1994: 179, figs. 719-720).
Style: Plain Failaka Style.

Type 24A (figs. 418-419): Closed plain cylindrical bowl, rim sloping slightly inwards with rounded lip.
Form code: RC1, k
Size: 170 mm
Stone type: 8
Decoration: Plain
Manufacture: -
Use: Internal and external surfaces worn.
Quantity: 2
Comparanda: -
Style: Miscellaneous

Type 24B (fig. 422-423): Closed plain cylindrical bowl, rim sloping slightly inwards with rounded lip.
Form code: RC1, k
Size: 140-160 mm
Stone type: 1
Decoration: Plain
Manufacture: -
Use: Internal and external surfaces worn.
Quantity: 2
Comparanda: -
Style: Miscellaneous

Type 25A (figs. 350-354): Closed plain ellipsoidal bowl, incurved rim with flattened lip. Associated with a flat base with rounded base edge, cf. type 42C.
Form code: RC2, c
Size: 190-420 mm
Stone type: 3 and 4
Decoration: Plain, cuneiform script.
Manufacture: External surface finely polished. One vessel possibly finished on a lathe.
Use: Internal and external surfaces worn. One sherd has a repair hole, another had semi-circular secondary carvings on its internal surface.
Quantity: 5
Comparanda: -
Style: Plain Failaka Style.

Type 25B (fig. 355): Closed plain ellipsoidal bowl, incurved rim with flattened lip.
Form code: RC2, c
Size: 270 mm
Stone type: 11
Decoration: Plain
Manufacture: -
Use: Internal and external surfaces worn.
Quantity: 1
Comparanda: -
Style: Plain Failaka Style.

Type 26 (figs. 53-54): Closed figuratively decorated conical bowl, inverted rim with rounded lip.
Form code: RC1, g
Size: 160-180 mm
Stone type: 1
Decoration: Whorl and bevelled squares.
Manufacture: -
Use: Wear marks on external surfaces. One bowl has a repair hole. Both bowls were cut secondarily and broken edges smoothed.
Quantity: 2

Comparanda: Jiroft, Iran (Cleuziou 2003: 125, fig. 75); Tepe Yahya, Iran (IVB) (Lamberg-Karlovsky 1988: 74-75, fig. 1.d, 78, fig. 3.b); Tarut, KSA, Shahr-I Sokhta, Iran (Kohl 1975: 28, figs. 1 and 2).
Style: 3rd Millennium Figurative Style.

Type 27 (figs. 217-218): Closed figuratively decorated spherical bowl, incurved rim with externally thickened lip, associated with a flat base with rounded base edge, cf. type 41D.
Form code: RC4, f
Size: 140-150 mm
Stone type: -
Decoration: Guilloche, hatched band, bovine/caprid, feline and moon. One vessel is inscribed with cuneiform script on top of rim.
Manufacture: -
Use: Internal and external surfaces worn. One bowl has been exposed to heat.
Quantity: 2
Comparanda: -
Style: Figurative Failaka Style.

Type 28A (figs. 220-222): Closed figuratively decorated ellipsoidal bowl, inverted sloping to slightly inwardly sloping rim with externally thickened lip and indentation below.
Form code: RC4, g and RC1, l
Size: 80-160 mm
Stone type: 4
Decoration: Fish, bovine and human.
Manufacture: -
Use: Internal and external surfaces worn, but mainly the latter. One bowl cut secondarily.
Quantity: 3
Comparanda: -
Style: Figurative Failaka Style.

Type 28B (figs. 295-296): Closed geometrically decorated ellipsoidal bowl, inverted sloping rim with externally thickened lip.
Form code: RC4, g
Size: 190-230 mm
Stone type: 2 and 4
Decoration: Dot in double circle, herringbone and oblique lines.
Manufacture: Chisel marks apparent on the internal surface. External surface polished.
Use: Surfaces worn, mainly external. One bowl has a repair hole and both have been cut secondarily. One bowl has a graffito of a boat.
Quantity: 2
Comparanda: -
Style: Geometric Failaka Style.

Type 28C (figs. 332-333): Closed plain ellipsoid bowl, inverted sloping rim with externally thickened lip.
Form code: RC4, g
Size: 230-240 mm
Stone type: 3
Decoration: Plain
Manufacture: -

Use: Surfaces worn, but mainly the external surface which also displays traces of exposure to heat.
Quantity: 2
Comparanda: -
Style: Plain Failaka Style.

Type 29 (figs. 223-225): Closed figuratively decorated ovaloid to ellipsoidal bowl, slightly incurved rim with externally thickened rounded lip, associated with body sherd type 66A and base type 48C.
Form code: RC4, i
Size: 160-200 mm
Stone type: 4
Decoration: Hatched band, humans and rosettes.
Manufacture: -
Use: Internal and external surfaces worn. One bowl has secondary cuts.
Quantity: 3
Comparanda: -
Style: Figurative Failaka Style.

Type 30 (fig. 271): Closed figuratively decorated ellipsoidal jar, incurved rim with an externally thickened lip with centred indentation.
Form code: RC4, h
Size: 100 mm
Stone type: 4
Decoration: Feline
Manufacture: -
Use: Internal and external surfaces worn. The bowl was cut secondarily and polished along its damaged edges.
Quantity: 1
Comparanda: No exact stone vessel parallels, but the decoration of a feline with stars on its rear is comparable with decoration on a gold vessel from Kalardasht, Iran (Porada 1963: 88, fig. 62).
Style: Figurative Failaka Style.

Type 31A (figs. 78-79): Closed plain spherical bowl, incurved rim with indentation below rounded lip. Type 31A is a closed version of type 5A, the bell-shaped bowl.
Form code: RC1, h
Size: 160-180 mm
Stone type: 5
Decoration: Plain
Manufacture: -
Use: Internal and external surfaces worn. One bowl has a repair hole.
Quantity: 2
Comparanda:
Style: Undecorated 3rd Millennium Style.

Type 31B (fig. 80): Closed plain spherical bowl, incurved rim with indentation below rounded lip. Type 31B was made from a different stone type than type 31A. Type 31B is a closed version of type 5A.
Form code: RC1, h
Size: 120 mm
Stone type: 1
Decoration: Plain
Manufacture: Chisel marks on the internal surface, external surface finely polished.
Use: Internal and external surfaces worn.

Quantity: 1
Comparanda: Jiroft, Iran (Pittman 2003: 81, fig. 122).
Style: Undecorated 3rd Millennium Style.

Type 32A (figs. 108-111): Diverse closed decorated rim fragments with extensive horizontal decoration from a group of vases.
Form code: RC4, f, RC1, g and RC3, a
Size: 120-250 mm
Stone type: 3 and 4
Decoration: Thin to grooved horizontal lines.
Manufacture: -
Use: Internal and external surfaces worn. One bowl has traces of soot on its external surface, another has repair holes with copper wire *in situ*. One bowl was cut secondarily, and another has a graffito of a branch.
Quantity: 4
Comparanda: Tarut, Al-Rufay'a, KSA (Zarins 1978: pl. 66, no. 115); Hili Tomb North A, UAE (David 1996: 36, fig. 5.14, 2011: 190, fig. 227: DLA/m10, DLA/m7).
Style: Umm an-Nar Style.

Type 32B (figs. 420-421): Closed plain rim sherds. Rims are incurved with externally thickened lips.
Form code: RC4, f
Size: 135-150 mm
Stone type: 2 and 4
Decoration: Plain
Manufacture: -
Use: Internal and external surfaces worn.
Quantity: 2
Comparanda: -
Style: Miscellaneous

Type 33Aa (figs. 114-117): Closed geometrically decorated conical jar, inverted sloping rim with rounded lip.
Form code: RC1, i
Size: 58-110 mm
Stone type: 2, 3 and 4
Decoration: Dot in double circle, horizontal lines.
Manufacture: External surfaces polished prior to incised decoration.
Use: Internal and external surfaces worn. One jar has been exposed to fire and heat.
Quantity: 4
Comparanda: Decoration with circles and lines: Fariq al-Akhrash, Tarut, KSA (Zarins 1978: pl. 71, nos. 40, 594); Barbar temple, Bahrain (period IIb) (Andersen & Højlund 2003: 318-319, fig. 834). Decoration with horizontal lines: Hili North Tomb A, UAE (David 2011: 190, fig. 227: DLA/m7); Qala'at al-Bahrain, Excavation 520, Bahrain (period IIb) (Højlund & Andersen 1994: 387, fig. 1908).
Style: Umm an-Nar Style.

Type 33Ab (figs. 173-178): Closed geometrically decorated conical jar, inverted sloping rim with rounded lip.
Form code: RC1, i
Size: 75-150 mm
Stone type: 2, 3 and 4
Decoration: Dot in single circle, dot in double circle, horizontal lines, oblique lines.
Manufacture: -

Use: Surfaces, mainly external, worn. One jar has been exposed to heat and another has a repair hole. Several jars were cut secondarily and one has "scarification marks" close to the rim.
Quantity: 5
Comparanda: Shimal, Tomb SH 102, Ras al-Khaimah, UAE (Vogt *et al.* 1989: 68-69, fig. 8.8); Shimal, SH99, UAE (Vogt & Franke-Vogt 1987: fig. 33.7); Jebel al-Buhais, tomb BHD 2, UAE (Jasim 2006: 26, fig. 24.3).
Style: Wadi Suq Style.

Type 33B (fig. 179): Large closed geometrically decorated conical jar, inverted sloping rim with rounded lip.
Form code: RC1, i
Size: 340 mm
Stone type: 3
Decoration: Dot in single circle, horizontal lines.
Manufacture: -
Use: Internal and external surfaces worn.
Quantity: 1
Comparanda: Shimal, s.t.6, Ras al-Khaimah UAE (De Cardi 1988: 67, fig. 12.9).
Style: Wadi Suq Style.

Type 33C (fig. 168): Closed geometrically decorated conical jar, inverted sloping rim with rounded lip. This jar has a flat base with angular base edge, cf. type 43A.
Form code: RC1, i
Size: 72 mm
Stone type: 4
Decoration: Horizontal lines, oblique lines.
Manufacture: Internal surface shows traces of being hollowed out with chisel and punches. External surface finely polished prior to incised decoration.
Use: External surface worn and exposed to heat and fire; "scarification marks" close to the rim.
Quantity: 1
Comparanda: Shimal, Ras al-Khaimah, UAE (Velde 2003: 107, fig. 5.6).
Style: Wadi Suq Style.

Type 33D (figs. 200-201): Closed geometrically decorated conical jar, inverted sloping rim with rounded lip. Type 33D is the only jar type carved from stone type 7.
Form code: RC1, i
Size: 120-160 mm
Stone type: 7
Decoration: Horizontal and oblique lines.
Manufacture: -
Use: Internal and external surfaces worn.
Quantity: 2
Comparanda: -
Style: Late Bronze Age Style.

Type 33E (figs. 162-163, 180): Closed geometrically decorated conical jar with handles, inverted sloping rim with rounded lip. Type 33E consists of jars, two of them complete, with vertical pierced lug handles, cf. type 61A. Associated with flat or rounded bases (types 43A and 41C).
Form code: RC1, i, H1
Size: 48-70 mm
Stone type: 4

Decoration: Dot in single circle, dot in double circle, horizontal and oblique lines.
Manufacture: Chisel and punch marks on the internal sidewall and base. External surface finely polished prior to incised decoration.
Use: Wear marks on external surface. One jar cut secondarily, another has "scarification marks" close to the rim.
Quantity: 3
Comparanda: Shimal, Ras al-Khaimah, UAE (Velde 2003: 107, fig. 5.1-5); Shimal, Ras al-Khaimah, UAE (David 1996: 40, fig. 6.6); Shimal, SH101, 102, UAE (Vogt & Franke-Vogt (eds.) 1987: figs. 5.2, 5.3 15.3).
Style: Wadi Suq Style.

Type 33F (fig. 202): Closed geometrically decorated conical jar, vertical rim with rounded lip.
Form code: RC1, g
Size: 120 mm
Stone type: 3
Decoration: Dot in double circle, herringbone and ladder.
Manufacture: -
Use: Internal and external surfaces worn.
Quantity: 1
Comparanda: -
Style: Late Bronze Age Style.

Type 33G (fig. 203): Closed geometrically decorated cylindrical jar, vertical rim with pointed lip.
Form code: RC3, a
Size: 70 mm
Stone type: 4
Decoration: Horizontal lines and herringbone.
Manufacture: Chisel marks on internal surface.
Use: Internal and external surfaces worn.
Quantity: 1
Comparanda: -
Style: Late Bronze Age Style.

Type 34A (fig. 270): Closed figuratively decorated ovaloid jar, inverted sloping rim with rounded lip.
Form code: RC1, i
Size: 100 mm
Stone type: 4
Decoration: Ram and moon.
Manufacture: -
Use: Internal and external surfaces worn. Large vertical secondary cut on the external surface followed by intentional breakage.
Quantity: 1
Comparanda: -
Style: Figurative Failaka Style.

Type 34B (fig. 68): Closed decorated ovaloid jar, inverted sloping rim with rounded lip.
Form code: RC1, i
Size: 130 mm
Stone type: 2
Decoration: Thick zigzag band, horizontal and oblique lines.
Manufacture: -
Use: Internal and external surfaces worn. Incised decoration on the lower part of the vessel body, i.e. horizontal and oblique lines, was carved using a different technique

and tool than the thick zigzag band close to the rim and is possibly secondary.
Quantity: 1
Comparanda: Gonur 1, Turkemenistan (Potts 2003: 80-81, fig. 1.4).
Style: Zigzag variant.

Type 35A (figs. 394-396): Closed plain ovaloid jar with either a flat or rounded lip. One or two indentations close to the rim on the external surface.
Form code: RC2, d
Size: 110-200 mm
Stone type: 2 and 4
Decoration: Plain
Manufacture: -
Use: Internal and external surfaces worn.
Quantity: 3
Comparanda: -
Style: Plain Failaka Style.

Type 35B (figs. 318-321): Closed geometrically decorated ovaloid jar with rounded lip. One or two indentations close to rim on external surface.
Form code: RC1, m and RC2, d
Size: 70-140 mm
Stone type: 4 and 3
Decoration: Dot in single circle, horizontal lines. Three of the jars have a simple decoration on top of the rim.
Manufacture: -
Use: Internal and external surfaces worn. One jar has traces of soot.
Quantity: 4
Comparanda: -
Style: Geometric Failaka Style.

Type 36 (fig. 112): Closed geometrically decorated cylindrical vase, vertical rim with indentation below rounded lip, normally associated with base type 43B.
Form code: RC1, c
Size: 90 mm
Stone type: -
Decoration: Dot in double circle and horizontal lines.
Manufacture: -
Use: External surface worn and cut secondarily.
Quantity: 1
Comparanda: Tarut, al-Rufay'a (Zarins 1978: pl. 71, no. 332); Ur, Mesopotamia (Reade & Searight 2001: 161-163, fig. 8).
Style: Umm an-Nar Style.

Type 37 (fig. 55): Closed figuratively decorated conical vase, outwardly sloping rim with out-curved rounded lip.
Form code: RO1, a
Size: 140 mm
Stone type: 1
Decoration: Guilloche and thick zigzag band.
Manufacture: -
Use: Internal and external surfaces worn.
Quantity: 1
Comparanda: Jiroft, Iran (Madjidzadeh 2003: 29-35, figs. 39a, 61b, 114d, 13b, 90c, 14, 13, 90, 93, 87, 60); Susa, Iran (Miroschedji 1973: 53, fig. 5.1 and 5.3). Parallels from Jiroft and Susa have similar vessel shape, size and structural

elements (plain raised bands), but the actual decoration elements differ.
Style: 3rd Millennium Figurative Style.

Type 38 (figs. 397-398): Closed plain straight to slightly inwardly sloping rim with indentation below rounded lip. Type 38 probably corresponds to necks of vases.
Form code: RC1, l
Size: 45-70 mm
Stone type: 2 and 4
Decoration: Plain
Manufacture: -
Use: Internal and external surfaces worn.
Quantity: 2
Comparanda: -
Style: Plain Failaka Style.

Type 39A (fig. 84): Closed plain rim, sloping inwards, with rounded lip.
Form code: RC1, i
Size: 180 mm
Stone type: 9
Decoration: Plain
Manufacture: -
Use: Internal and external surfaces worn.
Quantity: 1
Comparanda: -
Style: Undecorated 3rd Millennium Style.

Type 39B (fig. 85): A closed plain vase, vertical rim with externally thickened lip.
Form code: RC4, a
Size: 130 mm
Stone type: 9
Decoration: Plain
Manufacture: -
Use: Internal and external surfaces worn.
Quantity: 1
Comparanda: Nippur, Ur, Tell Brak, Mesopotamia (c. 2315 BC) (Potts 1994: 228-232, tab. 6.2, fig. 1).
Style: Undecorated 3rd Millennium Style.

Type 39C (fig. 86): A closed plain vase, horizontal everted rim with rounded lip.
Form code: RC1, j
Size: 165 mm
Stone type: 9
Decoration: Plain
Manufacture: -

Use: Internal and external surfaces worn.
Quantity: 1
Comparanda: Susa, Iran and Ur, Mesopotamia (Casanova 1991: 35, tables 9-10, pl. 5, no. 56); Sippar, Mesopotamia (Potts 1994: 228-232, tab. 6.2, fig. 2).
Style: Undecorated 3rd Millennium Style.

Type 40A (fig. 407): Plain square box with straight vertical walls and symmetrical thickened lip. Type 40A has a flat base with rounded base edge, cf. type 53A.
Form code: Bx1
Size: 100 × 40 mm
Stone type: 4
Decoration: Plain
Manufacture: Chisel marks on the internal surface. The box was left unfinished.
Use: Secondary cuts on external base. Heat and fire traces on the internal surface.
Quantity: 1
Comparanda: Al-Khidr, Failaka, Kuwait (Benediková *et al.* 2010: 99, fig. 86c-d).
Style: Plain Failaka Style.

Type 40B (fig. 272): Figuratively decorated square box with vertical walls and round lip. Combined with flat base of type 53B.
Form code: Bx2
Size: 25 × 35 mm
Stone type: -
Decoration: Boat and human.
Manufacture: -
Use: Internal and external surfaces worn.
Quantity: 1
Comparanda: -
Style: Figurative Failaka Style.

Type 40C (fig. 122): Square box with vertical walls, bi-angular rim to accommodate a square lid.
Form code: Bx5
Size: 35 × 37 mm
Stone type: 1
Decoration: Dot in single circle.
Manufacture: -
Use: Internal and external surfaces worn. A hole was carved in the external side.
Quantity: 1
Comparanda: -
Style: Umm an-Nar Style?

Bases (types 41-58)

A total of 99 base fragments (22.8 %) were divided into five basic shapes: flat bases, round bases, disk bases, ring bases and stump bases. These were then grouped into 18 types. These base sherds originate from a number of bowls, vases, jars, plates, boxes, a goblet and miscellaneous items.

Type 41A (figs. 118-120): Plain round base with rounded base edge. Base type 41A comes from a type of closed ovaloid jar (cf. type 33A) and/or open spherical bowl (cf. type 10A).
Form code: Ba2 a
Size: 100-180 mm
Stone type: 2
Decoration: Plain

Manufacture: -
Use: Internal and external surfaces worn. External surface of bases had been exposed to heat and fire. Broken edges smoothed.
Quantity: 3
Comparanda: Tarut, Fariq al-Akhrash, KSA (Zarins 1978: pl. 71, nos. 40, 595).
Style: Umm an-Nar Style.

Type 41B (figs. 169-172): Decorated round base with rounded base edge. Type 41B probably comes from a type of closed ovaloid jar, cf. types 33Ab and 33E.
Form code: Ba2, a
Size: 90-145 mm
Stone type: 2, 3 and 4
Decoration: Horizontal lines, oblique and vertical lines.
Manufacture: One base has visible chisel marks. The external surface was polished prior to incised decoration.
Use: Internal and external surfaces worn.
Quantity: 4
Comparanda: Shimal, s.t.6, Ras al-Khaimah, UAE (De Cardi 1988: 67, figs. 12.4-12.5); Shimal, SH103, SH101, UAE (Vogt & Franke-Vogt (eds.)1987: figs. 5.2, 5.3, 25.5-6); Saar Settlement, Bahrain (Killick & Moon 2005: 205, 208-209, fig. 5.25.c).
Style: Wadi Suq Style.

Type 41C (fig. 162, 164): Decorated round base with rounded base edge and lug handles. Type 41C includes one complete closed ovaloid jar, which illustrates the connection between the round base type 41C, rim type 33E and lug handles type 61A.
Form code: Ba2, a
Size: 120-140 mm
Stone type: 2 and 4
Decoration: Horizontal and oblique lines.
Manufacture: Chisel marks on the internal surface, external surface polished before decoration incised.
Use: Internal and external surfaces worn.
Quantity: 2
Comparanda: Cf. type 41B.
Style: Wadi Suq Style.

Type 41D (fig. 218-219): Figuratively decorated flat base with rounded base edge. Type 41D comes from a decorated spherical bowl of type 27.
Form code: Ba1, a
Size: 150-160 mm
Stone type: 2 and ?
Decoration: Bovine, moon and hatched band.
Manufacture: -
Use: Internal and external surfaces worn. Bases have been exposed to heat. One cut secondarily.
Quantity: 2
Comparanda: -
Style: Figurative Failaka Style.

Type 41E (fig. 151): Plain flat base with rounded base edge from a closed vessel with a spout positioned at the rim, cf. types 21C and 60E.
Form code: Ba1, a
Size: 160 mm
Stone type: 3

Decoration: Plain
Manufacture: -
Use: Internal and external surfaces worn. Broken edges smoothed.
Quantity: 1
Comparanda: -
Style: Wadi Suq Style?

Type 41F (fig. 210): Geometrically decorated round base with rounded base edge.
Form code: Ba2, a
Size: 60 mm
Stone type: 3
Decoration: Dot in single circle, horizontal and oblique lines.
Manufacture: -
Use: Internal and external surfaces worn.
Quantity: 1
Comparanda: -
Style: Late Bronze Age Style.

Type 42A (figs. 181-182): Geometrically decorated flat base with rounded base edge.
Form code: Ba1, a
Size: 120-180 mm
Stone type: 2
Decoration: Dot in double circle, horizontal and oblique lines.
Manufacture: -
Use: Internal and external surfaces worn. One base has been exposed to heat and has a repair hole.
Quantity: 2
Comparanda: Shimal, s.t.6, Ras al-Khaimah UAE (De Cardi 1988: 67, fig. 12.1); Shimal, SH103, UAE (Vogt & Franke-Vogt (eds.) 1987: figs. 25.7-25.10).
Style: Wadi Suq Style.

Type 42B (figs. 256, 263-264): Figuratively decorated flat base with rounded base edge; from a closed vessel, e.g. vase or jar.
Form code: Ba1, a
Size: 80-160 mm
Stone type: 4
Decoration: Thick zigzag, hatched band, bovine, fish, humans, sun/moon and branches.
Manufacture: Internal surface has marks from chisels and punches.
Use: Internal and external surfaces worn. One vessel has repair holes.
Quantity: 2
Comparanda: -
Style: Figurative Failaka Style.

Type 42C (fig. 350): Plain flat base with rounded base edge. Associated with rim type 25A.
Form code: Ba1, a
Size: 210 mm
Stone type: 4
Decoration: Plain
Manufacture: -
Use: Internal and external surfaces worn. External surface has been exposed to fire and heat.
Quantity: 1

Comparanda: -
Style: Plain Failaka Style.

Type 42D (fig. 424): Plain flat base with rounded base edge.
Form code: Ba1, a
Size: 200 mm
Stone type: 4
Decoration: Plain
Manufacture: -
Use: Internal and external surfaces worn. The external surface has been exposed to fire and heat. The internal surface has traces of a residue.
Quantity: 1
Comparanda: -
Style: Miscellaneous

Type 43A (figs. 163, 168, 183-188): Geometrically decorated flat base with angular base edge. Two complete closed ovaloid jars with this base are connected with rim types 33C and 33E.
Form code: Ba1, c
Size: 48-180 mm
Stone type: 2, 3 and 4
Decoration: Dot in single circle, horizontal lines and oblique lines.
Manufacture: -
Use: Internal and external surfaces worn. Three bases have been exposed to heat and fire, of which two show a residue on their internal surface. One base has been cut secondarily and smoothed on damaged edges.
Quantity: 8
Comparanda: Shimal, SH101, 102, 103, UAE (Vogt & Franke-Vogt (eds.) 1987: figs. 5.1, 15.3, 25.9-10); Tell Abraq, UAE (Potts 1991: 63, fig. 77).
Style: Wadi Suq Style.

Type 43B (fig. 113): Flat base with angular base edge from a vase with geometric decoration, cf. rim type 36.
Form code: Ba1, c
Size: 110 mm
Stone type: 2
Decoration: Dot in double circle, horizontal line.
Manufacture: -
Use: Internal and external surfaces worn.
Quantity: 1
Comparanda: Hili, North tomb A, UAE (David 2011: 190, fig. 227: DLA/m91, DLA/m70, DLA/m117); Al-Rufay'a, Tarut, KSA (Zarins 1978: pl. 71, no. 547).
Style: Umm an-Nar Style.

Type 43C (fig. 265): Large figuratively decorated flat base with angular base edge.
Form code: Ba1, c
Size: 360 mm
Stone type: 4
Decoration: Scorpion and bovine.
Manufacture: -
Use: Wear marks on external surface.
Quantity: 1
Comparanda: -
Style: Figurative Failaka Style.

Type 43D (fig. 425): Plain oval flat base with angular base edge.
Form code: Ba1, c
Size: c.180-190 mm
Stone type: 4
Decoration: Plain
Manufacture: Internal base has chisel and punch marks.
Use: Internal and external surfaces worn.
Quantity: 1
Comparanda: -
Style: Miscellaneous

Type 44 (fig. 33): Figuratively decorated flat base with rounded base edge. Type 44 is from an open cylindrical bowl, cf. type 17B.
Form code: Ba1, a
Size: 90 mm
Stone type: 1
Decoration: Feline and inlay.
Manufacture: -
Use: External surface has wear marks, especially on the base, and secondary cuts.
Quantity: 1
Comparanda: Jiroft, Iran (Madjidzadeh 2003: 44-46, figs. 78, 82, 80).
Style: 3rd Millennium Figurative Style.

Type 45 (fig. 56): Figuratively decorated flat base with rounded base edge. Although little is preserved, it is suggested that base type 45 is from a vase.
Form code: Ba1, a
Size: 90 mm
Stone type: 1
Decoration: Bevelled squares.
Manufacture: -
Use: Wear marks on external surface, especially on base.
Quantity: 1
Comparanda: Jiroft, Iran (Madjidzadeh 2003: 29-35, figs. 39a, 61b, 114d, 13b, 90c, 14, 13, 90, 93, 87, 60); Tarut, KSA (Burkholder 1971: pl. III no. 4).
Style: 3rd Millennium Figurative Style.

Type 46 (figs. 27, 28, 30): Decorated flat base with semi-angular base edge from a cylindrical bowl. Complete profiles demonstrate that base type 46 is associated with rim type 17A.
Form code: Ba1, b
Size: 90-160 mm
Stone type: 1
Decoration: Basketry
Manufacture: -
Use: Wear marks on external surface. Secondary cuts and intentional breakage on two bases.
Quantity: 3
Comparanda: Susa, Iran (Miroschedji 1973: 53, fig. 5.9).
Style: 3rd Millennium Figurative Style.

Type 47 (fig. 51): Decorated flat base with semi-angular base edge. The complete profile of a large cylindrical bowl is preserved. Type 47 is associated with rim type 16.
Form code: Ba1, b
Size: 300 mm
Stone type: 4

Decoration: Scorpions
Manufacture: -
Use: Wear marks on external surface.
Quantity: 1
Comparanda: Tarut, al-Rufay'a, KSA. Comparable vessel shapes, size and panels for decoration; however, decoration elements differ (Zarins 1978: pl. 68, nos. 542, 545).
Style: 3rd Millennium Figurative Style.

Type 48A (figs. 381-392, 446): Plain disk base with rounded base edge. Type 48A bases could originate from a number of different vessels, but one example suggests an association with type 20C.
Form code: Ba3, a
Size: 50-140 mm
Stone type: 2, 3 and 4
Decoration: Plain
Manufacture: One vessel possibly finished on a lathe. Other vessels finished with fine to medium-rough polish.
Use: Internal and external surfaces worn; on six of the vessels mainly on the external surface. Four of the vessels have been exposed to heat and fire as evident from traces on the base. One vessel has repair holes with copper wire *in situ*. A few were cut secondarily, and one has a graffito of a ram.
Quantity: 12
Comparanda: -
Style: Plain Failaka Style.

Type 48B (fig. 313): Geometrically decorated disk base with rounded base edge.
Form code: Ba3, a
Size: 200 mm
Stone type: 2
Decoration: Oblique lines.
Manufacture: External surface polished prior to incised decoration
Use: Internal and external surfaces worn.
Quantity: 1
Comparanda: -
Style: Geometric Failaka Style.

Type 48C (figs. 223, 228, 267): Figuratively decorated disk base with rounded base edge. Little is preserved of the bases, but base type 48C is associated with a number of body sherds, cf. 66A and rim types, cf. 29.
Form code: Ba3, a
Size: 80-180 mm
Stone type: 4
Decoration: Bovine/caprid, undefined creature (bull-man?) and humans.
Manufacture: -
Use: Internal and external surfaces worn. One base cut secondarily, then intentionally broken and smoothed along its edges.
Quantity: 2
Comparanda: -
Style: Figurative Failaka Style.

Type 49A (fig. 393): Plain disk base with angular base edge.
Form code: Ba3, b
Size: 60 mm

Stone type: 3
Decoration: Plain
Manufacture: -
Use: Internal and external surfaces worn. Base cut secondarily and smoothed on broken edges.
Quantity: 1
Comparanda: -
Style: Plain Failaka Style.

Type 49B (figs. 314-315): Geometrically decorated disk base with angular base edge.
Form code: Ba3, b
Size: 70-75 mm
Stone type: 4
Decoration: Horizontal and oblique lines.
Manufacture: External and internal surfaces polished.
Use: Internal and external surfaces worn. One base has secondary cuts and was then intentionally broken.
Quantity: 2
Comparanda: -
Style: Geometric Failaka Style.

Type 50A (figs. 361-365): Disk base with rounded base edge. Concentric stepped ridges characterise the wall profile. These ridges are confined to the lower part of the vessels. Type 50A is associated with types 20A and 68A.
Form code: Ba3, a
Size: 80-100 mm
Stone type: 4
Decoration: Plain. One base is inscribed with cuneiform script.
Manufacture: Finely polished.
Use: Internal and external surfaces worn.
Quantity: 5
Comparanda: No exact parallels, but concentric stepped ridges appear on stone vessels from: Qala'at al-Bahrain, Bahrain (period IIIb1) (Højlund & Andersen 1997: 70, fig. 296); Ebla, tomb of the Princess, Syria (Bevan 2007: 111, fig. 6.9, 216, 220, fig. L11). A number of Iranian bronze vessels also have similar concentric ridges, but do not share the overall shape: Shahdad, cemetery B, Iran (Bellelli 2002: pl. 16, fig. 68, pl. 24, fig. 149).
Style: Plain Failaka Style.

Type 50B (fig. 268): Disk base with rounded base edge. Concentric stepped ridges characterise the wall profile. Ridges are confined to the lower part of the vessels and above these is figurative decoration.
Form code: Ba3, a
Size: 40 mm
Stone type: 2
Decoration: Fish
Manufacture: -
Use: Internal and external surfaces worn.
Quantity: 1
Comparanda: See type 50A for references.
Style: Figurative Failaka Style.

Type 51A (figs. 366-370): Plain ring base with angular base edge. Concentric stepped ridges characterise the wall profile. These ridges are confined to the lower part of the vessels. Type 51A is associated with types 20A and 68A.
Form code: Ba4, a

Size: 50-100 mm
Stone type: 3 and 4
Decoration: Plain
Manufacture: -
Use: Internal and external surfaces worn. Two bases have repair holes and one has copper wire *in situ*. One base has been exposed to fire.
Quantity: 5
Comparanda: See type 50A for references.
Style: Plain Failaka Style.

Type 51B (fig. 266): Decorated ring base with angular base edge. The lower part of type 51B is decorated with concentric stepped ridges. Type 51B has a spherical vessel shape. As the rim was damaged secondarily, the original shape of the complete vessel is difficult to assess, but it seems to come from either a bowl or a vase.
Form code: Ba4, a
Size: 20 mm
Stone type: 1
Decoration: Hatched band.
Manufacture: -
Use: Internal and external surfaces worn. Smoothed along broken edges.
Quantity: 1
Comparanda: See type 50A for references.
Style: Figurative Failaka Style.

Type 51C (fig. 269): Figuratively decorated ring base with angular base edge.
Form code: Ba4, a
Size: 70 mm
Stone type: 4
Decoration: Hatched band, fish and humans.
Manufacture: Chisel marks on internal surface.
Use: External surface worn.
Quantity: 1
Comparanda: See type 50A for references.
Style: Figurative Failaka Style.

Type 51D (fig. 374): Large plain ring base with angular base edge. Concentric stepped ridges on lower part.
Form code: Ba4, a
Size: 120 mm
Stone type: 4
Decoration: Plain
Manufacture: -
Use: Internal and external surfaces worn. External surface has been exposed to heat.
Quantity: 1
Comparanda: See type 50A for references.
Style: Plain Failaka Style.

Type 51E (fig. 255): Geometrically and figuratively decorated ring base with angular base edge. Concentric stepped bands on lower part. Type 51E is associated with rim type 1F.
Form code: Ba4, a
Size: 120 mm
Stone type: 6
Decoration: Dot in single circle, branch.
Manufacture: External surface finely polished.
Use: Internal and external surfaces worn.

Quantity: 1
Comparanda: See type 50A for references.
Style: Figurative/Geometric Failaka Style.

Type 52A (figs. 399-401): Flat base with rounded base edge. Base type 52A is associated with rim type 18A, from a large thick-based plate with outwardly sloping walls.
Form code: Ba1, a
Size: 140-250 mm
Stone type: 3 and 4
Decoration: Plain
Manufacture: -
Use: Internal and external surfaces worn. One plate has been exposed to heat and fire on its external surface.
Quantity: 3
Comparanda: See type 18A for references.
Style: Plain Failaka Style.

Type 52B (figs. 404-405): Flat base with rounded base edge. Type 52B is associated with rim type 18B, from a large thick-based plate with concave walls.
Form code: Ba1, a
Size: 185-210 mm
Stone type: 2
Decoration: Plain
Manufacture: -
Use: External and internal wear marks. One plate has been exposed to heat and fire on its external surface.
Quantity: 2
Comparanda: See type 18B for references.
Style: Plain Failaka Style.

Type 53A (fig. 407): Plain flat base with rounded base edges. From a plain square box with everted sloping walls, cf. type 40A.
Form code: Bx1
Size: 100 × 40 mm
Stone type: 4
Decoration: Plain
Manufacture: Chisel marks on the internal surface. Box was left unfinished.
Use: Secondary cuts on external base.
Quantity: 1
Comparanda: Al-Khidr, Failaka, Kuwait (Benediková 2010: 99, fig. 86c-d).
Style: Plain Failaka Style.

Type 53B (fig. 272): Figuratively decorated flat base with rounded base edges. Base type 53B is from a square box with vertical walls and round lip, cf. type 40B.
Form code: Bx2
Size: 25 × 35 mm
Stone type: -
Decoration: Human and boat.
Manufacture: -
Use: Internal and external surfaces worn.
Quantity: 1
Comparanda: -
Style: Figurative Failaka Style.

Type 53C (figs. 81-82): Plain square box with closed walls. Flat base with rounded base edges; box corners are slightly raised. Walls curve inwards and towards the rim the vessel

becomes rounded (not square as at the base). Very organic shape possibly inspired by basketry or a leather bag. Box type 53C is associated with lid type 62E.
Form code: Bx3
Size: 60 × 60, 45 × 55 mm
Stone type: 4
Decoration: Plain
Manufacture: Chisel marks. One box has a possible suspension hole.
Use: Internal and external surfaces worn. Both boxes have been exposed to heat and a blackish residue is preserved on the internal surface of one of them.
Quantity: 2
Comparanda: Tarut, Al-Rufay'a, KSA (Zarins 1978: pl. 64, no. 21).
Style: Undecorated 3rd Millennium Style.

Type 53D (fig. 60): Figuratively decorated square box with vertical walls and flat base with a semi-angular base edge. Associated with box lid type 62D.
Form code: Bx4
Size: 30x15 mm
Stone type: 1
Decoration: Guilloche
Manufacture: -
Use: Internal and external surfaces worn. A hole was made in one box corner. The function of this hole is unclear. Secondary cuts are visible on external base. Broken edges smoothed.
Quantity: 1
Comparanda: Jiroft, Iran (*DA 2003:* 139, fig. 142).
Style: 3rd Millennium Figurative Style.

Type 54A (fig. 375): Ring base with rounded base edge. Too little remains to enable the overall vessel shape to be assessed.
Form code: Ba4, b
Size: 80 mm
Stone type: 4
Decoration: Plain
Manufacture: Finished on a lathe.
Use: Wear marks on external surface along with secondary cut marks.
Quantity: 1
Comparanda: -
Style: Plain Failaka Style.

Type 54B (figs. 376-377): Ring base with rounded base edge. Too little remains to enable the vessel shape to be assessed.
Form code: Ba4, b
Size: 160-200 mm
Stone type: 2
Decoration: Plain
Manufacture: -
Use: Internal and external surfaces worn.
Quantity: 2
Comparanda: -
Style: Plain Failaka Style.

Type 55 (fig. 97): Round base with rounded base edge. Type 55 comes from an open small bowl with carinated shoulders and externally thickened lip, cf. type 3.

Form code: Ba2, a
Size: -
Stone type: 10
Decoration: Plain
Manufacture: External surfaces highly polished.
Use: No significant wear marks.
Quantity: 1
Comparanda: Shahdad, Cemetery A, Iran (Hakemi 1997: 608, figs. Ff.2, Ff.7, Ff.8); Girsu, Mesopotamia (Potts 1994: 239).
Style: Undecorated 3rd Millennium Style.

Type 56 (fig. 199): Geometrically decorated disk base with angular base edge. Type 56 has everted sloping walls from an open bowl, which is probably associated with rim type 1G.
Form code: Ba3, b
Size: 180 mm
Stone type: 2
Decoration: Dot in double circle, horizontal lines, vertical lines and herringbone.
Manufacture: Polished prior to incised decoration.
Use: External surface worn.
Quantity: 1
Comparanda: Shimal, UAE (David 1996: 40, fig. 6.12; Franke-Vogt 1991: fig. 5.8).
Style: Late Bronze Age Style.

Type 57 (fig. 196): Plain flat base with rounded base edge. Type 57 is from an open bowl with everted sloping rims and rounded lips, cf. type 19C.
Form code: Ba1, a
Size: 70 mm
Stone type: 3
Decoration: Plain
Manufacture: -
Use: Internal and external surfaces worn.
Quantity: 1
Comparanda:
Style: Late Bronze Age Style?

Type 58A (fig. 87): Plain flat base with rounded base edge. Base type 58A comes from a cylindrical vase.
Form code: Ba1, a
Size: 75 mm
Stone type: 9
Decoration: Plain
Manufacture: The interior was hollowed out by a grinding slot. External surface finely polished.
Use: Internal and external surfaces worn.
Quantity: 1
Comparanda: Susa, Iran and Puzris-Dagan, Mesopotamia (Potts 1994: 234-237, tables 6.3, 6.4, fig. 1); Barbar temple, Bahrain (Casanova 2003: 285-287: figs. 761, 763).
Style: Undecorated 3rd Millennium Style.

Type 58B (fig. 95): Plain tall stump base, possibly from goblet.
Form code: Ba5, a
Size: 60 mm
Stone type: 9
Decoration: Plain
Manufacture: -

Use: Internal and external surfaces worn.
Quantity: 1
Comparanda: Quetta, Pakistan (Possehl 2002: 234-235, fig. 12.38); Shahdad, Iran (Hakemi 1997: 611.Fi.10).
Style: Undecorated 3rd Millennium Style.

Type 58C (fig. 89): Plain short stump base from jar.
Form code: Ba5, b
Size: 60 mm

Stone type: 9
Decoration: Plain
Manufacture: -
Use: Internal and external surfaces worn.
Quantity: 1
Comparanda: Girsu, Mesopotamia (Potts 1994: 234-237, tables 6.3, 6.4, fig. 5); Aali, mound 215, Bahrain (Højlund 2007: 83, fig. 159).
Style: Undecorated 3rd Millennium Style.

Spouts (type 60)

Spouts are represented by 15 fragments and comprise 3.4 % of the diagnostic sherds. Five different spout types could be established on the basis of morphology and decoration. Spouts are associated with a number of different bowls.

Type 60A (figs. 334-335): Plain square spout positioned horizontally at the top of vessel as a part of rim. The spout is open upwards and its underside slopes downwards. Type 60A is from a type of open bowl, cf. type 1D.
Form code: S1
Stone type: 3 and 4
Decoration: Plain
Manufacture: -
Use: Internal and external surfaces worn.
Quantity: 2
Comparanda: See type 1D for references.
Style: Plain Failaka Style.

Type 60B (fig. 123): Square spout positioned horizontally at the top of vessel as a part of rim. The spout is open upwards.
Form code: S2
Stone type: 4
Decoration: Dot in single circle.
Manufacture: Finely polished prior to incised decoration.
Use: Internal and external surfaces worn. Spout was cut secondarily.
Quantity: 1
Comparanda: -
Style: Umm an-Nar Style?

Type 60C (figs. 150, 152, 153): Squarish spout with exterior and interior rounded corners. These open spouts are positioned horizontally at the top of the vessel as a part of the rim. Type 60C is associated with rim types 12B, 13B and 22C.
Form code: S3
Size: 130-200 mm
Stone type: 3 and 4
Decoration: Dot in single circle, horizontal lines, oblique lines and vertical lines.
Manufacture: Polished prior to incised decoration.
Use: Internal and external surfaces worn. One spout with a repair hole and several cut secondarily.
Quantity: 3
Comparanda: See types 12B and 13B for references.
Style: Wadi Suq Style.

Type 60D (fig. 155): Trapezoid spout with internal square corners. This open spout is positioned at the top of vessel as part of rim.
Form code: S4
Stone type: 4
Decoration: Horizontal lines.
Manufacture: Polished prior to incised decoration.
Use: Internal and external surfaces worn. Traces of residue and secondary cut marks.
Quantity: 1
Comparanda: -
Style: Wadi Suq Style.

Type 60E (figs. 107, 148-149, 151, 157-158, 215, 429): Round spout positioned as part of rim. This open spout stems from bowls with rounded rims, cf. types 7B, 9C, 13B and 21C/41E. Most spouts have deep incised vertical or oblique grooves on their external surface.
Form code: S5
Stone type: 2 and 4
Decoration: Plain, oblique lines, vertical lines.
Manufacture: Polished prior to incised decoration.
Use: Internal and external surfaces worn. Two spouts have been exposed to heat and fire and two were cut secondarily, then broken intentionally. Some were smoothed along broken edges. Two spouts have repair holes.
Quantity: 7
Comparanda: Shimal, Ras al-Khaimah, UAE (Velde 2003: 107, fig. 5.11); Saar Settlement, Bahrain (Killick & Moon, 2005: 205, 208-209, pl. 5.25.d).
Style: Wadi Suq Style and Figurative Failaka Style.

Handles (type 61)

Handles are represented by 15 fragments and make up 3.4 % of the diagnostic assemblage. Five different handle types were identified, derived from jars, cooking pots and large open bowls.

Type 61A (figs. 160-166, 180): Pierced or non-pierced rectangular lug handle with rounded corners. Oval holes have been either drilled from two sides, meeting at an angle, or from one side along a vertical line. Lug handles are placed on the lower part of the vessel body, except for one vessel. Handle type 61A is associated with a closed jar of types 33E, 41C and 43A.
Form code: H1
Stone type: 2, 3 and 4
Decoration: Vertical lines and herringbone pattern.
Manufacture: Polished prior to incised decoration.
Use: Internal and external surfaces worn. Polished along broken edges.
Quantity: 8
Comparanda: Shimal, SH 99, UAE (Häser 1991: 224, fig. 2.a); Saar Settlement, Bahrain (Killick & Moon, 2005: 205, 208-209, fig. 5.25.f).
Style: Wadi Suq Style.

Type 61B (fig. 167): Pierced square lug handle with angular corners. The handle has been pierced vertically.
Form code: H2
Stone type: 2
Decoration: Plain
Manufacture: -
Use: Internal and external surfaces worn. All broken or cut edges smoothed secondarily.
Quantity: 1
Comparanda: Shimal, UAE (Velde 2003: 107, fig. 5.1-2).
Style: Wadi Suq Style.

Type 61C (figs. 322-323): Vertical geometrically decorated cylindrical handle protruding from the rim.
Form code: H3
Stone type: 3 and 5
Decoration: Horizontal lines, oblique lines.
Manufacture: -
Use: Internal and external surfaces worn. Has been exposed to heat and fire and shows secondary cut marks.
Quantity: 2
Comparanda: -
Style: Geometric Failaka Style.

Type 61D (fig. 159): Vertical decorated square handle carved at the upper part of the vessel protruding from the rim.
Form code: H4
Size: 220 mm
Stone type: 3 and 4
Decoration: Dot in single circle, horizontal lines, oblique lines and vertical lines.
Manufacture: -
Use: Internal and external surfaces worn.
Quantity: 2
Comparanda: -
Style: Wadi Suq Style.

Type 61E (figs. 316-317): A geometrically decorated half-ellipsoid loop handle. Type 61E rises vertically from the top of a rounded rim of an oval open bowl, cf. type 15.
Form code: H5
Stone type: 4
Decoration: Oblique lines.
Manufacture: -
Use: Internal and external surfaces worn.
Quantity: 2
Comparanda: See type 15 for references.
Style: Geometric Failaka Style.

Lids (type 62)

Lids constitute 2.3 % of the diagnostic fragments, being represented by 10 lids and lid fragments. Five variations were identified based on morphological characteristics. A number of circular lids with stem handles fit with a type of closed jars. A square lid corresponds to a square box and a circular lid fits an oval box. Occasionally the lids have holes which made it possible to tie the lid to the vessel.

Type 62A (fig. 426): Large circular lid with a cylindrical stemmed handle and two suspension holes.
Form code: L1
Size: 110 mm
Stone type: 3
Decoration: Dot in single circle, horizontal lines.
Manufacture:
Use: Internal and external surfaces worn. "Scarification marks" on the external surface.
Quantity: 1

Comparanda: -
Style: Miscellaneous.

Type 62B (figs. 189-194): Circular lid with stemmed knob handle. Upper surface of lid varies from flat to curved, the bottom is flat and the edge bi-angular.
Form code: L2
Size: 50-110 mm
Stone type: 2, 3 and 4
Decoration: Dot in single circle, dot in double circle, horizontal and vertical lines.
Manufacture: -
Use: Internal and external surfaces worn. Two lids with graffiti.
Quantity: 6
Comparanda: Shimal, SH 103, Ras al-Khaimah, UAE (Vogt 1989: figs. 5:5, 5:4, 27:1, 35:3); Shimal, Ras al-Khaimah, UAE (David 1996: 40, figs. 6.14, 6.18, 6.22); Shimal, s.t.6,

Ras al-Khaimah, UAE (De Cardi 1988: 67, fig. 12.13); Saar Settlement, Bahrain (Killick & Moon, 2005: 210-211, fig. 5.26.a-f, p. 212-213, fig. 5.27.a).
Style: Wadi Suq Style.

Type 62C (fig. 121): Circular lid likely with knob handle. Upper surface of lid is curved and geometrically decorated, the bottom is concave and the edge is bi-angular.
Form code: L3
Size: 100 mm
Stone type: 3
Decoration: Dot in double circle.
Manufacture: -
Use: Internal and external surfaces worn.
Quantity: 1
Comparanda: Hili Tomb UAE (David 2011: 194, fig. 230, DLA/m75).
Style: Umm an-Nar Style.

Type 62D (fig. 60): Figuratively decorated square box lid with rounded corners. Associated with box type 53D.
Form code: L4

Stone type: 1
Decoration: Guilloche
Manufacture: -
Use: External surface worn.
Quantity: 1
Comparanda: Jiroft, Iran (*DA 2003*: 139, fig. 142).
Style: 3rd Millennium Figurative Style.

Type 62E (fig. 83): Plain oval box lid. Could fit into box type 53C.
Form code: L.5
Size: 70 × 80 mm
Stone type: 4
Decoration: Plain
Manufacture: Chisel marks on internal surface. Multiple holes carved.
Use: Internal and external surfaces worn.
Quantity: 1
Comparanda: Barbar temple, 'pit of offering' temple II, Bahrain, circular lid made from alabaster (Casanova 2003: 283-286, fig. 762).
Style: Undecorated 3rd Millennium Style.

Body sherds (types 63-71)

A total of 75 body sherds, corresponding to 17.3 % of the diagnostic fragments, were grouped into nine types and further sub-divided into variants. With the exception of types 68A-B, which were defined on their morphological properties, these types were primarily established on the basis of decorative elements and stone type. The body sherds are associated with cylindrical, ovaloid to ellipsoidal bowls and conical and ovaloid jars and vases of various sizes.

Type 63A (figs. 38-50, 448): Body sherds from cylindrical bowls decorated with a hut motif. Type 63A has two size groups: 1) six sherds from vessels with a small diameter (100-160 mm) associated with rim type 17A, and 2) nine body sherds from a cylindrical vessel type with a larger diameter (200-220 mm).
Form code: Bo.
Size: 100-220 mm
Stone type: 1 and 5
Decoration: Hut
Manufacture: -
Use: Internal and external surfaces worn. One sherd has a repair hole. A few type 63A sherds were cut secondarily and the broken edges smoothed. One sherd has a graffito.
Quantity: 13
Comparanda: Jiroft, Iran (Madjidzadeh 2003: 48-49, figs. 73, 67; Vallat 2003: 91, figs. 70a, 71b); Susa, Iran (Amiet 1966: 166); Tepe Yahya, Iran (IVB) (Lamberg-Karlovsky 1988: 74-75, fig. 1.c, f; Lamberg-Karlovsky 1970: pl. 23j, fig. 21i, pl. 23j, fig. 21g); Adab, Mesopotamia (ED II) (Delougaz 1960: pl. IX.c); Tarut, KSA (Burkholder 1971: pl. IV nos. 7-8; Zarins 1978: pl. 66, nos. 109, 273, 568).
Style: 3rd Millennium Figurative Style.

Type 63B (figs. 59, 61): Body sherds with figurative decoration comprised of bevelled squares. From two different vessel shapes, a conical and an ovaloid vase.
Form code: Bo.
Size: 110-140 mm
Stone type: 1 and 5
Decoration: Bevelled squares and thick zigzag.
Manufacture: -
Use: Internal and external surfaces worn.
Quantity: 2
Comparanda: Susa, Iran (Miroschedji 1973: 53, fig. 5.13); Ur, Mesopotamia (Reade & Searight 2001: 156-157, fig. 1); Tarut, al-Rufay'a, KSA (Zarins 1978: pl. 66, no. 57; Cleuziou 2003: 117, fig. 4.7).
Style: 3rd Millennium Figurative Style.

Type 63C (figs. 62-63): Body sherds of different vessel shapes with figurative decoration of basketry.
Form code: Bo
Size: 80-180 mm
Stone type: 1
Decoration: Basketry
Manufacture: -
Use: Internal and external surfaces worn.
Quantity: 2
Comparanda: Jiroft, Iran (Pittman 2003: 85).
Style: 3rd Millennium Figurative Style.

Type 63D (figs. 57, 64): Body sherds with figurative decoration and inlay holes for semi-precious stones. One sherd is from a slender vase, another is too small for the shape of the vessel to be assessed, but it had a large diameter (c. 220 mm).
Form code: Bo
Size: 80-220 mm

Stone type: 1
Decoration: Inlay holes for decoration, undefined animal and snake.
Manufacture: -
Use: Internal and external surfaces worn.
Quantity: 2
Comparanda: Jiroft, Iran (Madjidzadeh 2003: 29, fig. 90c, 44-45, figs. 78, 82); Tarut, al-Rufay'a, KSA (Burkholder 1971: pl. VII nos. 17-21; Zarins 1978: pl. 67, nos. 135, 140, 58); Mesopotamia (Aruz 2003: 335-338, nos. 232-235).
Style: 3rd Millennium Figurative Style.

Type 63E (fig. 65): Body sherd decorated with a date palm. Its diameter is quite small, possibly a narrow neck from a vase.
Form code: Bo
Size: 60 mm
Stone type: 1
Decoration: Date palm.
Manufacture: -
Use: Internal and external surfaces worn.
Quantity: 1
Comparanda: Kerman province, Iran (Rossignol-Strick 2003: 11-13, figs. 128, 111, 110).
Style: 3rd Millennium Figurative Style.

Type 63F (fig. 58): Body sherd decorated with a tree and recumbent bovine/caprid; from a slender cylindrical vase.
Form code: Bo
Size: 80 mm
Stone type: 1
Decoration: Ungulate and branch.
Manufacture: -
Use: Internal and external surfaces worn. Broken edges smoothed.
Quantity: 1
Comparanda: -
Style: 3rd Millennium Figurative Style.

Type 64A (fig. 66): Body sherd decorated with a guilloche and zigzag pattern.
Form code: Bo
Size: 120 mm
Stone type: 5
Decoration: Guilloche and zigzag.
Manufacture: -
Use: Internal and external surfaces worn.
Quantity: 1
Comparanda: -
Style: 3rd Millennium Figurative Style.

Type 64B (fig. 67): Body sherd decorated with a zigzag pattern; from a slender cylindrical vase.
Form code: Bo
Size: 70 mm
Stone type: 1
Decoration: Thick zigzag.
Manufacture: -
Use: Internal and external surfaces worn. Sherd was cut secondarily and broken edges smoothed.
Quantity: 1

Comparanda: Kalba, tomb K2, Sharjah (David & Phillips 2008: 120, fig. 3). Various zigzag genre 1 vessels (Potts 2003: 77-91).
Style: Zigzag variant.

Type 65A (fig. 229): Figuratively decorated body sherd with a spherical shape, probably from a vase.
Form code: Bo.
Size: 110 mm
Stone type: 4
Decoration: Hatched band.
Manufacture: -
Use: Wear marks on external surface and secondary cut marks.
Quantity: 1
Comparanda: No exact stone vessel parallels, but the hatched band occurs on a vessel from Qala'at al-Bahrain, Excavation 519, Bahrain (period IIIb1) (Højlund & Andersen 1997: fig. 327).
Style: Figurative Failaka Style.

Type 65B (figs. 230-235): Figuratively decorated body sherds from a group of spherical or ellipsoid bowls. Type 65B is grouped here because of similar decorative elements (hatched band and processional scenes) and stone type. Type 65B has a smaller diameter than type 65C.
Form code: Bo
Size: 100-160 mm
Stone type: 4
Decoration: Hatched band, bovine/caprid, fish, undefined animal, humans, rosette and bird.
Manufacture: -
Use: Internal and external surfaces worn. One sherd has secondary cut marks and was smoothed along damaged edges.
Quantity: 6
Comparanda: -
Style: Figurative Failaka Style.

Type 65C (figs. 236-240): Figuratively decorated body sherds from a group of spherical or ellipsoid bowls with a larger diameter than type 65B.
Form code: Bo
Size: 160-360 mm
Stone type: 2 and 4
Decoration: Hatched band, bovine/caprid, undefined animals/creatures, bird and snake.
Manufacture: -
Use: Internal and external surfaces worn. One sherd has been exposed to heat. Two sherds have a blackish residue and one has been incised with a graffito.
Quantity: 6
Comparanda: -
Style: Figurative Failaka Style.

Type 66A (figs. 223-226): Figuratively decorated body sherds from a group of ovaloid to ellipsoidal bowls decorated with humans in procession. Associated with rim type 29 and base type 48C.
Form code: Bo
Size: 140-200 mm
Stone type: 4
Decoration: Humans and rosettes.

Manufacture: -
Use: Wear marks on external surface, also some on the interior. Three sherds were secondarily cut, then intentionally broken.
Quantity: 8
Comparanda: -
Style: Figurative Failaka Style.

Type 66B (figs. 242-243): Figuratively decorated body sherds, one with cuneiform inscription, probably from the same vessel. The two sherds have been lost and only photos exist.
Form code: Bo
Size: -
Stone type: -
Decoration: Bovine/caprid, humans, branch and cuneiform.
Manufacture: -
Use: -
Quantity: 2
Comparanda: -
Style: Figurative Failaka Style.

Type 67A (figs. 244-248): Body sherds figuratively decorated with a moon or a combination of a sun, star and moon.
Form code: Bo
Size: 100-160 mm
Stone type: 4
Decoration: Undefined animal/creature, humans, sun, star and moon.
Manufacture: -
Use: Internal and external surfaces worn. One sherd has been exposed to heat and one has had its broken edges smoothed.
Quantity: 5
Comparanda: -
Style: Figurative Failaka Style.

Type 67B (figs. 249-252): Body sherds figuratively decorated with bovines, caprids and undefined animals.
Form code: Bo
Size: 120-160 mm
Stone type: 4
Decoration: Bovines, caprids and undefined animal.
Manufacture: -
Use: Internal and external surfaces worn. Two sherds have secondary cut marks and were then smoothed along broken edges. One sherd has a graffito.
Quantity: 4
Comparanda: -
Style: Figurative Failaka Style.

Type 67C (figs. 253-254): Body sherds figuratively decorated with scorpions.
Form code: Bo
Size: 160-220 mm
Stone type: 4
Decoration: Scorpions
Manufacture: -
Use: Internal and external surfaces worn.
Quantity: 2
Comparanda: -
Style: Figurative Failaka Style.

Type 68A (figs. 371-373): A group of plain body sherds with concentric ridges stepped ridges. Associated with vessel types 20A, 50A, 51A, 51B, and 51D.
Form code: Bo
Size: 80-120 mm
Stone type: 2 and 4
Decoration: Plain
Manufacture: -
Use: Internal and external surfaces worn. One sherd has been exposed to fire, one has repair holes and two were cut secondarily and smoothed along the edges.
Quantity: 3
Comparanda: No exact parallels, but concentric stepped ridges appear on the following stone vessels: Qala'at al-Bahrain, Bahrain (period IIIb1) (Højlund & Andersen 1997: 70, fig. 296); Ebla, tomb of the Princess, Syria (Bevan 2007: 111, 216, 220).
Style: Plain Failaka Style.

Type 68B (fig. 303): One geometrically decorated body sherd with concentric stepped ridges.
Form code: Bo
Size: c.100-130 mm
Stone type: 3
Decoration: Dot in single circle.
Manufacture: -
Use: Internal and external surfaces worn.
Quantity: 1
Comparanda: -
Style: Geometric Failaka Style.

Type 69 (figs. 408-409): Body sherds with cuneiform inscription.
Form code: Bo
Size: 200 mm
Stone type: 3 and 4
Decoration: Inscribed with cuneiform script.
Manufacture: -
Use: Internal and external surfaces worn. One sherd has a repair hole and shows secondary cut marks and intentional breakage.
Quantity: 2
Comparanda: -
Style: Plain Failaka Style.

Type 70 (figs. 204-209): Body sherds with geometric decoration, some fragments apparently come from a conical jar type.
Form code: Bo
Size: 80-280 mm
Stone type: 2, 3 and 4
Decoration: Dot in single circle, horizontal lines, oblique lines, vertical lines and net.
Manufacture: -
Use: Wear on internal and external surfaces, especially the latter. One sherd has been exposed to heat and fire, another has secondary cut marks and two sherds were smoothed along broken edges.
Quantity: 6
Comparanda: Qusais, Qattara, Rumeilah, Nizwa, Shimal, UAE (Velde 2003: figs. 6.6, 6.8, 6.10 and 6.11); Ur, Mesopotamia (Reade & Searight 2001: 164-165, fig. 11); Shimal, SH102, UAE (Vogt & Franke-Vogt 1987: fig. 15.8).
Style: Late Bronze Age Style.

Type 71A (figs. 90-94): Plain body sherds from a group of spherical vases with a narrow neck and a stump base of type 58C.
Form code: Bo
Size: 90-240 mm
Stone type: 9
Decoration: Plain, but one sherd has part of a cuneiform inscription
Manufacture: Traces of polishing on external surface. One sherd was hollowed out with grinding slots.
Use: Internal and external surfaces worn.
Quantity: 5
Comparanda: Ur, Girsu, Susa, Tepe Hissar, Bactria, Mundigak (ED III-Ur III) (Potts 1994: 241, fig. 4).
Style: Undecorated 3rd Millennium Style.

Type 71B (fig. 88): A plain body sherd from a cylindrical vase (cf. types 58A and 39A).
Form code: Bo
Size: 140 mm
Stone type: 9
Decoration: Plain
Manufacture: -
Use: Internal and external surfaces worn.
Quantity: 1
Comparanda: Mari, Girsu, Ur, Bahrain, Susa, Shahdad, Mundigak, Kulli, Bactria (Casanova 1991: 38-39, tables 9-10, fig. 3: 41, 46, fig. 4: 47; Bahrain, Barbar temple (Temple II) (Casanova 2003: 283-288, figs. 761, 763-764, 766); Susa, Puzris-Dagan (Potts 1994: 234-237, tables 6.3, 6.4, fig. 1).
Style: Undecorated 3rd Millennium Style.

2.3. Decoration

The Failaka stone vessel corpus is decorated in two fundamentally different ways: figuratively and geometrically. These can be described via the decorative elements listed below. The diagnostic assemblage also includes an undecorated group, and a small number of sherds from all three groups are inscribed with cuneiform script (fig. 20).

There is a significant difference in how figurative and geometric decoration was applied to the vessels. Figurative decoration was created by removing the surface around the motifs, thereby making the decoration stand out in a low relief, whereas geometric decoration was incised into the surface. This reflects differences in craftsmen's traditions related to specific regions and periods and also differences in how much time and effort was invested in the vessels.

Decoration	N
Figurative decoration	107
Geometric decoration	139
Plain	137
Cuneiform	13

Fig. 20. Frequency of decoration types in the diagnostic assemblage.

2.3.1. Figurative decoration

About a quarter of the diagnostic sherds (fig. 20) show figurative decoration and this has been divided up into the 23 decorative elements (F1-F23) listed below.[2]

When describing the vessels bearing figurative decoration, the author has drawn on Rice's terminology of decorative styles e.g. 1) *Representational, naturalistic or realistic* representations, which refer to a style that depicts concrete things (e.g. humans, animals, objects), 2) *Abstract, iconic or geometric* representations, which refer to styles in which "the subject has been reduced to a selection of particular features regarded in some way (usually in symbolic content) as essential or basic". Furthermore, Rice's terminology of design is used to describe the distribution of decoration on the vessels: *Configurative design* (realistic likeness, little distortion), *Distributive design* (horror vacui, great distortion) and *Expansive design* (some distortion of the image, but less horror vacui) (Rice 1987: 247-248).

Stone vessels with *distributed* and *expansive design* are seen with predominantly decorative elements that have been transformed or distorted to some extent. Although these decorative elements are taken from actual things, such as animals (e.g. scorpions) and architecture, they are dissolved into abstract, iconic or geometric elements. These distributed and expansive designs are associated with a group of vessels in the so-called 3rd Millennium Figurative style, carved from stone types 1 and 5.

Configurative design is predominant in a group of vessels in the so-called Figurative Failaka Style, dating from the 2nd millennium BC, as the majority of the figurative elements are representational and naturalistically positioned on the vessel with little distortion. This type of design implies a great emphasis on shape with an attempt being made to depict things as accurately as possible. The stylistic representational elements include plants, boats, scorpions, ungulates, fish, snakes, birds, felines and humans. Humans are portrayed in such detail that clothing and hairstyles can be identified and differentiated. Empty space is left around the naturalistic decorative elements, which are often positioned on a horizontal hatched band. Naturalistic elements are sometimes combined with iconic celestial symbols and mythical creatures. The representation of celestial symbols (i.e. sun, moon and star, F18), which appear on 9.4 % of the figurative vessels, is often seen associated with humans walking in procession, branches, ungulates and mythical creatures. Together they present scenarios of action seemingly related to cultic practices. This design style is associated with vessels in the Figurative Failaka Style that were made from stone types 2 and 4.

In general, the most frequent figurative decorative elements are those depicting humans (F17, 26.4 %), the hatched band (F12, 23.6 %), ungulates (F13, 21.6 %) and the hut motif (F2, 13.2 %).

As for the stone types used to produce the figurative vessels, these are predominantly stone types 1 (35.8 %) and 4 (35 %) and, to a lesser degree, types 2 (7.5 %), 5 (2.8 %) and 6 (1 %) (fig. 21).

---

[2] A number of terminological phrases have been borrowed from Kohl, e.g. scorpion, date palm, whorl, mat, hut, imbricate, bevelled square, rosette (1978: 465-466).

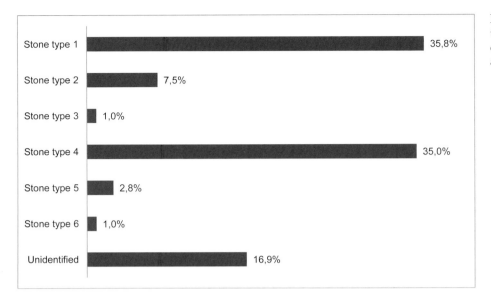

Fig. 21. Frequency of stone types within the figurative decorated diagnostic assemblage (Σ 107).

It is noteworthy that there is a specific relationship between certain decorative elements and certain stone types (fig. 22). Distributive and expansive designs, occasionally with abstract iconic elements, occur exclusively on vessels made from stone types 1 and 5, whereas configurative design, displaying decorative elements as naturalistic representations of either concrete or imaginary components, mainly occurs on vessels carved from stone types 2 and 4. This strong relationship between different design representations and stone types is significant as it defines various figurative stone vessel styles described in the following chapter.

Some decorative elements, e.g. scorpions, birds, felines and the rosette, occur on vessels carved from both stone types 1 and 4, but the design and carvings are entirely different. On stone type 1 vessels these specific decorative elements are typically carved in either a distributive or expansive design and all, except the scorpion, have inlay holes. On stone type 4 vessels the above-mentioned decorative elements are represented in a configurative design by a more naturalistic likeness.

Figurative decorative elements

F1. Scorpion

Scorpions occur in two different design representations: one is naturalistic and representational, being carved in a configurative design, whereas the other displays tightly-packed animals depicted in an abstract and iconic fashion (distributive design). The scorpion is primarily portrayed unaccompanied, with one exception when it is associated with a bovine (F13). The scorpion is represented on 4.7 % (N: 5) of the figuratively decorated vessels.

	F1: Scorpion	F2: Hut	F3: Whorl	F4: Imbricate	F5: Basketry	F6: Inlay	F7: Date Palm	F8: Bevelled square	F9: Textile	F10: Guilloche	F11: Thick zig-zag	F12: Hatched band	F13: Ungulate	F14: Fish	F15: Feline	F16: Undefined animal/creature	F17: Human	F18: Celestial symbol	F19: Boat	F20: Branch	F21: Rosette	F22: Bird	F23: Snake
Stone type 1	X	X	X	X	X	X	X	X	–	X	X	–	X	–	X	–	–	–	–	–	X	X	X
Stone type 5	–	X	–	–	–	–	–	X	–	X	X	–	–	–	–	–	–	–	–	–	–	–	–
Stone type 2	–	–	–	–	–	–	–	–	–	X	X	X	X	–	X	X	X	–	X	–	X	X	
Stone type 4	X	–	–	–	–	–	X	–	–	–	X	X	X	X	X	X	X	X	X	X	X	–	–
Stone type 6	–	–	–	–	–	–	–	–	–	–	–	–	–	–	–	–	–	–	–	X	–	–	–

Fig. 22. Correlation between stone types and figurative decoration elements (diagnostic assemblage).

F2. Hut

The hut motif occurs in distributive designs. This motif, which is apparently derived from actual architecture, is reproduced in an abstract and iconic fashion. The hut motif includes several elements, the most predominant of which is the hut façade, described as an architectural façade or poles supporting a curved roof lintel. Associated decorative elements are geometrised zigzags, steps, stars, bevelled squares and criss-crossed ornamentation. The hut is represented on 13.2 % (N: 14) of the figurative vessels.

F3. Whorl

Stylised entwined whorls in a repeated pattern. The whorl motif is rarely represented on the figuratively decorated vessels (0.9 %, N: 1).

F4. Imbricate

The imbricate motif can be described as scales or tiles set in a repeated distributive pattern, arranged in a horizontal manner and covering the entire surface of a vessel. Imbricate decoration is represented on 0.9 % (N: 1) of the figuratively decorated vessels.

F5. Basketry

A naturalistic representation of woven basketry in a configurative design. This covers the entire surface of a vessel, bordered at the rim and base by a plain horizontal or zigzag band (F11). Basketry decoration is represented on 5.7 % (N: 6) of the figurative vessels.

F6. Inlay

Circular or elliptical cut-outs for inlays of semi-precious stones. No *in situ* stone inlays are preserved. This decorative element is combined with abstract and iconic animal representations of a caprid (F13), feline (F15), snake (F23) and bird (F22). Only the snake and bird representations have diamond-shaped inlay holes. Decorative motifs with inlay holes are carved in an expansive design. This ornamentation technique is represented on 6.6 % (N: 7) of the figuratively decorated vessels.

F7. Date palm

Date palms are rendered in either a naturalistic or an iconic representation, displayed in an expansive design. Although few complete trees are preserved, tree trunks and clusters of dates are seen. The date palm is represented on 3.8 % (N: 4) of the figuratively decorated vessels.

F8. Bevelled square

Distributive design of small bevelled squares arranged in horizontal lines and covering the entire surface. The bevelled square resembles brickwork and appears in association with the hut façade (F2).

On some vessels this motif is seen separated by plain bands and zigzags (F11). Bevelled squares are represented on 2.6 % (N: 3) of the figurative vessels.

F9. Textile

A seemingly naturalistic representation of textile or weaving displayed in a configurative design. Textile decoration is represented on 0.9 % (N: 1) of the figurative vessels.

F10. Guilloche

Guilloche is a rounded, interlocking repetitive pattern presented in single or multiple horizontal bands. It occurs either just below the rim or on the middle of the body, or it can cover an entire surface as seen on a box and box lid. Guilloche is not strictly speaking a figurative decoration element, but as it is often combined with figurative decorations, such as animals and celestial symbols, it is incorporated here. The guilloche motif described here is dissimilar to the guilloche motif with inlays published by Kohl (1978). Guilloche is represented on 4.7 % (N: 5) of the figuratively decorated vessels.

F11. Thick zigzag

The thickened zigzag appears as a horizontal band positioned either below the rim or on the shoulder to middle of the body, occasionally delimited on each side by plain bands. Like guilloche, the thickened zigzag is not figurative in itself, but is often associated with figurative decoration elements, such as the hut (F2), basketry (F5) and bevelled squares (F8), and is therefore listed here. As the zigzag motif is a rather simple element, it is not surprising to find it on various styles of stone vessels. The thick zigzag, which appears in raised relief, should be distinguished from the thin incised zigzag (G10), which is part of the geometric decorative repertoire described below. The thick zigzag is represented on 5.7 % (N: 6) of the figurative vessels.

F12. Hatched band

A narrow hatched band often appears below the rim and just above the base of a vessel, and also in between, dividing the surface into horizontal panels of figurative scenes. The hatched band is important since it ties several figurative decorative elements together: ungulate (F13), bird (F22), fish (F14), feline (F15), undefined or mythical creature (F16), guilloche (F10), humans (F17) in processional scenes, celestial symbols (F18) and the rosette (F21).

The hatched band is the second most frequent figurative element and is represented on 23.6 % (N: 25) of the figuratively decorated vessels.

F13. Ungulates

This decorative element ranges from naturalistic to abstract and iconic representations of bovines, caprids and rams. The ungulates are carved in a configurative design. The bovines appear to be predominant within this group, but several representations are difficult to identify because the heads of the animals are missing and only the lower part of body or the hooves survive.

There are two different shapes of bovine horns: one curving outwards, the other inwards. The frontal part on some bovines has a vertical band with hatched lines, possibly representing a fleece. This feature is not present on all bovines and never on caprids. The level of detail invested in the decoration varies greatly. Some of the ungulates have carefully depicted fur, while others are simple and undecorated. This decorative element is associated with hatched bands (F12), fish (F14), (attacking) feline (F15), celestial symbols (F18), processional or worship scenes and cuneiform script. Ungulates are represented on 21.6 % (N: 23) of the figuratively decorated vessels.

F14. Fish
Naturalistic representations of fish with varying levels of detail, from fine naturalistic renditions, including scales and fins, to more iconic depictions with a simple outline. The fish is placed in a configurative design. It is associated with various decorative elements including the hatched band (F12), rosette (F21), humans (F17) and ungulates (F13). Fish are represented on 6.6 % (N: 7) of the figuratively decorated vessels.

F15. Feline
The feline motif is carved in an abstract and iconic fashion and appears in both configurative and expansive designs. It is present on only a few fragments and all scenes with felines differ radically from one another. One scene shows an attacking feline biting the neck of a caprid. On another fragment a feline is portrayed in profile, as it is being bit at the neck by a snake. A third sherd depicts the rear end of a feline decorated with incised stars. The feline is represented on 3.8 % (N: 4) of the figuratively decorated vessels.

F16. Undefined animals and creatures
Several fragments display undefined animals or fictitious creatures, all in a configurative design. The category undefined animals include both animals where too little is preserved for them to be identified and also unknown animals. Several vessels are decorated with the motif of an animal depicted in profile with a fleece, pointed ears and a curved braided band (ram's horns?) below its eyes. The undefined animals are primarily associated with plain bands, hatched band (F12), crescent moon (F18) and humans (F17). Fictitious or mythical creatures include bull-men, a vomiting animal kept on a leash

and a creature with human legs and a curled tail. A large human face with a beard and long hair is portrayed full-face with a large circular disc over the head. This representation seems likely to have been associated with some kind of worship or cultic practice, as humans are seen approaching from both sides with hands folded as if in prayer. All mythical creatures are associated with the hatched band (F12). This decorative category is represented on 7.5 % (N: 8) of the figurative vessels.

F17. Human
Naturalistic human representations are the most common figurative decorative element seen in the assemblage. Humans are portrayed in a configurative design. Some are nude, others wear knee-length skirts or long dresses which also cover the upper torso. Hairstyles also vary widely, ranging from bald to long-haired with hair bands and some figures wear skullcaps. Many of the humans have raised arms sometimes with palm fronds being held in front of their chest. They are walking or standing in close lines approaching stylised poles, altars or possible deities. Humans are often associated with the rosette (F21), hatched band (F12) ungulates (F13), undefined animals/creatures (F16), celestial symbols (F18), branches (F20) and fish (F14). They are represented on 26.4 % (N: 28) of the figuratively decorated vessels.

F18. Celestial symbols
A number of fragments are decorated with various combinations of astral and lunar symbols in a configurative design. These include a low-lying crescent moon carried on the back of ungulates (F13), a combination of the sun, moon and star that occasionally is seen carried on the back of ungulates, with humans (F17) walking towards it in procession and a combination of the sun and a star in association with a bull-man (F16). Celestial symbols are represented on 9.4 % (N: 10) of the figuratively decorated vessels.

F19. Boat
A naturalistic representation of a boat with an up-curved stern, associated with a human figure. The boat is rarely represented on the figuratively decorated vessels (0.9 %, N: 1).

F20. Branch
Naturalistic branch positioned on a horizontal line together with humans and animals and, in one case, being held in the hands of humans walking in procession. The branch differs from the more stylised date palm (F7), due to its different shape and lack of a trunk and date clusters. The branch is represented on 6.6 % (N: 7) of the figuratively decorated vessels.

F21. Rosette
The rosette motif is associated with human representations (F17) and is often positioned close to their heads. The rosette appears only on vessels decorated in a configurative design and is also associated with the hatched band (F12) and fish (F14). It is represented on 4.7 % (N: 5) of the figuratively decorated vessels.

F22. Bird
The bird is modestly represented by two examples. One fragment illustrates a representational bird with a crooked beak, long neck and extended wings. The general design is configurative. On this vessel the bird is associated with humans (F17), ungulates

(F13) and hatched band (F12). On another fragment only a wing is preserved and this has carved inlay holes. The bird is represented on 1.8 % (N: 2) of the figuratively decorated vessels.

F23. Snake
The snake appears primarily in the group of vessels with inlay holes. One fragment shows the body and a second depicts a snake biting a feline (F15) at the neck. A third fragment is a more realistic representation of a snake, seen biting the neck of a bovine (F13). The design context of the snake ranges from configurative to expansive.

The snake is represented on 2.8 % (N: 3) of the figuratively decorated vessels.

2.3.2. Geometric decoration

About a third of the diagnostic sherds have geometric decoration (fig. 20). Eleven different decorative elements were identified (G1-G11) and these are combined in various ways. Decorative elements are either limited to a zone close to the rim or they cover the entire surface. In general, there is an increase in the intensity of geometric decorative elements from the late 3rd millennium through the 2nd millennium.

The decorative elements are distributed according to certain rules. Horizontal lines and dots in circles (G1, G2, G3) often occur together, arranged in horizontal stripes and forming a continuous band encircling primarily the upper part of the vessel. Oblique and vertical lines (G4, G6) always appear on the lower part of the vessel body and never close to the rim, except in a few instances where they occur

directly on top of the rim. Decoration on top of rim includes simple lines, oblique lines, dot in single circle, zigzag or a combination of these elements (fig. 23).

Horizontal lines (G3) constitute the predominant decoration element, being represented on 69.7 % of the diagnostic geometrically decorated sherds. The next most common decorative elements are oblique lines (G4, 48.9 %) and the dot in single circle (G1, 39.6 %); the latter is more common than the dot in double circle (G2, 25.2 %). Dot in single circle and dot in double circle never occur on the same vessel in the Falaika assemblage.

The dominant stone types used for diagnostic vessels with geometric decoration are types 4 (38.1 %), 3 (25.2 %), 2 (23.7 %) and, to a lesser degree, 1 (0.7 %), 5 (0.7 %), 6 (0.7 %), 7 (1.4 %) and 11 (0.7 %) (fig. 24).

Geometric decorative elements

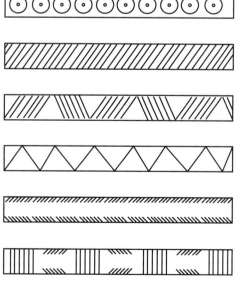

Fig. 23. Geometric decoration on top of rims.

G1. Dot in single circle
Dots in single circles are primarily arranged in a horizontal line and only rarely arranged vertically. Sometimes several rows of dot in circles follow each other, in some instances divided by horizontal lines. This decorative element is primarily positioned on the upper part of the vessel and, to a lesser degree, on the lower part of the body. One rim is incised on top with continuous dot in single circles. This motif is represented on 39.6 % (N: 55) of the geometrically decorated vessels.

G2. Dot in double circle
Dot in two circles occurs in the same decorative composition as described above and is represented on 25.2 % (N: 35) of the geometrically decorated vessels.

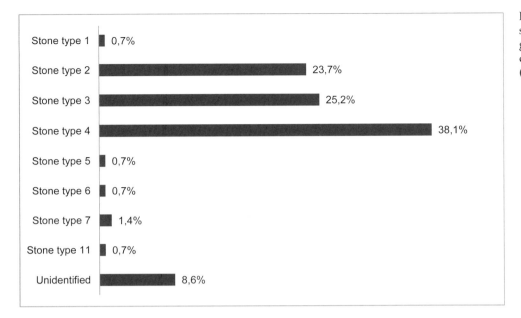

Fig. 24. Frequency of stone types within the geometric decorated diagnostic assemblage (Σ139).

G3. Horizontal lines

Horizontal lines encircling the entire vessel range from a single line to multiple lines arranged in groups. These simple lines are used to separate different decorative elements. Horizontal lines are the most frequent geometric decorative element and are represented on 69.7 % (N: 97) of the geometrically decorated vessels.

G4. Oblique lines

Alternating bunches of oblique parallel lines are seen primarily on the lower part of the vessel body but are, in a few cases, also found on the top of rims. Oblique lines are the second most frequent geometric decorative element and are represented on 48.9 % (N: 68) of the geometrically decorated vessels.

G5. Vertical lines

Vertical lines range from a single line to a group of lines, arranged primarily on the lower part of the vessel body. Vertical lines are represented on 7.9 % (N: 11) of the geometrically decorated vessels.

G6. Herringbone

The herringbone decoration consists of alternating rows of short oblique strokes positioned between lines. The pattern can occur as single or multiple rows or bands arranged in both a horizontal and a vertical fashion, even on the same vessel. When present horizontally, the herringbone pattern forms a single band that encircles the vessel, often just below the rim or below a set of dotted circles. When oriented vertically, the pattern occurs in groups which cover the lower part of the vessel body. This decorative element is represented on 4.3 % (N: 6) of the geometrically decorated vessels.

G7. Triangle with horizontal lines

Triangles filled with horizontal lines. This decorative element occurs both close to the rim and on the central part of the body. Triangles filled with horizontal lines are rare in the assemblage, being only represented on 1.4 % (N: 2) of the geometrically decorated vessels.

G8. Ladder

The ladder decorative element consists of two lines with the space between them occupied by short strokes. Ladder decoration often forms a horizontal band encircling the vessel just below the rim, but in one case it is oriented vertically on the middle of the body. The motif is represented on 2.8 % (N: 4) of the geometrically decorated vessels.

G9. Net

Horizontal and vertical lines crossing each other on the lower middle to lowest part of the body. The net motif is rare on the geometrically decorated vessels (1.4 %, N: 2).

G10. Thin zigzag

The thin zigzag motif occurs predominantly as a single line, but in one instance a number of zigzag lines are arranged parallel to each other. The motif is seen either on the middle of the body, between horizontal lines (G3), or on the top of rims. It is represented on 2.8 % (N: 4) of the geometrically decorated vessels.

G11. Semicircle

This decoration is seen exclusively on the surface of spouts and ranges from thin to thick grooved lines. It is represented on 5.8 % (N: 8) of the geometrically decorated vessels.

2.3.3. Plain

Vessels without decoration constitute a large part of the diagnostic assemblage (fig. 20). Undecorated vessels were predominantly made from stone types 4 (38.7 %), followed by 2 (19.7 %), 3 (13.1 %) and 1 (7.3 %) (fig. 25). A number of stone types used for the undecorated vessels are not represented in the figu-rative and geometrically decorated groups. Some of these stone types have a distinctive appearance, e.g. stone types 9 (8 %) and 10 (1.5 %), while others seem less suited to the application of decoration (e.g. stone types 8 (1.5 %) and 11 (0.7 %).

2.3.4. Cuneiform inscriptions

Thirteen sherds bear cuneiform inscriptions, ten of which have been published previously (Glassner 2008), and the remaining three are undecipherable. Cuneiform inscriptions are associated with undec-orated, geometrically and figuratively decorated bowls and plates. The inscriptions mainly occur on the vessel body itself, but two examples show writing on the rim and one sherd is inscribed externally on its base. Vessels bearing these inscriptions were made from stone types 4, 3, 9 and 11.

The inscriptions mention the god Enki, the god Inzak of Akarum and a lesser divinity PA.NI.PA, a temple of Inzak, 'old temple' (Egalgula) and various names. As the inscriptions refer to religious devo-tion, it seems likely that they were an original part of the design rather than later additions, at least in the cases where figurative decoration actually depicts worship.

KM1296 (fig. 354). A type 25A sherd with three lines of text. Mentions the Amorite name of: *ᴵIa-mi-ú*. Dated to the Isin-Larsa/Old Babylonian/Kassite period (Glassner 1984: 38, no. 29, fig. 7).

KM1517 (fig. 215). Five lines of text on a rim sherd with spout of type 7B/60E.

[…]-*mu-um*-ᵈ[x]-*ši-ta*-[…]
[…]x-*si-É-kar-ra* […]
[…]-*am.* ⁽ᵈ⁾PA.NI.[PA…]
[…] *ta! am bi* […]
[…] *an* […]

These are proper names: "*[…] mum-ᵈ..šita[…], […] si-Hakara and […] am-PA.NI.PA*" (Glassner 2008: 185, 202, no. 33, 1984: 39, fig. 9).

KM1518 (fig. 365). End of inscription on a flat base of type 50A.

…
[…] x
[ᵈ*In-z*]*a-ak*
[*šá A-kà*]-*rum*

"…*Inzak of Akarum*". Inzak was the tutelary god of Dilmun and Akarum refers to a geographical lo-

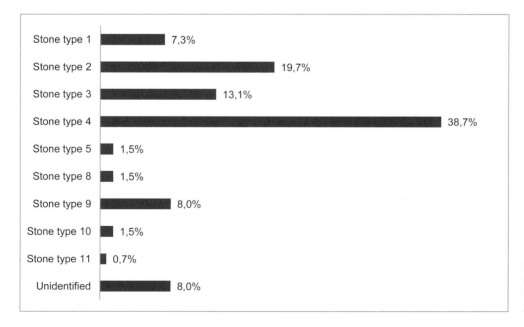

Fig. 25. Frequency of stone types within the plain diagnostic assemblage (Σ 137).

Stone type 1 — 7,3%
Stone type 2 — 19,7%
Stone type 3 — 13,1%
Stone type 4 — 38,7%
Stone type 5 — 1,5%
Stone type 8 — 1,5%
Stone type 9 — 8,0%
Stone type 10 — 1,5%
Stone type 11 — 0,7%
Unidentified — 8,0%

cation or ethnic group in Eastern Arabia (Glassner 2008: 185, 202, no. 34, 1984: 40, fig. 10).

KM1520 (fig. 216). Inscription on top of rim of type 20B.

[é].gal.gu.la x […]

Égalgula, "old temple". In an inscription on a stamp seal this temple is connected with Inzak of Agarum (Glassner 2008: 186, 202, no. 35, 1984: 40 and 48, no. 33).

KM1522 (fig. 408). Body sherd (type 69) bearing two lines of text. The signs *ki* and *a* are preserved (Glassner 2008: 186, 202, no. 36, 1984: 41, fig. 12).

KM1642 (fig. 402). Two lines preserved close to rim of type 18Ab.

[…] gal […]
[…]ni an […]
…

Maybe possible to restore to [é].gal.[gula], "old temple" (Glassner 2008: 186, 203, no. 37, 1984: no. 35).

KM1645 (fig. 302). The beginning of a single line on a type 6B rim sherd.

^{I}Ba-^{d} […]

Translated as "*Iqīš…*" (Glassner 2008: 187, 203, no. 38, 1984: 41, fig. 14).

KM1649 (fig. 406). A few undecipherable cuneiform signs incised on rim sherd of type 18C.

KM1728 (fig. 92). Three lines of undecipherable cuneiform script on a type 71A body sherd.

KM3051-3082-1394 (fig. 218). A few undecipherable cuneiform signs incised on a type 27/41D bowl.

F3.138/881.HU (fig. 242). Body sherd of type 66B with inscription between two humans in procession on top of a bovine figure.

[é].gal ^{d}*In-za-ak*.

Translated as "the temple of Inzak" (Glassner 2008: 187, 203, no. 39, 1984: 42; Bibby 1970: fig. 20A).

KM3528 (fig. 409). Seven lines on the lower body of a vessel (type 69).

[*a-na*^{d}] *En-ki*
[lug] al.a.ni.ir
[…] x si DI a
[é].gal ^{d}*In*
[…] x x an
[…] ^{d}*In-za*
[…] bur ú še

Translated as: "*For Enki, my lord, …, the temple of Inzak, …, Inzak, …vessel…*". (Glassner 2008: 188, 203 no. 40, 1984: 42, fig. 15).

KM3529 (fig. 360). Six lines are preserved below the rim of a small shallow bowl of type 20A.

[…é].gal
[…] en!!? NI!-TUK!!?
[…] x x
[…] ni
[…^{d}*In*]- *za-a*[k]
[…] x […]
…

The cuneiform inscription is translated as: "*…the temple, …lord of Dilmun (??), …, …, …Inzak,..*" (Glassner 2008: 188, 203, no. 41, 1984: 43, fig. 16).

3. Stone vessel styles

Based on a typological analysis of the stone, morphology and decoration of the 387 diagnostic stone vessel fragments, these have been grouped into eight different styles (fig. 26), which can be dated to a period extending from the middle of the 3rd millennium to the late 2nd millennium BC. Five of these styles are known from the literature: 1) *3rd Millennium Figurative Style* also named *Série Ancienne,* 2) *3rd Millennium Undecorated Style,* 3) *3rd Millennium Umm an-Nar Style* (also named *Série Recente),* 4) *2nd Millennium Wadi Suq Style* (also named *Série Tardive),* and 5) *2nd Millennium Late Bronze Age Style,* also named *Série Intermediaire.*

Further to these are three new styles, presented here at some length, only one of which has been sporadically mentioned previously in the literature. These styles date from the middle of the 2nd millennium BC and are termed 6) *Figurative Failaka Style,* 7) *Geometric Failaka Style* and 8) *Plain Failaka Style.* Finally, a group of miscellaneous pieces.

Vessel styles	N
3rd millennium Figurative Style	44
3rd millennium Undecorated Style	29
3rd millennium Umm an-Nar Style	26
2nd millennium Wadi Suq Style	70
2nd millennium Late Bronze Age Style	16
2nd millennium Figurative Failaka Style	61
2nd millennium Geometric Failaka Style	38
2nd millennium Plain Failaka Style	86
Miscellaneous	17
Total	387

Fig. 26. Frequency of the eight vessel styles in the diagnostic assemblage.

3.1. 3rd Millennium Figurative Style

A total of 44 diagnostic fragments are assigned to the *3rd Millennium Figurative Style* (David 1996: 32), known elsewhere as *Série Ancienne* (Miroschedji 1973), *Intercultural Style* (Kohl 1978: 30) or *Jiroft Style* (Muscarella 2005: 177. Perrot 2003: 11).

3rd Millennium Figurative Style vessels are elaborately carved with figurative motifs such as combat scenes between beasts and snakes (sometimes inlayed with semi-precious stones), scorpions, huts, date palms or imitations of basketry, textiles and masonry. It is generally assumed that these vessels were produced in south-eastern Iran, and the island of Tarut, Saudi Arabia, is no longer seen as a likely production site (Potts 2010: 178).

Vessels with figurative motifs similar to those from Failaka presented below have predominantly been recovered from funerary or temple contexts in Iran, Mesopotamia and Tarut. Comparative material derives from many sites and was found in contexts dating to c. 2600-2300 BC.

The 3rd Millennium Figurative Style vessels from Failaka include the following vessel shapes: cylindrical and conical bowls, vases, a square box and box lid, besides a number of body sherds. They have been divided up into 14 different types. The decoration includes figurative elements such as scorpion, hut, whorl, imbricate, basketry, date palm, bevelled square, textile and guilloche. A number of figuratively decorated sherds have holes for inlays, a decoration technique widely used in the general Figurative Style, but no inlays are preserved in the Failaka material. Nine out of Kohl's twelve established decorative groups (1978: 465-66) were identified in the Figurative Style material from Failaka.

In the following, the various Figurative Style vessel types will be described and general parallels provided. Individual parallels for each type are given in chapter 2.

Bowls

Figuratively decorated cylindrical bowls occur in three sizes: small, medium and large. The small and medium-sized (types 17A, 17A/46, 17B, 17B/44 and 63A, figs. 27-50) have close parallels at several Iranian sites (e.g. Susa, Jiroft, Bampur and Tepe Yahya), Gulf sites (e.g. al-Rufay'a, Sharm and Saar) and a few sites in Mesopotamia (e.g. Nippur, Mari and Adab). These bowls are decorated with a number of different elements: hut, basketry, scorpion, textile, feline, snake, bird, ungulate and date palm. Some have inlay holes for semi-precious stones.

With respect to morphology, size and decorative panels, a large cylindrical bowl decorated with scorpions (type 16/47, fig. 51) resembles vessels from al-Rufay'a (Tarut), although the individual decorative elements are different. A large open ovaloid bowl (type 11C, fig. 52) has similar decoration, a date palm, to an example from al-Rufay'a, but differs in shape and size.

Types 16/47 and 11C were produced in a golden softstone (stone type 4), very different from the greenish softstone (stone type 1) used for the small and medium-sized cylindrical bowls described above.

Two conical bowls (type 26, figs. 53-54) decorated with whorl and bevelled square motifs resemble a number of Iranian vessels from Jiroft, Tepe Yahya and Shahr-I Sokhta, as well as an example from Tarut.

Vases

Two types of vase are decorated in the Figurative Style: 1) a slender conical vase represented by rim, base and body sherds, decorated with basketry and thick zigzag bands (type 37, fig. 55), bevelled squares (type 45, fig. 56), undefined animal and snake with inlay holes (type 63D, fig. 57) and ungulate, rosette and branch (type 63F, fig. 58); 2) one body sherd is from an ovaloid vase decorated with bevelled squares (type 63B, fig. 59).

These vase sherds have parallels at Jiroft, Susa, Ur and Al-Rufay'a (Tarut).

Box and box lid

A square box (type 53D, fig. 60) and a box lid (type 62D, fig. 60), both decorated with a guilloche motif have exact parallels in a grave at Jiroft.

Body sherds

Body sherds of types 63B, 63C, 63D, 63E and 64A (figs. 61-66) are decorated with a number of different decoration elements, bevelled squares, date palm, basketry, inlay, undefined animals, thick zig-zag and guilloche, but too little remains of them for the overall vessel shape to be assessed.

There is a definite consistency in the shapes, decorative elements, iconography and stone types within the general Figurative Style repertoire and this can also be recognised in the Failaka assemblage. After the recent appearance of hundreds of vessels in this style in the Jiroft plain it is likely that vessels of this style were produced in south-eastern Iran (Potts 2010: 178).

The stone vessels from Tarut and the Iranian sites share many common features, but a few differences should be mentioned. Figurative Style vessels were carved from a soft dark green to dark grey stone on Tepe Yayha (Zarins 1978: 66; Miroschedji 1973: 9. Kohl 1975: 20), whereas a number of Figurative Style vessels from Tarut were produced from a soft light grey-beige or golden stone and possibly worked on a lathe (Burkholder 1971: 306-322; Zarins 1978: 67). The divergent stone types and manufacturing techniques may suggest different production centres within south-eastern Iran.

This exploitation of different stone types was also recognised in Failaka's 3rd Millennium Figurative Style material. 85.7 % (N: 36) was made from stone type 1 (green softstone), whereas type 5 (light grey talc?) (7.1 %, N: 3) and type 4 (golden softstone) (4.7 %, N: 2) were employed to a lesser degree.

Although it seems likely that all 3rd Millennium Figurative Style vessels found on Failaka, the most typical in dark green stone type 1, derive from south-eastern Iran, a smaller percentage in the light grey-beige stone type 4 was possibly produced in an area in south-eastern Iran with easier access to stone from Arabia. This is based on the observation that the later Wadi Suq Style vessels, originating from the Oman Peninsula, were produced from the exact same stone type.

The 3rd Millennium Figurative Style material does not seem to have been employed at a domestic level since vessels rarely show any significant traces of use, e.g. soot discolouration, traces of heating or wear on the inside. The interiors of these vessels are rarely affected and are normally preserved in a good condition, whereas the external side of the bases may show some patina eller wear, probably resulting from moving and placing them on various surfaces.

30 % of the Figurative Style sherds excavated on Failaka have secondarily applied features, such as cut marks and intentional fractures which subsequently were smoothed along the broken or cut edges, evidence that raw material of the broken vessels was reused.

Zigzag variant

A bodysherd (Type 64B, fig. 67) from a vase and several rim and body fragments from a jar (Type 34B, fig. 68) were decorated with a thick zigzag band on an otherwise plain vessel body (the vase) or combined with horizontal and oblique lines on the lower part of the vessel (the jar) which may have been added at a later date.

The thick zigzag band occurs on 3rd Millennium Figurative Style vessels accompagnied by decoration elements such as bevelled squares or guilloche, but though dealt with in this context and counted with the 3rd Millennium Figurative Style the shape and decoration of the two vessels described here are rather related to "Zigzag genre 1" bowls produced in the late 3rd and early 2nd millennium BC in southeastern Iran (Potts 2003). An exact parallel for the vase was found at Kalba, UAE (David & Phillips 2008: 118-123, fig. 3). The jar resembles vessels with similar zigzag decoration (but without the decoration on the lower part) distributed from Turkmenistan over Iran to the Arabian Gulf (e.g. Susa, Tepe Yayha, Tell Abraq, Gonur 1 and Bampur) and excavated in contexts dating to 2300-1600 BC (Potts 2003: 80-87, fig. 1.4).

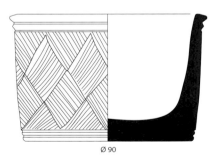

Ø 90

Fig. 27. Type 17A/46 (KM367).

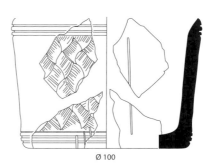

Fig. 28. Type 17A and 46
(KM3027-3028).

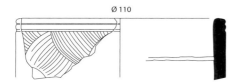

Fig. 29. Type 17A (KM3024).

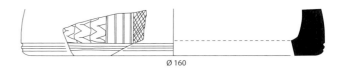

Fig. 30. Type 46 (KM3019).

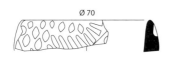

Fig. 31. Type 17B
(KM3004).

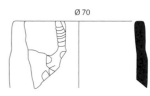

Fig. 32. Type 17B
(KM3104).

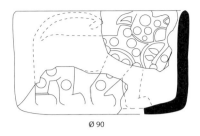

Ø 90

Fig. 33. Type 17B/44
(KM3040-3043).

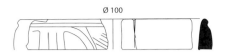

Ø 100

Fig. 34. Type 17B (KM3086).

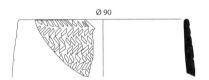

Ø 90

Fig. 35. Type 17B (KM3097).

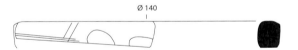

Ø 100

Fig. 36. Type 17B (KM3007).

Ø 140

Fig. 37. Type 17B (KM3085).

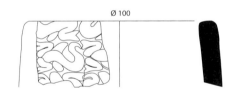

Fig. 38. Type 63A (KM3093/02, 3022, 3107).

Fig. 39. Type 63A (KM3012).

Fig. 43. Type 63A (KM3013).

Fig. 40. Type 63A (KM3074).

Fig. 41. Type 63A (KM3018).

Fig. 44. Type 63A (KM3073).

Fig. 42. Type 63A (KM3100/02).

Fig. 45. Type 63A (KM3100/01).

Fig. 46. Type 63A (KM3011).

Fig. 48.Type 63A (KM3065).

Fig. 47. Type 63A (KM3014).

Fig. 50. Type 63A (KM3105).

Fig. 49. Type 63A (KM3010).

Ø 300

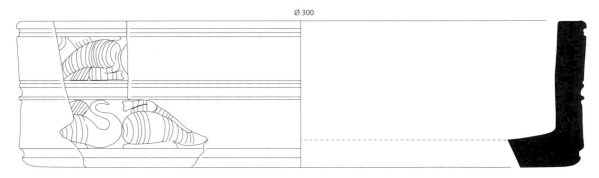

Fig. 51. Type 16/47 (KM422).

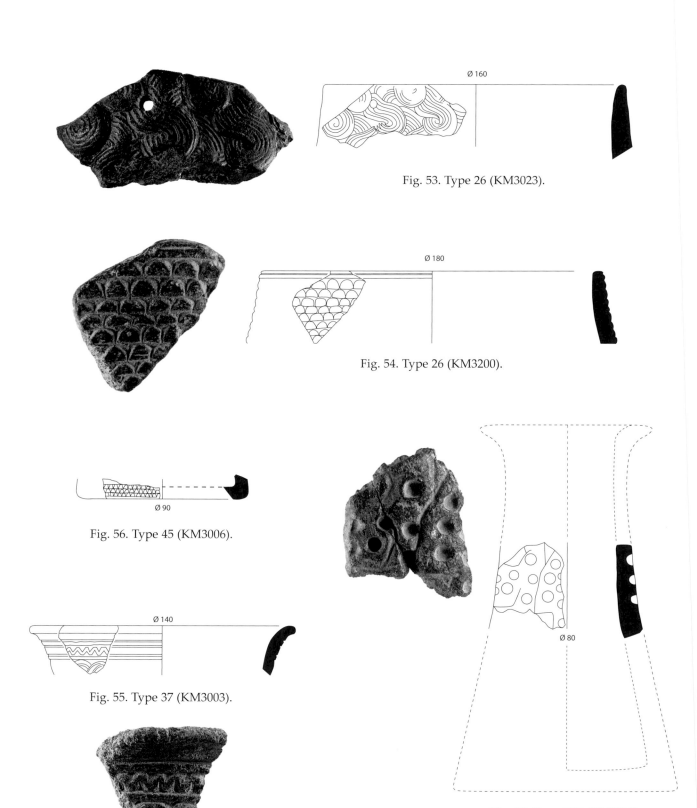

Fig.52. Type 11C (KM 3081-3114).

Fig. 53. Type 26 (KM3023).

Fig. 54. Type 26 (KM3200).

Fig. 56. Type 45 (KM3006).

Fig. 55. Type 37 (KM3003).

Fig. 57. Type 63D (KM3041).

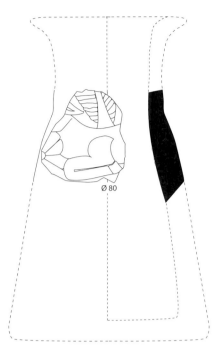

Fig. 58. Type 63F (KM3112).

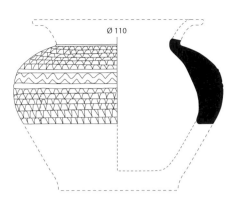

Fig. 59. Type 63B (KM3002).

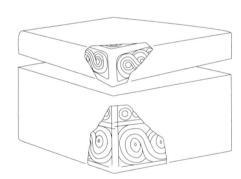

Fig. 60. Types 53D (KM3115) and 62D (KM3150).

Fig. 61. Type 63B (KM3111).

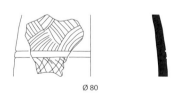

Fig. 62. Type 63C (KM3026).

Ø 180

Fig. 63. Type 63C (KM3025).

Ø 220

Fig. 64. Type 63D (KM3042).

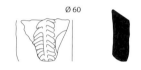

Ø 60

Fig. 65. Type 63E (KM3072).

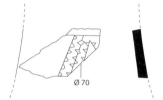
Ø 70

Fig. 67. Type 64B (F6 822).

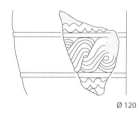
Ø 120

Fig. 66. Type 64A (KM3017).

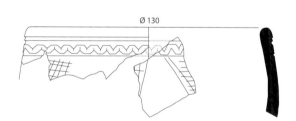
Ø 130

Fig. 68. Type 34B (KM3001-3005).

3.2. 3rd Millennium Undecorated Style

A total of 29 diagnostic fragments, distributed between nine different types, have been identified as a 3rd Millennium Undecorated Style. They have parallels from sites in Iran, Mesopotamia and the Arabian Gulf, dated to between 2600 and 1800 BC (Casanova 2003: 283-288; Zarins 1978).

Their circulation was thus contemporaneous or, at least, overlapped chronologically with the *3rd Millennium Figurative Style*. They have been excavated in mortuary contexts in Iran and in South Mesopotamia, e.g. the Royal tombs at Ur. They apparently derive from Iran, as they have been found on a number of production sites, e.g. Shahdad, attested by unfinished vessels found together with copper tools (Hakemi 1997: 15-82; Salvatori & Tosi 1997: 126).

Four different stone types are represented: a dark greenish stone, type 1 (34.5 %, N: 10), a light soft talc stone, type 5 (6.9 %, N: 2), a white-beige banded calcite, type 9 (41.4 %, N: 12) and a black stone with white spots, type 10 (6.9 %, N: 2). These stone types are associated with different vessel forms.

The 3rd Millennium Undecorated Style consists of three distinct groups described below: 1) Plain bell-shaped bowls, 2) White-beige banded calcite vessels and 3) Black and white spotted vessels.

3.2.1. Plain bell-shaped bowls

Bowls

The bell-shaped bowls are either open or closed. The open examples (type 5A, figs. 69-77) show morphological similarities with bowls excavated at cemetery sites such as Shahdad, Jiroft, Rufay'a, Ur and Hili North Tomb A. Furthermore, similar bowls were found at Tepe Yahya and the Barbar Temple on Bahrain.

A closed variant was found alongside the open bowls at Jiroft. This closed form was also recognised among the diagnostic sherds from Failaka (type 31A, figs. 78-79 and type 31B, fig. 80), which were produced from two different stone types: 1 and 5.

Bell-shaped bowls from Tepe Yahya and Tarut were carved from a soft dark green stone and their surfaces were highly polished (Zarins 1978: 70, pl. 64.43; Kohl 1975: 20). This manufacturing technique, and the use of a dark green stone (stone type 1), is likewise observed in the bell-shaped bowls from Failaka. As the contemporary Iranian Figurative Style vessels, the bell-shaped bowls were produced from stone types 1 and 5. Furthermore, they seem to occur on similar sites (e.g. Jiroft, Tarut, Ur) and in similar contexts (e.g. tombs).

In Iranian and Mesopotamian contexts bell-shaped bowls are dated to c. 2650-2100 BC (Hakemi 1997; Potts 1994: 247).

The bell-shaped bowls on Failaka show far more wear marks than vessels in the Figurative Style, and several bowls have repair holes, suggesting a different context of use. One bowl shows signs of having been recut with the intention of reuse.

Box and box lid

Two distinctive base fragments derived from boxes with square bases (type 53C, figs. 81-82) which may represent imitations of beakers woven from palm leaves (Højlund 1995: 100-102, fig. 2; Højlund & Andersen 1997: fig. 327). One box has a hole carved partly through its wall.

A lid seems to fit this box type (type 62E, figs. 83). A parallel to the box is known from al-Rufay'a (Zarins 1978: pl. 64, no. 21). These boxes and associated lid were produced from a golden softstone (stone type 4). The boxes have been exposed to heat and one has a blackish residue preserved on its internal surface.

3.2.2. White-beige banded calcite vessels

Twelve white-beige vessel fragments in the Failaka assemblage were identified as calcite (stone type 9). All have a plain, highly-polished exterior, and one sherd is inscribed with a few cuneiform symbols. All the calcite sherds show wear to some extent. None seem to have been exposed to fire and none show any secondary cut marks that could suggest reuse.

The calcite fragments derive from a diverse collection of cylindrical vases, globular jars, a bowl and a goblet. The geographical distribution of calcite vessels broadly coincides with that of the 3rd Millennium Figurative Style (Potts 1993: 387), and these vessels were in circulation in the period 2600-1800 BC (Casanova 2003: 283-288. Potts 1994: 192). Parallels are found in Bahrain, Tarut, Mesopotamia and Iran, and they are known to have been manufactured at sites in south-east Iran such as Shahdad and Shahr-I Sokhta (Ciarla 1979: 319-335; Hakemi 1997: 80-82; Casanova 2003: 286-288).

Bowl

A rim sherd (type 39A, fig. 84) possibly derives from a bowl, though too little remains for its overall shape to be assessed and no parallels have been found.

Vase

A number of tall cylindrical vases (types 39B, 39C, 58A and 71B, figs. 85-88) with flat bases, named *Série IVa* by Casanova (1991: fig. 3: 41-46, 2003: 283-288), have parallels from a wide range of sites, including Mari, Tell Brak, Girsu, Ur, Nippur, Bahrain, Susa, Shahdad, Mundigak, Kulli and Bactria.

Jar

Several fragments originate from globular jars (type 58C, figs. 89 and type 71A, figs. 90-94), which have parallels at Ur, Girsu, Susa, Tepe Hissar, Bactria, Mundigak and Aali. One body fragment is inscribed with a few cuneiform signs.

No vessels bearing cuneiform inscriptions have yet been found in Iran. This practice seems only to apply to vessels imported into Mesopotamia. Many calcite vessels were dedicated to Mesopotamian deities and deposited in the temples of Nippur, Girsu, Adab and Ur. Numerous of them were taken as war booty from foreign countries, in particular from the 'land of Elam', by the kings of Mesopotamia (Potts 1989; Potts 1993: 388).

Goblet

A base, possibly from a goblet (type 58B, figs. 95), has parallels at Shahdad and Quetta.

3.2.3. The black and white spotted vessels

Bowls

Two bowls with carinated shoulders (types 3/55 and 3, figs. 96-97) were produced in a black/grey limestone with white spots (stone type 10). These bowls have parallels in the cemetery at Shahdad in Iran, at Tarut and in Girsu in Mesopotamia. In the latter case, the bowl was inscribed with the name of Ur-Baba, the father-in-law of Gudea, ruler of Lagash (c. 2093-2080 BC) (Potts 1994: 239).

The stone type is rare and not heavily exploited in the 3rd – 2nd millennium stone vessel repertoire. The vessel form, however, is common in a group of whitish calcite bowls, called *série I* (Casanova 1991: fig. 1). It seems reasonable to suggest that the black and white spotted vessels were produced in the same region as the white calcite vessels, because of their great similarity in shape and the fact that they date to the same period, the middle to late 3rd millennium BC.

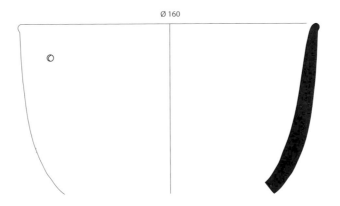

Fig. 69. Type 5A (KM3196/05).

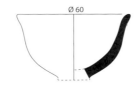

Fig. 70. Type 5A (F6.443/1129.HK).

Fig. 71. Type 5A (KM6065/03).

Fig. 72. Type 5A (KM6062/10).

Fig. 73. Type 5A (881.ACJ).

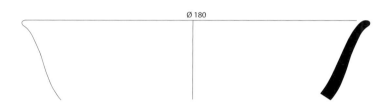

Fig. 74. Type 5A (881.ALT).

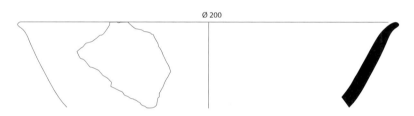

Fig. 75. Type 5A (881.AHS).

Fig. 76. Type 5A (881.ASS).

Fig. 77. Type 5A (KM6064/01).

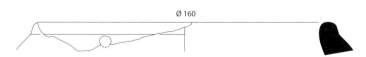

Fig. 78. Type 31A (KM3196/03).

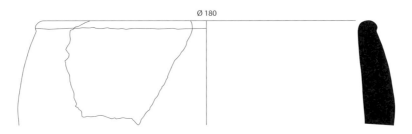

Fig. 79. Type 31A (KM6065/04).

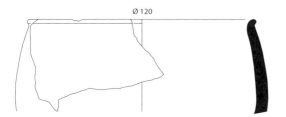

Fig. 80. Type 31B (KM1519).

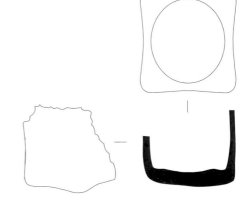

Fig. 81. Type 53C (KM3155).

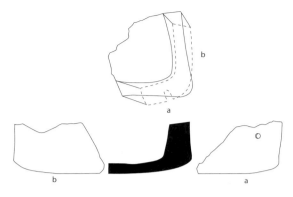

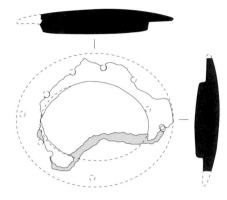

Fig. 82. Type 53C (881.BUK).

Fig. 83. Type 62E (881.ZR).

Fig. 85. Type 39B (KM1733).

Fig. 84. Type 39A (1732/02).

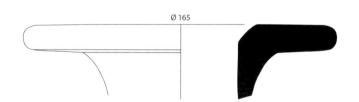

Fig. 86. Type 39C (KM1727).

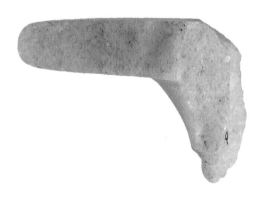

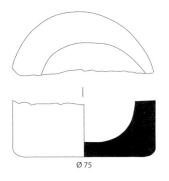

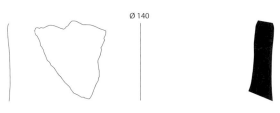

Fig. 88. Type 71B (KM1729/02).

Ø 75

Fig. 87. Type 58A (KM1731).

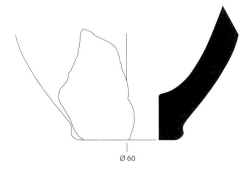

Ø 60

Fig. 89. Type 58C (KM1730).

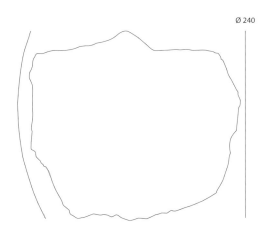

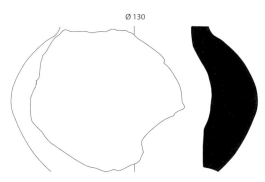

Ø 130

Fig. 91. Type 71A (KM1736).

Ø 240

Fig. 90. Type 71A (KM1726).

67

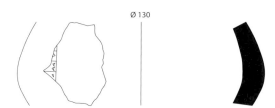

Fig. 92. Type 71A (KM1728).

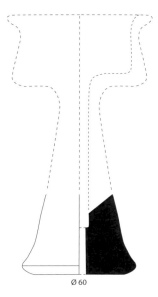

Fig. 95. Type 58B (KM1729/03).

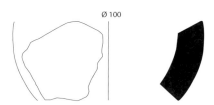

Fig. 93. Type 71A (KM1729/01).

Fig. 94. Type 71A (KM1732/01).

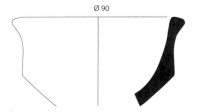

Fig. 97. Type 3 (KM1737).

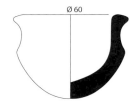

Fig. 96. Type 3/55 (KM1735).

3.3. 3rd Millennium Umm an-Nar Style

A total of 26 fragments in the diagnostic Failaka assemblage can be identified as belonging to the *Umm an-Nar Style*, dating from 2300-2000 BC (Miroschedji 1978; Potts 1993; Killick & Moon 2005: 205). These have been divided up into twelve types.

Umm an-Nar vessels have predominantly been excavated in burial contexts on the Oman Peninsula (David 1996: 34-35) and occur sparsely across the Middle East, from the Indus Valley to Central Iran and Mesopotamia, but in much smaller numbers than the previously described 3rd millennium stone vessel styles.

The Umm an-Nar Style differs from the preceding 3rd millennium styles in several other ways: vessel shapes, stone types and decorative elements. Umm an-Nar vessels have decoration incised into the surface, in simple geometric patterns, in contrast to the preceding relief-carved figurative decoration.

The Umm an-Nar vessels from Failaka were produced from an assortment of soft grey-toned stone types (stone type 3 represented by 34.6 % (N: 9), stone type 2 with 23 % (N: 6) and stone type 4 with 19.2 % (N: 5)) with the exception of one sherd in a soft greenish stone (stone type 1, 3.8 %). The remaining 15.4 % comprised unidentified stone types.

The various types and their general parallels are described below.

Bowls

Bowls are either plain (types 9A and 19A, figs. 98-101) or decorated with a single band of geometric decoration (e.g. dot in single circle or dot in double circle and horizontal lines) below the rim (types 10A, 10A/41A, and 22A, figs. 102-106). Bowls are of spherical, ellipsoid and ovaloid form. One ellipsoid bowl with a single geometric band below the rim has a spout (type 10B/60E, fig. 107). Similar bowls were excavated at Susa (Iran), Ur (Mesopotamia), al-Rufay'a (Tarut) and Saar (Bahrain).

Vases

A few vases (types 32A, 36 and 43B, figs. 108-113) were noted. Type 32A is decorated all over its surface with horizontal lines and can be compared with vases from al-Rufay'a and Hili Tomb North A. Types 36 and 43B derive from the same cylindrical vase type, decorated with dot in double circles, and they have parallels from al-Rufay'a, Hili Tomb North A and Ur.

Jars

A number of conical jars (type 33Aa, figs. 114-117) are decorated with either a band of dot in double circle and horizontal lines below the rim or horizontal lines all over the surface. Some undecorated jar bases (type 41A, figs. 118-120) appear related to the Umm an-Nar jar with a single decoration band below the rim. Similar jars were excavated at Fariq al-Akhrase (Tarut), the Barbar temple and Qala'at al-Bahrain and Hili North Tomb A.

Jar lid

A single jar lid (type 62C, fig. 121) has close parallels at Hili.

Box

A rim fragment from a box corner (type 40C, fig. 122) has no parallels. Its simple geometric decoration (dot in single circle) could be either Umm an-Nar or Wadi Suq Style, but since the material is stone type 1, otherwise only found in the 3rd millennium, it probably belongs to the Umm an-Nar category.

Spout

A unique spout (type 60C, fig. 123) should possibly also be grouped as Umm an-Nar, due to its characteristic decoration.

In general, the Umm an-Nar vessels recovered on Failaka are worn and sometimes have traces of soot and discolouration from heat, indicating that they have been involved in household activities. A few vessels have repair holes and *in situ* copper wire. Graffiti and secondary cut marks are also present, suggesting that Umm an-Nar vessels were reused to some extent for other purposes.

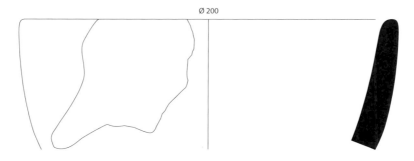

Fig. 98. Type 9A (KM3192/03).

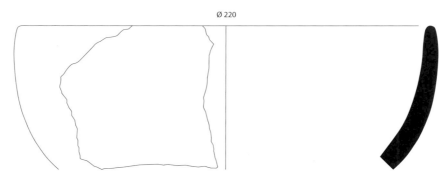

Fig. 99. Type 9A (KM6062/14).

Fig. 100. Type 19A (KM6065/02).

Fig. 101. Type 19A (KM6061/02).

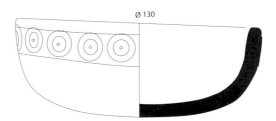

Fig. 102. Type 10A/41A (KM63).

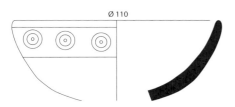

Fig. 103. Type 10A (881.AJB).

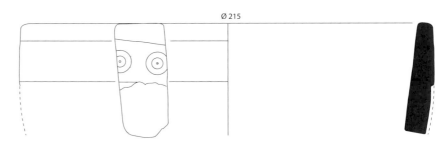

Fig. 105. Type 10A (KM8537).

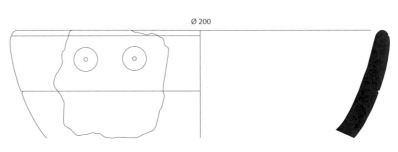

Fig. 104. Type 10A (KM3182/08).

Fig. 106. Type 22A (KM3178/06).

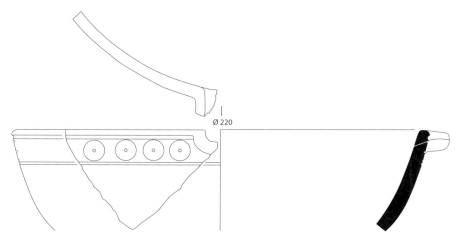

Fig. 107. Type 10B/60E (KM3130).

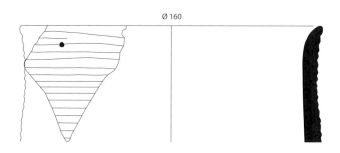

Fig. 108. Type 32A (KM6039).

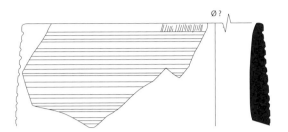

Fig. 109. Type 32A (KM6042/10).

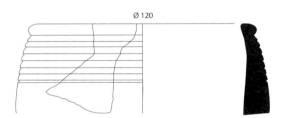

Fig. 110. Type 32A (KM6042/06).

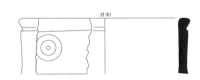

Fig. 112. Type 36 (F6.638).

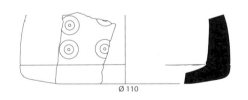

Fig. 113. Type 43B (881.ASN).

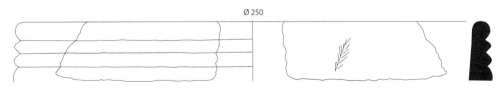

Fig. 111. Type 32A (KM6041).

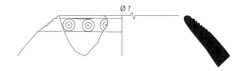

Fig. 114. Type 33Aa (KM3181/01).

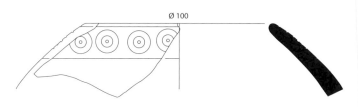

Fig. 115. Type 33Aa (KM3181/03).

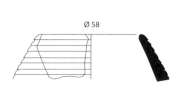

Fig. 116. Type 33Aa
(KM6042/08).

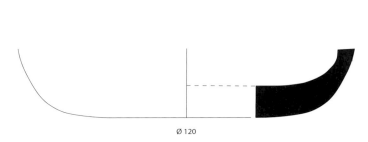

Fig. 117. Type 33Aa (KM6042/09).

Fig. 118. Type 41A (KM6100/02).

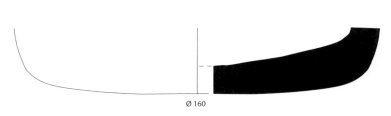

Fig. 119. Type 41A (KM6100/03).

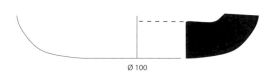

Fig. 120. Type 41A (KM6101/02).

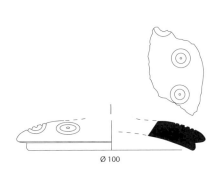

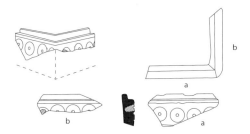

Fig. 122. Type 40C (KM3178/01-02).

Fig. 121. Type 62C (KM3126/01).

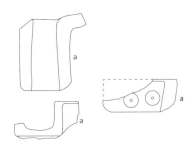

Fig. 123. Type 60B (KM3134).

3.4. 2nd Millennium Wadi Suq Style

In all 70 diagnostic sherds were assigned to the 2nd millennium *Wadi Suq Style*. This style emerged at the beginning of the 2nd millennium BC, when it replaced the Umm an-Nar Style. Wadi Suq vessels were also produced on the Oman Peninsula and were in circulation in the period c. 2000-1600 BC (Velde 2003).

The general shape of Wadi Suq vessels developed from the Umm an-Nar Style, but they are more diverse and have more extensive geometric decoration (David 1996: 39). On Failaka, Wadi Suq vessels are predominantly decorated, with only a small proportion being undecorated. The geometric decoration mainly consists of horizontal lines and dot in single or double circles set in bands below the rim, the lower parts of the bodies being ornamented with oblique lines.

Wadi Suq vessels are rarely found outside the Oman Peninsula, with only a few vessels in South Mesopotamia, Bahrain and along the Iranian coast and none in the Indus Valley (David 1996: 39).

Wadi Suq bowls excavated on Failaka often show marks of use, including soot, suggesting that they were used in household contexts, whereas most Wadi Suq vessels found on the Oman Peninsula derive from collective tombs, though they also occur in settlements (Potts 1991). The Failaka Wadi Suq bowls have a marked larger diameter (they range from 9.5 cm to 42 cm with an average of 23 cm) than those found on the Oman peninsula, a fact that may be related to their different contexts and uses.

The parallels used in comparison derive from sites on the Oman Peninsula, e.g. Shimal and Jebel al-Buhais, as well as Bahrain, e.g. Qala'at al-Bahrain and Saar, and from the Ur graves in Mesopotamia.

Three Wadi Suq style bowls had "scarification marks" close to the rim.

The material used to produce Wadi Suq vessels is normally described as soft, light grey stone (David 1996: 31-46, 2002: 317-335). This corresponds to the situation in the assemblage presented here, which includes three varieties of grey stone: type 2 with 32.8 % (N: 23), type 3 with 32.8 % (N: 23) and type 4 with 24.3 % (N: 17). The remaining 10 % (N: 7) could not be identified.

Wadi Suq vessels encompass the following 13 types and their overall parallels are referred to below.

Bowls

A number of bowls of ellipsoid (type 10C, figs. 124-126), spherical (types 9B, 13A, 13C, 21A, 21B, figs. 127-140) or ovaloid (types 12A and 22B, figs. 141-147) shape belong to the Wadi Suq repertoire. Occasionally these bowls have spouts, e.g. spherical bowls with spouts (types 9C/60E, 13B/60E, 13B/60C, 21C/41E/60E, figs. 148-151), ovaloid bowls with spouts (types 12B/60C, 22C/60C, figs. 152-153) or handles (types 12C/61D, fig. 154). Furthermore, a number of spouts (types 60D, 60E, figs. 155-158) and handles (type 61D, fig. 159) should likely be assigned to this group of Wadi Suq bowls due their overall similarity. The majority of the bowls are geometrically decorated and only a few are plain.

Rims are simple and either rounded, pointed or flattened. Flattened rims are occasionally incised with small dashes forming various decorative combinations.

Many of the bowls have well preserved manufacturing marks, e.g. chisel marks and polishing lines. The majority of the Wadi Suq bowl types have seen much exposure to heat and fire and some of these heat-exposed bowls have preserved residue on their internal surfaces. Vessel repairs are also well represented. Many of the sherds show cut marks and reworked edges resulting from later reuse.

Wadi Suq bowls found on Failaka have parallels at Shimal, Saar, Qala'at al-Bahrain and Ur.

Jars

A number of rim and base sherds derive from a group of ellipsoid jars that are decorated geometrically with horizontal lines and row(s) of dot in circle(s) below the rim and horizontal and oblique lines on the lower body; some jars have combinations of rare decorative elements (zigzag, oblique lines with dot in circle) (type 61A, figs. 160-161). Jars occur with lug handles (types 33E/41C/61A, 33E/43A/61A, 41C/61A, 61A, 61B, figs. 162-167) or without (types 33C/43A, 41B, figs. 168-172). In the case of a number of rim fragments, it could not be determined whether these jars had originally had lug handles or not (types 33Ab, 33B, figs. 173-179). Lug handles are normally located on the mid-lower to lower body, but in one case the lug handle was on the upper body (type 33E/61A, fig. 180). Furthermore, a number of bases (types 42A, 43A, figs. 181-188) have been assigned to this category, as they appear more likely to derive from jars than from bowls.

The Wadi Suq jars from Failaka occur in a variety of sizes, with a diameter ranging from 4.8 cm (the smallest) through c. 10-15 cm (medium), up to 34 cm (the largest).

Most of the vessels are worn from use; a few have repair holes and in rare instances show traces from heat. Some jars have cut marks and reworked edges, which are evidence of reuse.

The majority of comparanda for this group of jars comes from the tombs at Shimal and Jebel al-Buhais and a few of them have parallels from the settlement of Saar.

Jar lids

Six fragments of geometrically decorated circular lids with stemmed handles (type 62B, figs. 189-194) are likely partners for the jars with lug handles described above. Similar jar lids are known from tombs at Shimal and the Saar settlement.

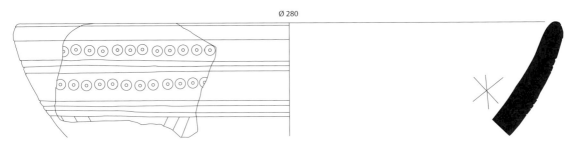

Ø 280

Fig. 124. Type 10C (KM3183/02).

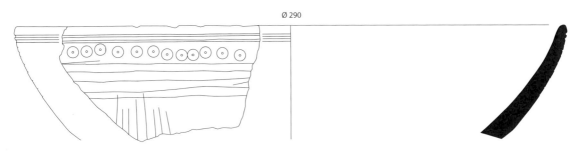

Ø 290

Fig. 125. Type 10C (KM3176/02).

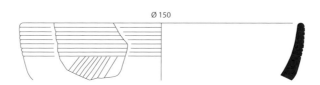

Fig. 126. Type 10C (KM3180/01).

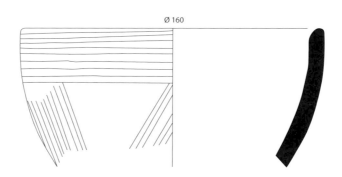

Fig. 127. Type 9B (KM6049/03).

Fig. 128. Type 9B (KM6048).

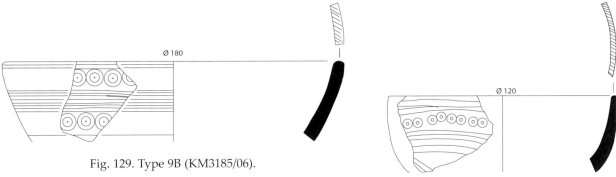

Fig. 129. Type 9B (KM3185/06).

Fig. 130. Type 9B (F6.736).

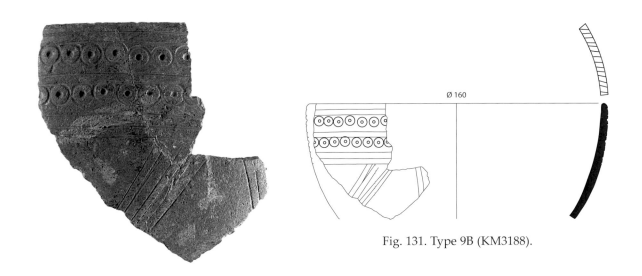

Fig. 131. Type 9B (KM3188).

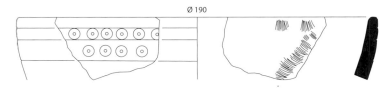

Fig. 132. Type 9B (KM3185/07).

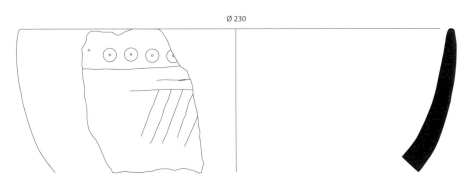

Fig. 133. Type 9B (KM3180/02).

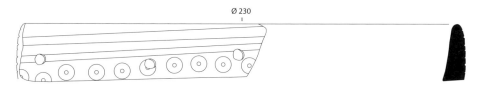

Fig. 134. Type 13A (KM3194/02).

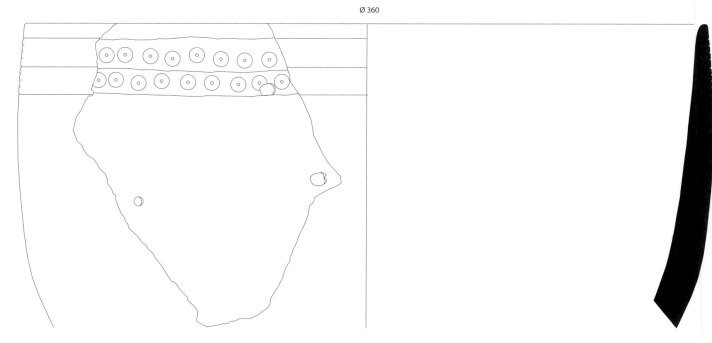

Fig. 135. Type 13C (KM3193/03).

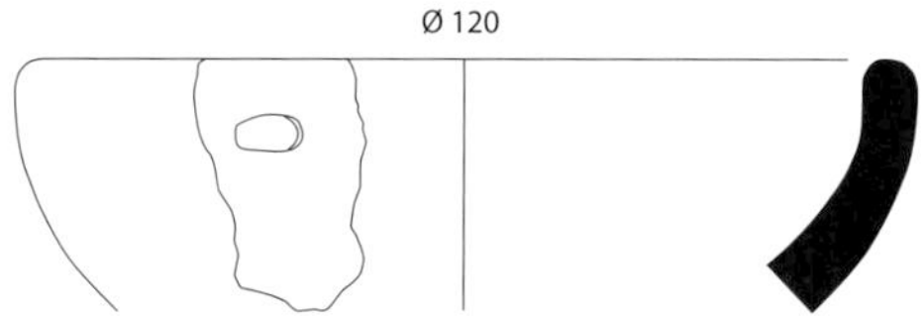

Fig. 137. Type 21A (KM3196/01).

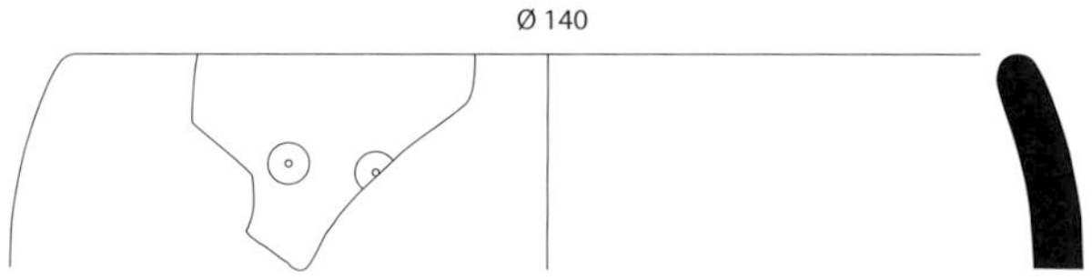

Fig. 139. Type 21B (KM3192/01).

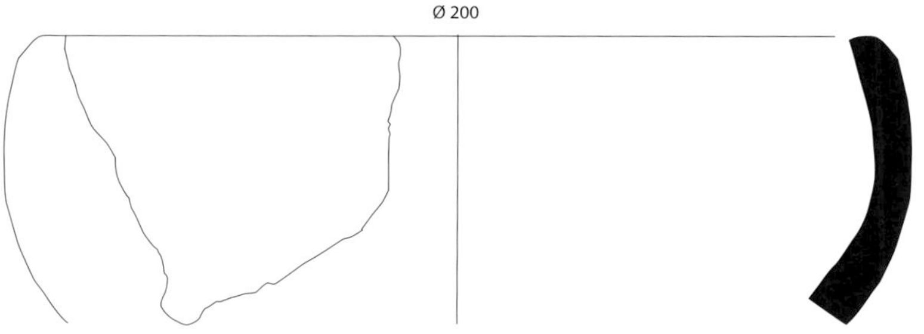

Fig. 138. Type 21A (KM6061/01).

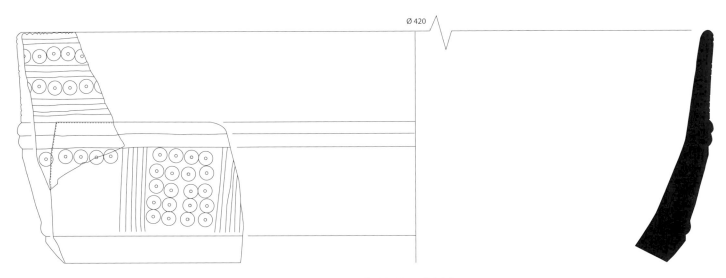

Fig. 136. Type 13C (KM3184/3186).

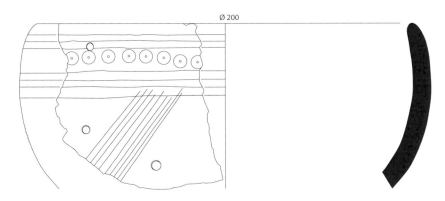

Fig. 140. Type 21B (881.BNC).

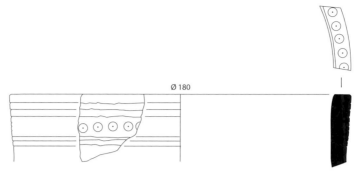

Fig. 141. Type 12A (KM3175).

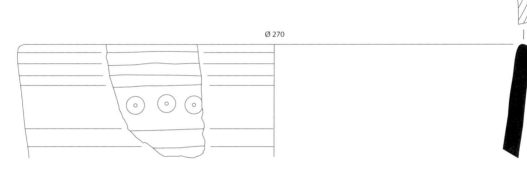

Fig. 142. Type 12A (KM3179/11).

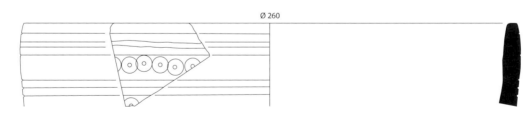

Fig. 143. Type 12A (KM3185/05).

Fig. 144. Type 22B (F6/1129.783).

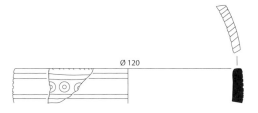

Fig. 145. Type 22B (KM3178/04).

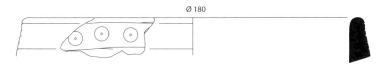

Fig. 146. Type 22B (KM3178/03).

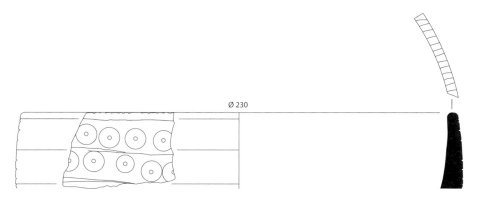

Fig. 147. Type 22B (KM3177/01).

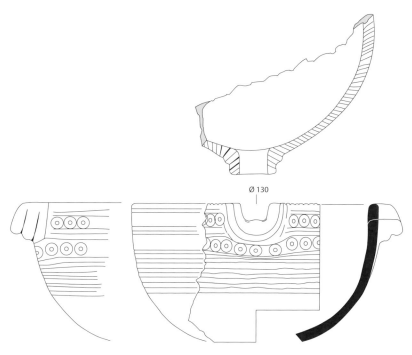

Fig. 148. Type 9C/60E (F6.732).

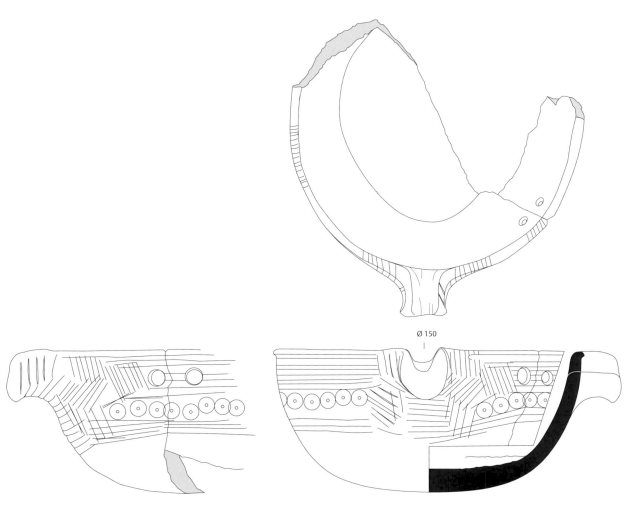

Ø 150

Fig. 149. Type 13B/60E (881.AVS, BBU).

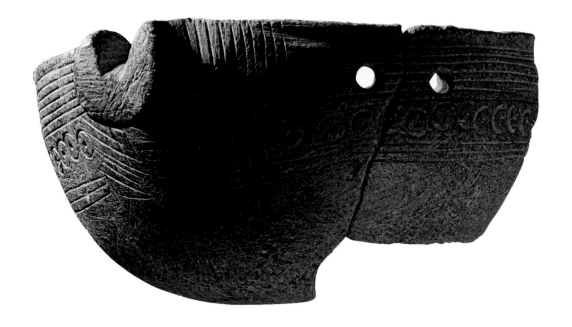

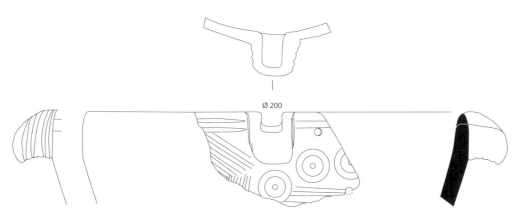

Ø 200

Fig. 150. Type 13B/60C (KM3128).

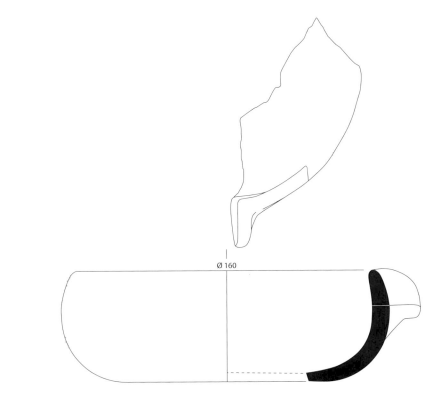

Ø 160

Fig. 151. Type 21C/41E/60E (KM6053).

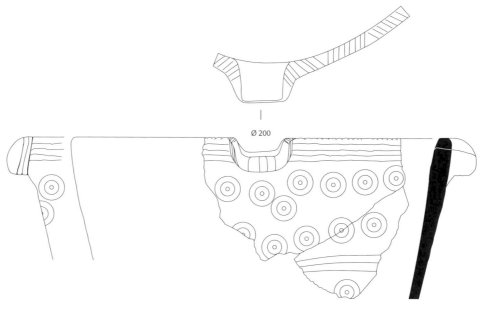

Fig. 152. Type 12B/60C (KM3129, 6076/04).

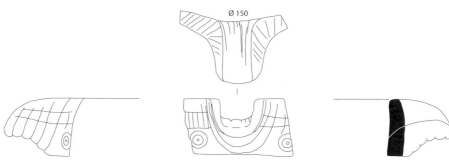

Fig. 153. Type 22C/60C (KM3131).

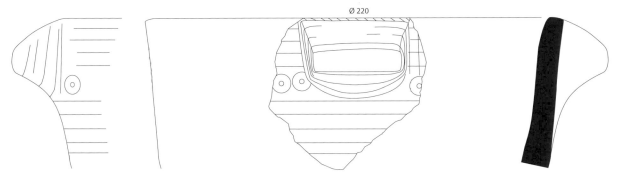

Fig. 154. Type 12C/61D (KM3141).

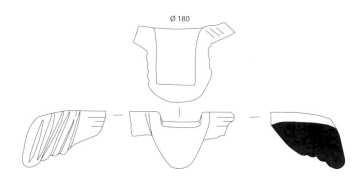

Fig. 155. Type 60D (KM3132).

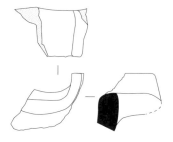

Fig. 156. Type 60E (KM3139).

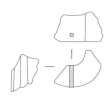

Fig. 157. Type 60E (KM1662).

Fig. 158. Type 60E (KM3133).

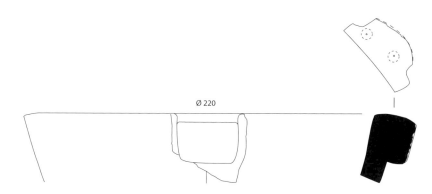

Ø 220

Fig. 159. Type 61D (KM3148/02).

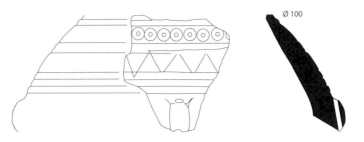

Fig. 160. Type 61A (KM3143).

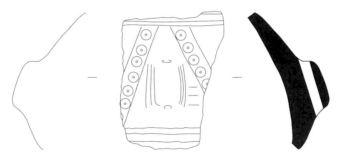

Fig. 161. Type 61A (KM3140).

Fig. 162. Type 33E/41C/61A (KM3123).

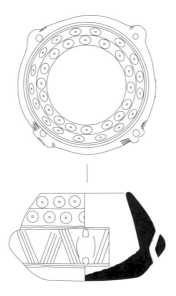

Fig. 163. Type 33E/43A/61A (KM59).

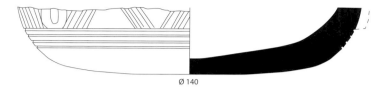

Ø 140

Fig. 164. Type 41C/61A (KM6090).

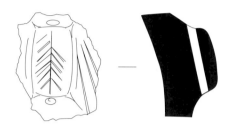

Fig. 165. Type 61A (881.AQH).

Fig. 166. Type 61A (KM3142).

Fig. 167. Type 61B (KM1493).

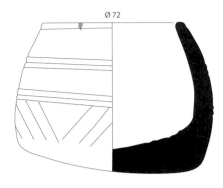

Ø 72

Fig. 168. Type 33C/43A (KM65).

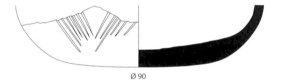

Ø 90

Fig. 169. Type 41B (KM6091/07).

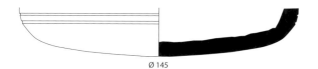
Fig. 170. Type 41B (KM6094).

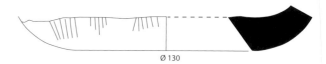
Fig. 171. Type 41B (KM6091/01).

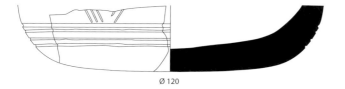
Fig. 172. Type 41B (KM6092/03).

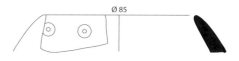
Fig. 173. Type 33Ab (KM3178/05).

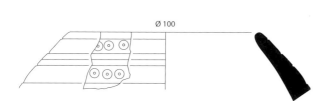
Fig. 174. Type 33Ab (KM3185/02).

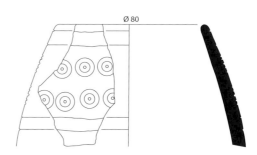
Fig. 177. Type 33Ab (KM3177/04).

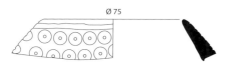
Fig. 176. Type 33Ab (KM3177/02).

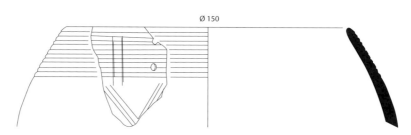
Fig. 178. Type 33Ab (KM6040).

Fig. 179. Type 33B (KM3192/02).

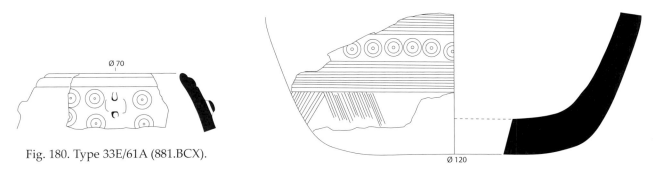

Fig. 180. Type 33E/61A (881.BCX).

Fig. 181. Type 42A (KM6068/01).

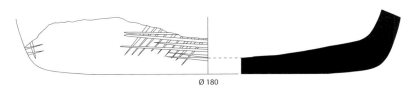

Fig. 182. Type 42A (KM6091/06).

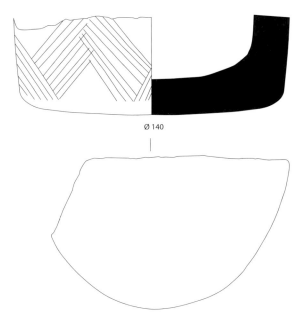

Fig. 183. Type 43A (881.AEI).

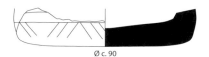

Fig. 184. Type 43A (KM6091/03).

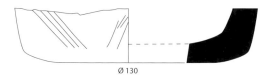

Fig. 185. Type 43A (KM6091/02).

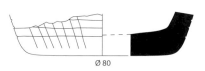

Fig. 186. Type 43A (KM6091/04).

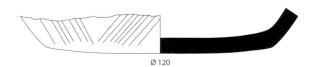

Fig. 187. Type 43A (KM6091/05).

Fig. 188. Type 43A (KM6101/04).

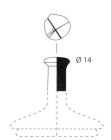

Fig. 189. Type 62B
(KM3124/01).

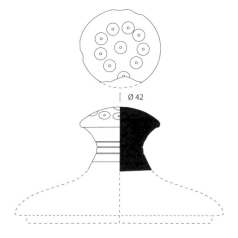

Fig. 190. Type 62B (KM3124/02).

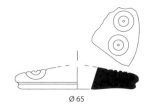

Fig. 191. Type 62B
(KM3126/02).

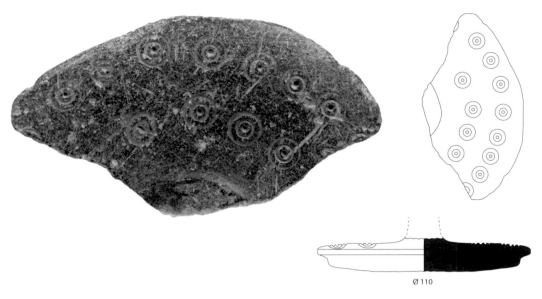

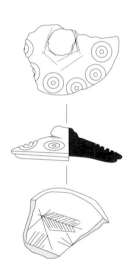

Fig. 192. Type 62B (KM3126/03).

Fig. 193. Type 62B (KM3124/03).

Fig. 194. Type 62B (KM3126/04).

3.5. 2nd Millennium Late Bronze Age Style

A total of 16 diagnostic fragments, distributed between seven types, can be referred to the *Late Bronze Age Style*, dating from 1600-1250 BC (Velde 2003: 112). The Late Bronze Age Style developed from the Wadi Suq repertoire but is more extensively decorated, with often the entire surface of the vessels being covered (Velde 2003).

Late Bronze Age types on Failaka include a number of extensively geometrically decorated bowls and jars. Only one bowl type is undecorated.

In general, these vessels show signs of being worn and a few have been repaired.

Two sherds had marks from secondary recutting followed by smoothing of the edges.

Parallels derive from Tell Abraq, Qusais, Qattara, Rumeilah, Nizwa, Shimal on the Oman Peninsula and from Ur, Mesopotamia.

Late Bronze Age vessels from Failaka are predominantly made from stone type 4 (43.8 %, N: 7), followed by type 3 (25 %, N: 4), type 2 (12.5 %, N: 2) and type 7 (12.5 %, N: 2); one sherd could not be identified. The only use of stone type 7 occurred in a Late Bronze Age type (type 33D).

The various types and their general parallels are described below.

Bowls

There are a number of undecorated conical bowl fragments (type 19C, figs. 195-196) with parallels at Tell Abraq, in addition to some densely geometrically decorated ellipsoid and spherical bowls (types 8B, 1G and 56, figs. 197-199) with parallels at Shimal.

Jars

Most of the Late Bronze Age sherds could be assigned to geometrically decorated conical (types 33D and 33F, figs. 200-202) or cylindrical jars (type 33G, fig. 203). A number of body sherds (type 70, figs. 204-209) and a single base (type 41F, fig. 210) are also associated with these jars.

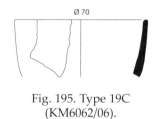

Fig. 195. Type 19C
(KM6062/06).

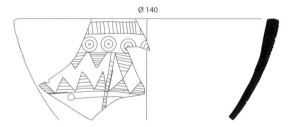

Fig. 197. Type 8B (KM3172).

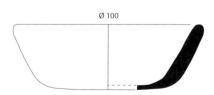

Fig. 196. Type 19C/57 (KM6054/02).

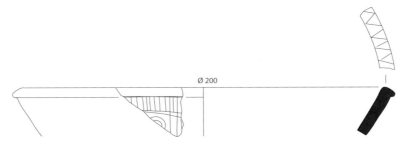

Fig. 198. Type 1G (KM3108).

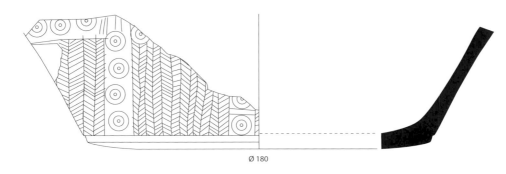

Fig. 199. Type 56 (KM1478).

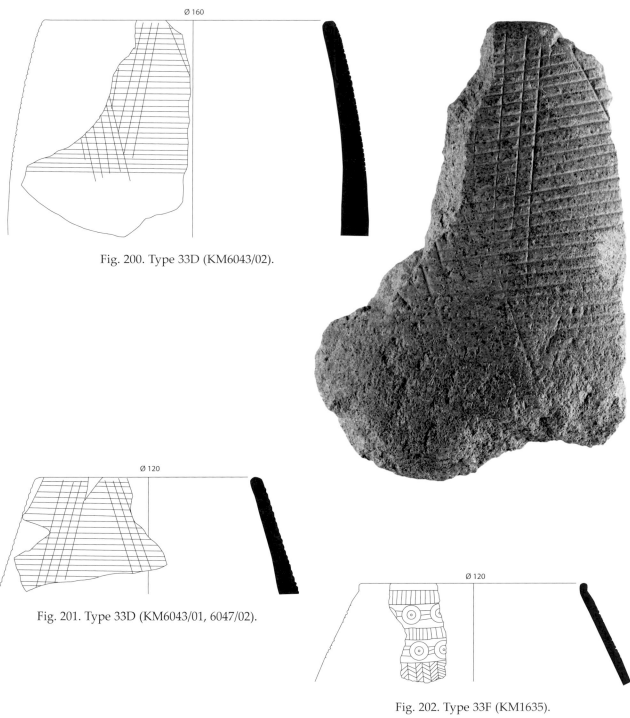

Fig. 200. Type 33D (KM6043/02).

Fig. 201. Type 33D (KM6043/01, 6047/02).

Fig. 202. Type 33F (KM1635).

Fig. 203. Type 33G (881.ZV).

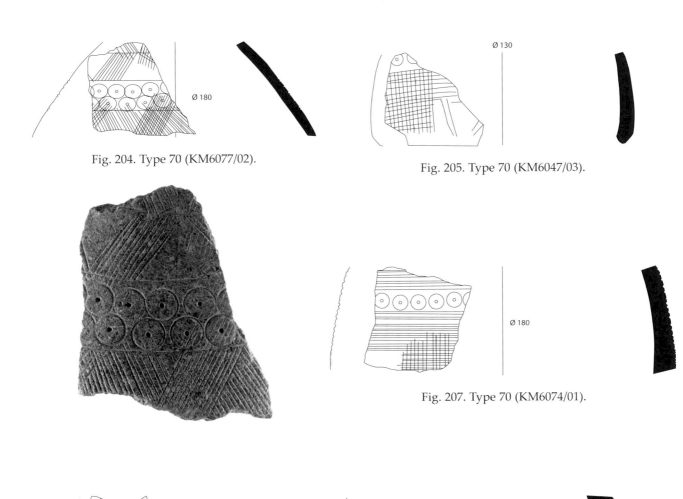

Fig. 204. Type 70 (KM6077/02).

Ø 180

Ø 130

Fig. 205. Type 70 (KM6047/03).

Ø 180

Fig. 207. Type 70 (KM6074/01).

Ø 280

Fig. 206. Type 70 (KM6074/02).

Ø 80

Fig. 208. Type 70 (KM6077/03).

Ø 80

Fig. 209. Type 70 (KM6077/01).

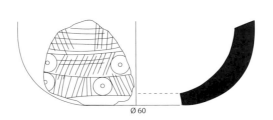

Ø 60

Fig. 210. Type 41F (881.AHU).

3.6. 2nd Millennium Figurative Failaka Style

Three new soft-stone vessel styles have been identified in the Failaka assemblage: *Figurative, Geometric* and *Plain Failaka Styles*. Despite the different types of decoration, some overall morphological characteristics and stone types link these three styles together. The dating range of the styles is problematic, but it will be argued below that they belong in the mid second millennium BC.

61 figuratively decorated sherds fall outside the definition of the *3rd Millennium Figurative Style* described above. The existence of such a special group has previously been suggested by Kjærum (pers. comm.), and Howard-Carter reported that Al-Gailani Werr, acting as a consultant to the Kuwait National Museum, singled out a number of figuratively decorated vessel fragments excavated by the Danish team, which she termed 'Failaka Unique' and dated to the Ur III-Isin/Larsa or Old Babylonian periods (Howard-Carter 1989 p. 255, figs. 6-9).

In the course of the present analysis of the complete stone vessel assemblage excavated by the Danish team, the significance of this 2nd millennium stone vessel style has become increasingly clear and it is proposed to name it the *Figurative Failaka Style*.

The Figurative Failaka Style has a decorative layout and a set of decorative elements and figurative themes that are unknown in the 3rd Millennium Figurative Style. The entire surface of the 3rd Millennium Figurative Style vessels is covered with decoration from rim to base in an unbroken flow, whereas the Figurative Failaka Style vessels are divided into illustrative panels separated by horizontal encircling hatched bands. The 3rd Millennium Figurative Style vessels on Failaka are primarily cylindrical flat-based bowls and vases, whereas Figurative Failaka Style vessels are ellipsoidal or spherical bowls, often with rounded, disc or ring bases.

The decoration applied to the Figurative Failaka Style was carved in a similar fashion to the 3rd Millennium Figurative Style, with the surface around the motives being removed, making the actual decoration stand out in a low relief. However, a different set of decorative elements (such as a hatched band, branch, fish, ship and celestial symbol sometimes carried on the back of an animal) was used, rather than the decorative elements defined by Kohl for the 3rd Millennium Figurative Style. Humans are depicted on several 3rd Millennium Figurative Style vessels but always in scenes showing men wrestling with snakes or beasts. These combatant scenes involving humans are not represented in the Failaka Figurative Style. A number of elements, such as scorpion, ungulate, feline, bird and rosette do, however, appear in both groups.

The Figurative Failaka Style was predominantly manufactured using stone type 4 with 57.3 % (N: 35), followed by stone type 2 with 11.5 % (N: 7) and, to a lesser degree, stone types 1 (1.6 %, N: 1) and 6 (1.6 %, N: 1). Seventeen pieces (27.8 %) could not be identified. This distribution is completely different from that seen in the 3rd Millennium Figurative Style, which was primarily made using stone type 1. Stone types 2 and 4 were both also used to manufacture Wadi Suq vessels and this could suggest that the stone was obtained from the same or similar sources.

One third of the Failaka Figurative vessels (N: 20) show signs of having been reused to some extent, showing secondary cut marks, breaks and reworking of broken edges and there is at least one pendant which was reworked from a Figurative Failaka bowl (fig. 442).

It has not been possible to locate stone vessels from other sites that can serve as parallels for the Figurative Failaka style, but other types of comparanda, primarily from Failaka, will be referred to below, specifically Dilmun stamp seals in Style III.

This style comprises 61 diagnostic specimens (15.5 %), distributed between 19 different types which are described below with their general parallels.

Bowls

The majority of the Figurative Failaka vessels are bowls of spherical or ellipsoid shape. Some are open (types 5B, 7A and 7B/60E, figs. 211-215), others are closed (types 20B, 27, 27/41D, 41D, 28A, 29/48C/66A, figs. 216-228). Bowls have profiled protruding rims, often with a hatched or guilloche band just below. The hatched band is well represented and links a number of rims, body sherds and bases together. This motif is repeated several times on these bowls. Bases have rounded, disc or ring footings. A number of body sherds (types 65A, 65B, 65C, 66B, 67A, 67B, 67C, figs. 229-254) are associated with these figurative bowls, based on their similar shape and decoration. Bowls are occasionally inscribed in cuneiform script.

One bowl displays a hybrid combination of figurative and geometric elements (type 1F/51E, fig. 255).

It is decorated with a number of palm branches positioned between protruding horizontal ledges, as well as multiple dots in single circles on the body and oblique lines incised on top of the flattened rim. The morphology of the bowl and its stone type (type 6) are also without exact parallels, though there is a certain resemblance to the stepped ridges found on bases belonging to the Figurative, Geometric and Plain Failaka vessels, as well as the broad base with the special transition to the belly (e.g. fig. 269).

The Figurative Failaka Style bowls all show some degree of wear, but their interiors were less affected than the external surfaces. A few bowls have possibly been exposed to heat, but none show traces of soot.

Bases

A few base types are associated with the Figurative Failaka Style. Types 42B, 43C and 51B (figs. 256, 264-266) appear to be either from a jar or a vase, whereas the other bases (types 48C, 50B and 51C, figs. 267-269) more probably originate from bowls. Types 50B and 51C, the disk base with concentric stepped ridges and the ring base, are similar to base types found in the Geometric Failaka Style (e.g. Type 20C/48B, 68B) and the Plain Failaka Style (e.g. Types 20A/50A-51A, 48A, 68A), indicating contemporaneity between the three styles.

Jars

A few sherds are from jars. One is ovaloid with several incised horizontal lines below the rim (type 34A, fig. 270) and another is more ellipsoid (type 30, fig. 271). Both jars show evidence of reuse in the form of secondary cuts and breaks.

Box

A corner of a square box (type 40B/53B, fig. 272) in stone type 4 is decorated with a human figure and a boat.

The Figurative Failaka Style and Style III stamp seals

Stamp seals of Style III offer some interesting similarities to the Figurative Failaka Style, with respect to decorative elements and motifs, which are relevant to a discussion of the cultural provenience and dating of the Figurative Failaka Style.

Stamp seals are typical for the Dilmun area, occurring for the first time in the 21st century BC and continuing into the first half of the 2nd millennium. Several styles, IA, IB, II and III, have been distinguished by Kjærum on the basis of the seals found on Failaka and in Bahrain (Kjærum 1980, 1983, 1994,

2003).

A total of 22 Style III stamp seals (figs. 273-285) and 1 impression from Failaka have been published (Kjærum 1983: nos. 45-50, 302-304, 311, 344-351 and 366; Glassner 1984: figs. 4-6. Pic 1990 no. 18) and 12 seals are known from Bahrain (Denton 1997: 174-189; Al-Sindi 1999). They have been extensively discussed by Denton, who was the first to mention their similarities to decorated stone vessels found on Failaka (Denton 1997: 178).

Seals of Style III represent a complete departure from the earlier styles (I-II) in the Dilmun seal tradition. The radial and chaotic composition of the previous seals is completely absent and replaced by an arrangement of the motifs in vertical panels, into which cuneiform inscriptions are often integrated, clearly an influence from Babylonian cylinder seals (Højlund 1989: 11. Denton 1997: 176-177).

The fact that cuneiform inscriptions are clearly integrated into the design of the Style III seals is an important warning to treat the cuneiform inscriptions on the Failaka Figurative Style vessels as secondary. They are indeed an original part of the decoration.

The majority of Style III seals show humans and in one case bull-men in a gesture of worship (figs. 273-279, 284-285) (Kjærum 1983: nos. 45, 46, 49, 304, 345, 348, 350, 351), i.e. with both arms raised and the hands near the face, a well-known motif on Mesopotamian cylinder seals of the Isin-Larsa, Old Babylonian and Kassite periods (Collon 1987, nos. 140, 155-157, 166-172, 235-236, 245). On three seals the worshippers hold a branch in one hand (figs. 275-277) and sometimes they flank a central pole or staff (fig. 285).

The worshipper's physical appearance, i.e. gestures, clothing, hairstyle, branch, is strikingly similar to figures carved on Failaka Figurative Style bowls (figs. 213 (type 7A), 256-263 (type 42B), 233 (type 65B), 242-243 (type 66B), 239 (type 65C).

A horizontal hatched band is associated with these scenes, on both seals (figs. 272-278, 280, 283, 285) and vessels, and the same band is seen on a bowl of type 7B. This bowl is not decorated with worship scenes but it has a cuneiform script referring to the deity PA.NI.PA (fig. 215). This deity is also mentioned on two Style III seals where it is associated with the god Inzak of Agarum (Glassner 2008: 174, 196, nos. 3 and 5). The rounded decorated spout has close parallels to Wadi Suq spouts (type 60E) from the 2nd millennium BC.

A number of poles or standards are illustrated on the Failaka Style vessels, though their upper parts are rarely preserved (figs. 233, 234, 239) and found also on Style III seals. In one case (fig. 234) a pole has incised horizontal strokes, which are also seen on several Style III seals (fig. 276) (Kjærum 1983: 143, no. 351).

Three Style III seals show a garbed man with a

branch behind his back seated on a stool with concave seat and sides (figs. 276-278). Exactly the same motif is seen on a Failaka Figurative Style vessel (fig. 233). Compare the shape of the stool with the shape of a stone altar from Umm es-Sujur on Bahrain, dating from 2000-1800 BC (Konishi 1996; Lombard 1999, no. 118).

Several celestial symbols, star, sun and crescent moon, occur on both Style III seals (figs. 279-280, 284-285) and the Figurative Failaka Style vessels (figs. 213, 218, 236, 244-248, 256, 270). They are either worshipped by humans, carried on the back of animals or seen in combination with a bull-man. One particular sherd (fig. 245), with a combined symbol of sun, moon and star, has an exact parallel on a Style III seal excavated by Howard-Carter at Tell F5 (fig. 279).

These celestial symbols are well-known in 2nd millennium Mesopotamian iconography (e.g. Harper & Pittman 2005: 104-105, fig. 73, 19th-18th cent. BC. King 1912, no. XI, p. 76, pls. I-IV, 12th cent. BC), where they may represent deities. The sun represents the god of justice Shamash/Utu. He was the son of the moon god Sin/Nanna, who is represented by a full or crescent moon. The moon god can also be depicted as a bull or a cattle herder. He was worshipped in particular in the marshy areas of Southern Mesopotamia. Sin's daughter was the goddess of Inanna/Ishtar, a fertility goddess, whose symbol is the star of Venus, the morning and evening star. Together, these three gods formed a celestial triad of divinities worshipped in the 3rd and 2nd millennium BC (Nijhowne 1999: 31; Schneider 2011: 59; Jacobsen 1976: 121-127, 134-143)

A unique vessel (type 42B: figs. 256-257) has two panels showing processional scenes, in which a large bearded face is being worshipped. The face is full-frontal, unlike all other human representations in the Figurative Failaka Style, and there is a large rosette or disc over the head. In a repeating pattern, three people with their arms raised walk in procession towards the face. Low-lying crescent moons are positioned between the heads of the worshippers. The upper panel, demarcated by hatched bands, shows several bovines carrying a sun/moon on their backs. The face must represent a deity, although his identity is presently unknown.

The face does not appear on other Figurative Failaka Style vessels, but several other decorative elements seen on this specific vessel are shared with most of the Figurative Failaka Style vessels, e.g. the hatched band, a celestial symbol carried on back of a bovine and branches. This unique vessel was produced in stone type 4, which was used for more than half of the Figurative Failaka Style vessels.

A small terracotta head from Tell F3 (fig. 281) shows a similar oval face, with bushy eyebrows above large oval eyes and the lower face covered by a full beard. Comparable portraits with similar facial features were incised on two Style III stamp seals (figs. 282-283).

A number of other decorative elements seen on both Style III seals and Figurative Failaka Style vessels should be briefly noted: The palm branch (figs. 213, 233, 243, 256, 258) is rather common. Nashef (1986: 346) suggested that it represented the main god of Dilmun, Inzak of Agarum. This idea is interesting in relation to a specific sherd which displays humans in procession, associated with a branch and a cuneiform inscription mentioning *the Temple of Inzak* (fig. 242). Bull-men, bovines and rams (Types: 7A, 27, 30, 28A, 42B, 65B, 67B), rosettes (Type 29) and maritime life in the guise of water, fish and boats (Types: 28A, 42B, 42B, 50B, 51C, 65B, 40/53B) are also represented.

The majority of the Figurative Failaka Style vessels (e.g. type 65A, fig. 229) are decorated with horizontal hatched bands positioned either close to the rim or the base or used to separate decorative panels. A similar hatched band was carved on a soft stone vessel excavated at Qala'at al-Bahrain and dating from the Kassite period IIIb1, c. 1400 BC (Højlund & Andersen 1997: 83, fig. 327).

On Style III seals, one or two figures are occasionally seen standing on top of a horizontal rectangular hatched panel (figs. 273-278, 280, 283, 285), which may represent a temple platform or podium (Denton 1997: 178). Since there is a similarity between the themes depicted on Figurative Failaka Style vessels and those on Style III seals, i.e. in the form of figures walking in procession or standing in a gesture of worship on a hatched band, it can be suggested that the hatched bands on the Figurative Failaka vessels were likewise intended to evoke associations with a temple setting.

On one sherd (Type 65C, fig. 239) a big bird with a crooked beak and outfolded raised wings faced by an oxe (possibly the same bowl as fig. 240) is positioned below a standard or altar that is being worshipped by humans. The posture of the bird is similar to birds carved on six Style III seals (figs. 284-285) (Kjærum 1983 nos. 48, 289, 304). It should be noted that in the Sealand, Dilmun's neighbour to the north, several gods were worshipped who could take the form of a bird (Dalley 2009: 78).

Style III represents the final stage in the evolution of stamp seals in the Dilmun area, i.e. the upper Arabian Gulf. Considering the many detailed similarities in motives and elements between Style III and the Figurative Failaka Style, they must be contemporary and produced in the same cultural environment. There can be no doubt that Failaka was part of, if not the centre, of this cultural sphere. The number of Style III seals found on Failaka exceeds the number found on Bahrain and the Style III seals found in Bahrain are of inferior quality. This tallies with the fact that no Figurative Failaka Style vessels occur in Bahrain.

Unfortunately, none of the Style III seals have been found in good, stratified contexts, so their dating is still obscure. Denton reviewed the scanty evidence, including the orthography of the cuneiform inscriptions on some of the seals, and suggested that Style III seals should probably be dated to the terminal phase of Qala'at al-Bahrain period II or a very early phase of Qala'at al-Bahrain period IIIa (Denton 1997: 181), i.e. from the late Old Babylonian period or the Early Kassite period (fig. 2).

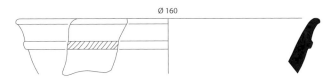

Fig. 211. Type 5B (KM3199).

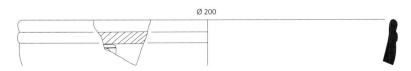

Fig. 212. Type 7A (KM3076).

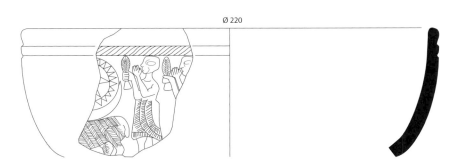

Fig. 213. Type 7A (KM1513).

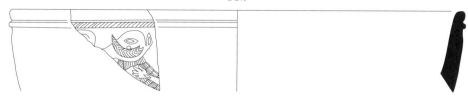

Ø 240

Fig. 214. Type 7A (KM3045).

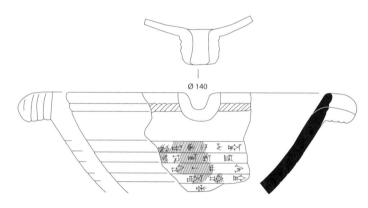

Ø 140

Fig. 215. Type 7B/60E (KM1517).

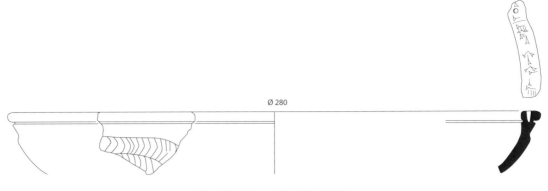

Fig. 216. Type 20B (KM1520).

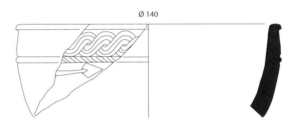

Fig. 217. Type 27 (KM3070).

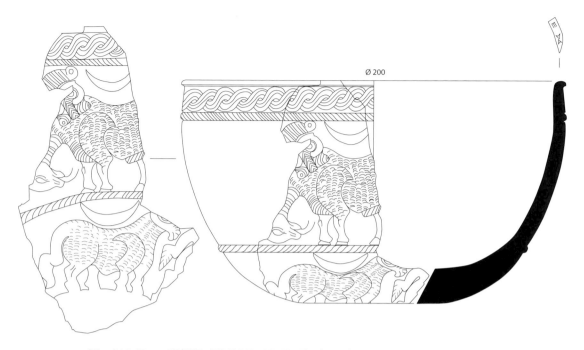

Fig. 218. Type 27/41D (KM3051, 3082). The base fragment (KM1394) derives from the Johns Hopkins University excavation at Tell F5.

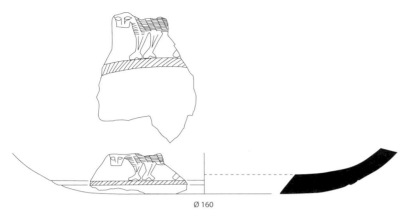

Fig. 219. Type 41D (KM3052).

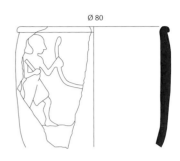

Fig. 220. Type 28A (KM3020).

Ø 130

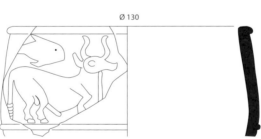

Fig. 221. Type 28A (KM3044).

Ø 160

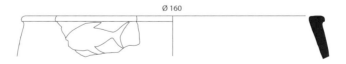

Fig. 222. Type 28A (KM3059).

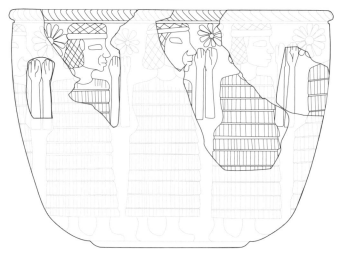

Ø 170

Fig. 223. Type 29/48C/66A. Reconstructed on the basis of KM371, 3008/01, 3008/02, 3036, 3037, 3075, 3101, 3008/03, 3038/01-03, and 2091.

Fig. 225. Type 29/66A (KM3008/01, 3037).

Fig. 224. Type 29/66A (KM371, 3008/02).

Fig. 226. Type 66A (KM3075).

Fig. 227. Type 66A (KM3036).

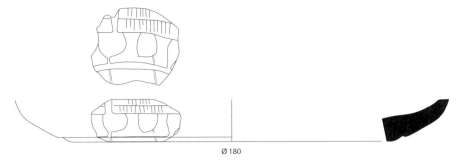

Ø 180

Fig. 228. Type 48C (KM3101).

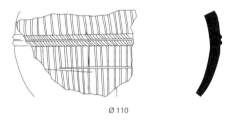

Ø 110

Fig. 229. Type 65A (KM3095).

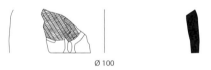

Ø 100

Fig. 231. Type 65B (KM3054).

Fig. 230. Type 65B (881.ALN, ABQ).

Ø 100

Fig. 233. Type 65B (KM3035).

Ø 100

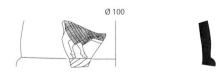

Fig. 232. Type 65B (KM3055).

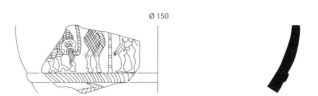

Fig. 234. Type 65B (KM3021).

Fig. 235. Type 65B (KM3049).

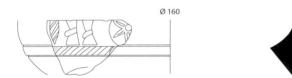

Fig. 236. Type 65C (KM3053).

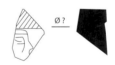

Fig. 237. Type 65C (KM3118).

Fig. 238. Type 65C (KM3033).

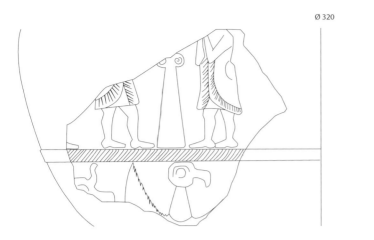

Fig. 239. Type 65C (KM3064).

Fig. 240. Type 65C (KM3000).

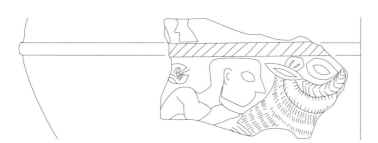

Ø 360

Fig. 241. Type 65C (KM1514).

Fig. 243. Type 66B (881.ABE).

Fig. 242. Type 66B (F3.138/881.HU).

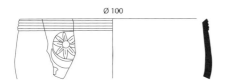

Fig. 244. Type 67A (KM3106).

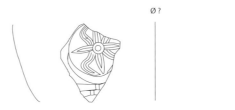

Fig. 245. Type 67A (KM3029).

Fig. 246. Type 67A (KM3102).

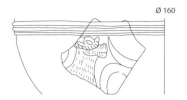

Fig. 247. Type 67A (KM3015).

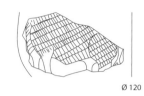

Fig. 248. Type 67A (KM3103).

Fig. 249. Type 67B (KM1637).

Fig. 250. Type 67B (881.R).

Fig. 251. Type 67B (KM3066).

Fig. 252. Type 67B (KM3046).

Fig. 253. Type 67C (KM3084).

Fig. 254. Type 67C (KM3056).

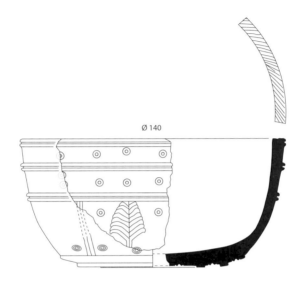

Fig. 255. Type 1F/51E (KM3063, A129-X454).

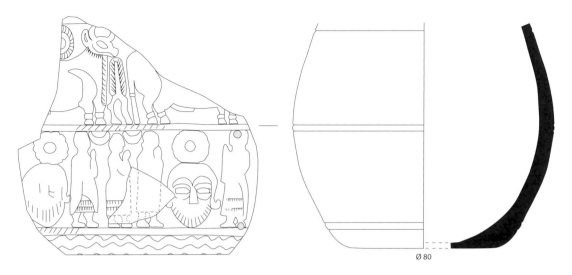

Fig. 256. Vessel with base of type 42B
(drawing based on KM372, 3030, 3031, 3032, 3099 and X147-A30).

Ø 80

Fig. 257. Vessel with base of type 42B, upper part
missing, with decoration reconstructed.

Fig. 258. Body sherd (KM372).

Fig. 259. Body sherd (KM3032).

Fig. 260. Body sherd (KM3031).

Fig. 261. Body sherd (KM3099).

Fig. 263. Type 42B (KM3030).

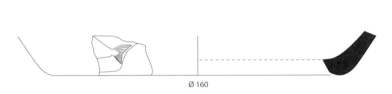

Ø 160

Fig. 264. Type 42B (KM3060).

Fig. 262. Body sherd (X147-A30).

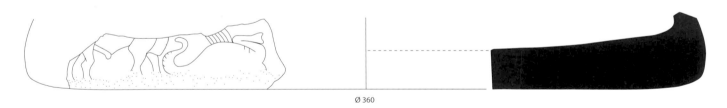

Ø 360

Fig. 265. Type 43C (KM3098).

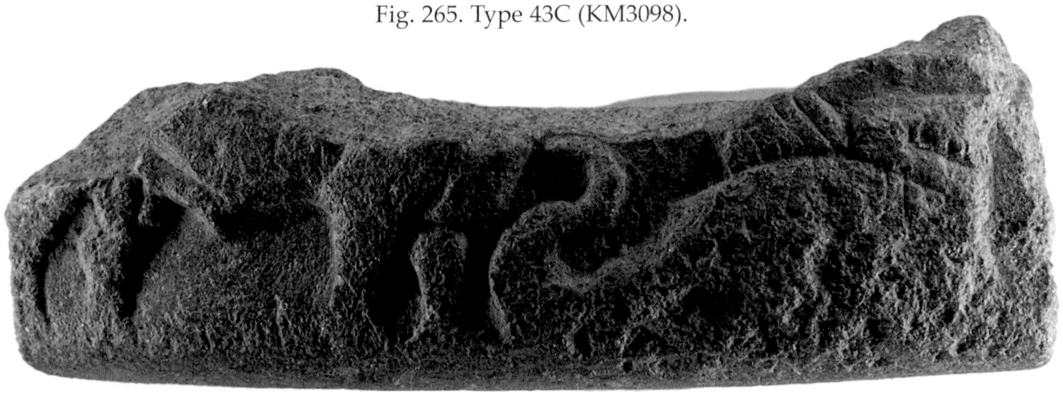

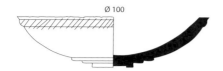

Fig. 266. Type 51B (KM6051, 6081/02).

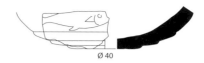

Fig. 268. Type 50B (KM3058).

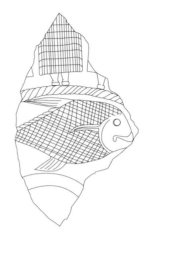

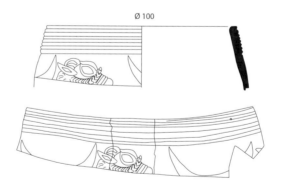

Fig. 267. Type 48C (KM1515).

Fig. 269. Type 51C (KM425).

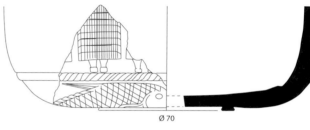

Fig. 270. Type 34A (KM3048, 3068, 3069).

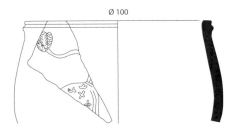

Ø 100

Fig. 271. Type 30 (KM3057).

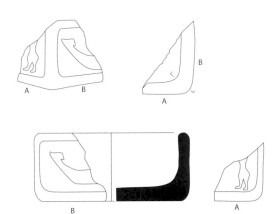

Fig. 272. Type 40B/53B (KM3062).

Fig. 273. Style III stamp seal. Persons in a gesture of worship. 2:1 (Kjærum 1983 no. 49) (Photographer Jozef Ďuriš, Kuwait-Slovak Archaeological Mission/KSAM).

Fig. 274. Style III stamp seal. Persons in a gesture of worship. 2:1 (Kjærum 1983 no. 345) (Photographer Jozef Ďuriš, Kuwait-Slovak Archaeological Mission/ KSAM).

Fig. 275. Style III stamp seal. Man in gesture of worship holding branch. 2:1 (Kjærum 1983 no. 350) (Photographer Jozef Ďuriš, Kuwait-Slovak Archaeological Mission/KSAM).

Fig. 276. Style III stamp seal, bifacial. Left: Men on boat in a gesture of worship. One man holding a branch. Right: Garbed man seated on stool facing worshipper. Pole or standard and branch behind seated person. 2:1 (Kjærum 1983 no. 351) (Photographer Jozef Ďuriš, Kuwait-Slovak Archaeological Mission/KSAM).

Fig. 277. Style III stamp seal. Garbed man seated on stool facing worhipper, placed on hatched panel. Behind persons branches. 2:1(Kjærum 1983 no. 302) (Photographer Jozef Ďuriš, Kuwait-Slovak Archaeological Mission/KSAM).

Fig. 278. Style III stamp seal. Garbed man seated on stool facing worshipper, placed on hatched panel. Behind seated person branch. 2:1 (Pic 1990 no. 18) (Photographer Jozef Ďuriš, Kuwait-Slovak Archaeological Mission/KSAM).

Fig. 279. Style III stamp seal, worshippers and celestrial symbols. 2:1 (Johns Hopkins excavations at Tell F5) (Photographer Jozef Ďuriš, KSAM).

Fig. 280. Style III stamp seal. Celestrial symbols above bull placed on hatched panel, reverse side of fig. 275. 2:1 (Kjærum 1983 no. 350)
(Photographer Jozef Ďuriš, KSAM).

Fig. 281. Bearded face in terracotta from Tell F3 (KM1492).

Fig. 283. Style III stamp seal with bearded face above bull; reverse side of fig. 274. 2:1 (Kjærum 1983 no. 345)
(Photographer Jozef Ďuriš, KSAM).

Fig. 282. Style III stamp seal with bearded face. 2:1 (Kjærum 1983 no. 347)
(Photographer Jozef Ďuriš, KSAM).

Fig. 284. Style III stamp seal. Birds with crooked beaks. 2:1 (Kjærum 1983 no. 48)
(Photographer Jozef Ďuriš, KSAM).

Fig. 285. Style III stamp seal. Birds, bull-men and men in a gesture of worship around central pole or standard. 2:1 (Kjærum 1983 no. 304)
(Photographer Jozef Ďuriš, KSAM).

3.7. 2nd Millennium Geometric Failaka Style

A total of 38 sherds were geometrically decorated, but could not be grouped with either Umm an-Nar, Wadi Suq or Late Bronze Age Styles due to their different vessel shapes and decoration layout. Their vessel shapes and the stone types used to produce them, however, are similar to those of the Figurative Failaka and the Plain Failaka Styles and a general contemporaneity between the three styles is assumed. This group was named *Geometric Failaka Style*. The style includes 14 types of bowls and a jar type; these were manufactured from several different stone types. The most common stone is type 4 with 66.7 % (N: 26), followed by stone types 2 (15.4 %, N: 6) and 3 (7.7 %, N: 3). The remaining stone types (11, 5 and 6) are each only represented by a single sherd (each 2.5 %) and one sherd could not be identified (2.5 %, N: 1).

Of the 38 Geometric Failaka style sherds, nine had been worked secondarily (cut marks and smoothed edges). One rim sherd (type 20C, 1129.BH.72) had thin incised ("scarification") lines.

The various types and their general parallels are described below.

Bowls

A group of medium to large spherical, ovaloid and ellipsoid bowls (types 1B, 1B/48A, 1E and 28B, figs. 286-296) have counterparts in the Plain Failaka Style types 1C and 28C. They are decorated with bands of horizontal lines with dot in single or double circles positioned in between. Herringbone patterns and zigzag decoration are also represented. The decoration tends to cover most of the vessel surface.

Type 1B/48B vessels are sooty and show repairs; they seem to have been used to the same extent and for similar purposes (cooking bowls?) as types 1C and 28C from the Plain Failaka Style. Types 1E and 28B are also worn, but do not appear to have been exposed to heat and fire.

Some vessels of types 1B/48B and 28B were repaired, and a sherd of type 28B (fig. 296) was decorated with a graffito. Two sherds had marks from reuse (secondary cuts).

A few parallels are available for this group: Type 1B appears to show some similarity to a bowl excavated at al-Hajjar, which is dated to around 1550 BC (Denton 1994: 139, fig. 36e), though the published drawing is neither very detailed nor to scale. Type 1E has a parallel recovered during the French excavations at Tell F6, from a context dated to the 14th century BC.

A number of smaller ellipsoid (type 20C, 20C/48A, figs. 297-299) and spherical bowls (types 6A and 6B,

figs. 300-302), with pronounced and occasionally decorated rims and disk bases have been identified. They have simple geometric decoration in a very similar manner to types 1B/48A, 1E, 28B described above. The same overall form of type 20C/48A is also found in a plain version, type 20A: However, the characteristic concentric ridges are not seen on any of these bowls. One geometric body sherd (type 68B, fig. 303) did, however, have these concentric ridges, so it is not unlikely than exact equivalents were produced in both geometric and plain versions. Type 6A was carved from a soft stone, whereas type 6B was made from a hard stone and was inscribed with cuneiform script on its external surface. The geometric decoration seen on type 6B appears to be limited to a number of oblique lines decorating the rim.

Types 4B and 4D (figs. 304-308) include a number of large ellipsoid bowls apparently bearing the same traits as their undecorated counterparts, i.e. types 4A and 4C: sooty exteriors and multiple repair holes, possibly suggesting use in a household context. Several of these had subsequently been cut and broken in order to reuse the stone for new purposes. The apparently closely related type 11B (figs. 309-312), consisting of ovaloid to ellipsoid bowls, is also seen in an undecorated version (type 11A).

A number of disk bases (types 48B and 49B, figs. 313-315) are apparently associated with the above described bowl types.

A unique ellipsoid bowl, with a vertical loop handle and geometric decoration just below the rim (types 15/61E, 61E, figs. 316-317), probably imitates bronze/ceramic/woven vessels. It has been exposed to heat and traces of a blackish residue are preserved on its interior. It is not possible to give any parallels in stone, but ceramic and metal examples are available throughout the 2nd millennium BC.

Jars

One ovaloid jar type (type 35B, figs. 318-321) was ascribed to the Geometric Failaka Style, as it could not be assigned to the Wadi Suq jars or their plain counterparts (type 35A). The geometric decoration is not extensive and consists predominantly of decorated rims with undecorated or occasionally sparsely decorated bodies.

Handles

One handle type (type 61C, figs. 322-323) positioned horizontally on a bowl or pan. Both examples have been exposed to heat and fire, particularly on one side, suggesting that they were positioned over a fire.

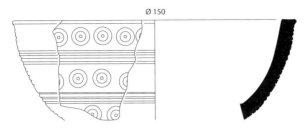

Fig. 286. Type 1B (KM3173).

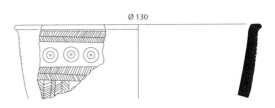

Fig. 287. Type 1B (KM3190).

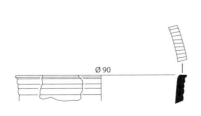

Fig. 289. Type 1E (KM6042/05).

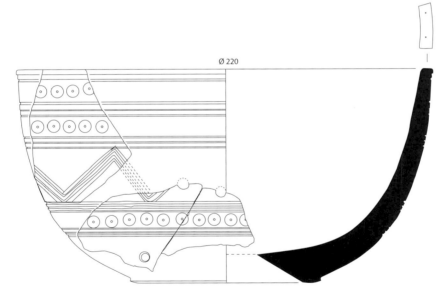

Fig. 288. Type 1B/48A (KM3183/01, 6069/01, 6069/03, 6092/02).

Fig. 290. Type 1E (KM6042/01).

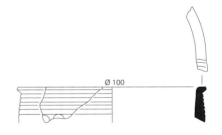

Fig. 291. Type 1E (KM6042/02).

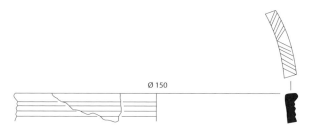

Fig. 292. Type 1E (KM6042/04).

Fig. 293. Type 1E (KM6042/03).

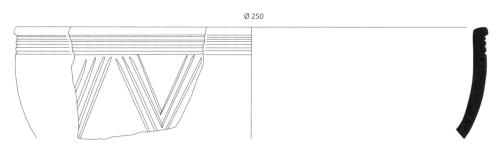

Fig. 294. Type 1E (KM1516).

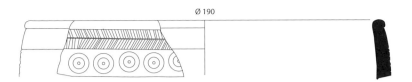

Fig. 295. Type 28B (KM3174).

Fig. 296. Type 28B (KM3113).

Fig. 297. Type 20C (881.AAJ).

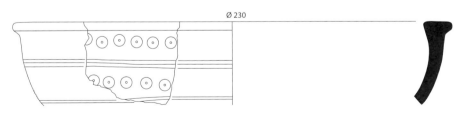

Fig. 298. Type 20C (F6.72).

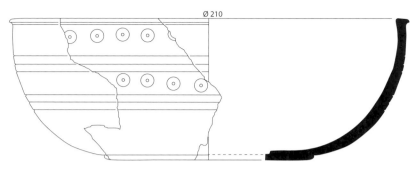

Fig. 299. Type 20C/48A (881.AQM, BEZ, ASE).

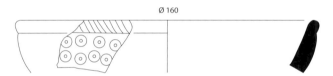

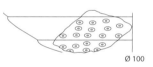

Fig. 300. Type 6A (KM3185/04).

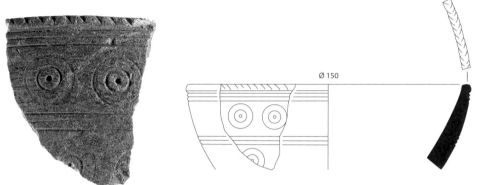

Fig. 301. Type 6A (KM3185/03).

Fig. 303. Type 68B (KM6071).

Fig. 302. Type 6B (KM1645).

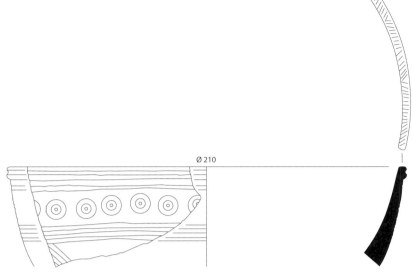

Fig. 304. Type 4B (KM3176/01).

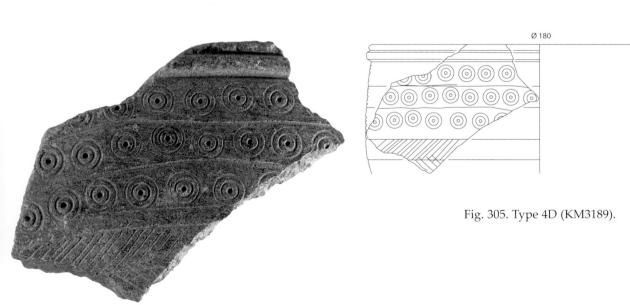

Fig. 305. Type 4D (KM3189).

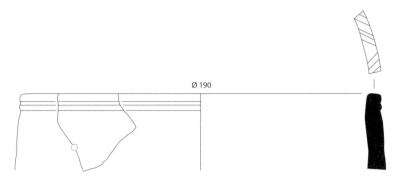

Fig. 306. Type 4D (KM6057/02).

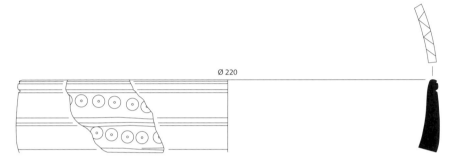

Fig. 307. Type 4D (KM3185/08).

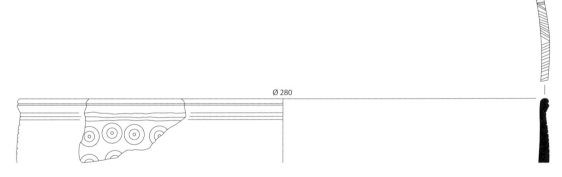

Fig. 308. Type 4D (KM3177/03).

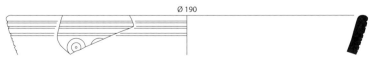

Fig. 309. Type 11B (KM3181/02).

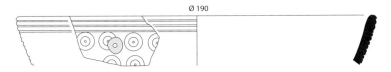

Fig. 310. Type 11B (KM3193/02).

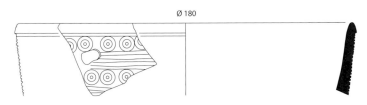

Fig. 311. Type 11B (KM3193/01).

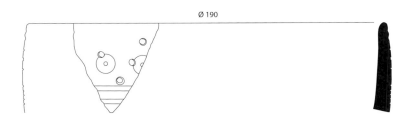

Fig. 312. Type 11B (KM3194/01).

Fig. 313. Type 48B (KM6102/05).

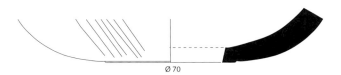

Fig. 314. Type 49B (KM6082/03).

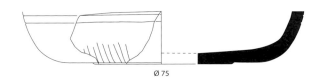

Fig. 315. Type 49B (KM3154).

133

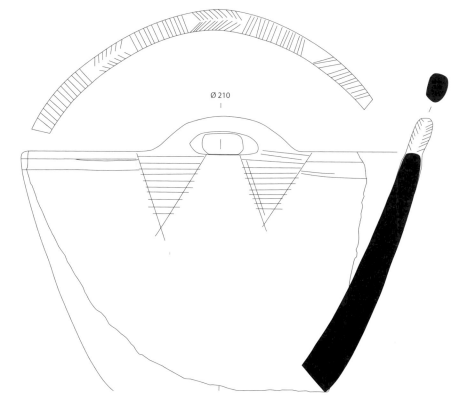

Fig. 316. Type 15/61E (KM6052).

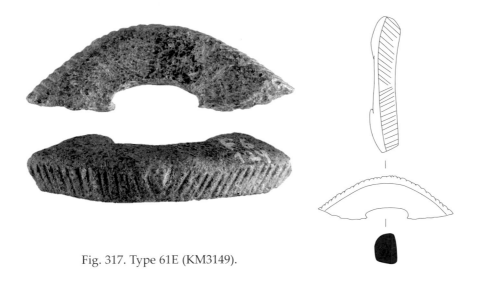

Fig. 317. Type 61E (KM3149).

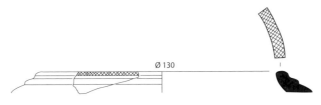

Fig. 318. Type 35B (881.BNX).

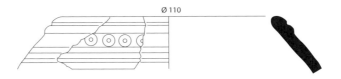

Fig. 319. Type 35B (881.BAR).

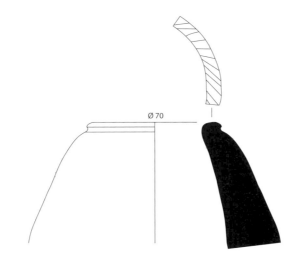

Fig. 321. Type 35B (881.BFF).

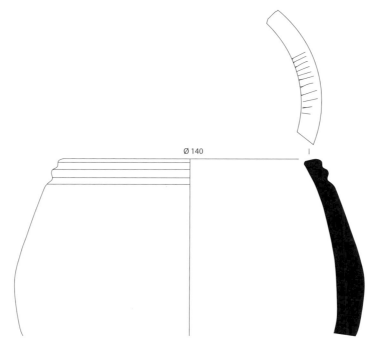

Fig. 320. Type 35B (1129.711).

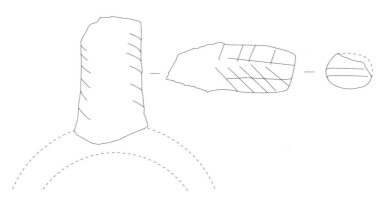

Fig. 322. Type 61C (KM3145).

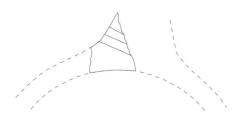

Fig. 323. Type 61C (KM6105/01).

3.8. 2nd Millennium Plain Failaka Style

A number of undecorated stone vessels, occasionally inscribed with cuneiform script, show similarities in morphology and stone types with vessels from both Figurative and Geometric Failaka Styles. A total of 86 diagnostic sherds have been referred to this Plain Failaka Style group. These were distributed between 23 types: bowls, jars, vases, plates and a box. The most common stone type was type 4 with 51.6 % (N: 44), followed by stone type 2 with 18.6 % (N: 16) and stone type 3 with 18.6 % (N: 16), together with two vessels made from the hard stone type 11 (2.3 %). A few sherds (9.3 %, N: 8) could not be identified.

The various types and their general parallels are described below.

Bowls

A group of large ellipsoid bowls (diameter c. 20-38 cm), with accentuated or externally thickened lips, occurs in an open version (type 1C, figs. 324-331) and a closed version (type 28C, figs. 332-333). Both versions are also found in the geometrically decorated style (see above). The same overall shape is found with a square spout (type 1D/60A, figs. 334-335).

The exteriors of these bowls have been exposed to heat and fire and this suggests that they were used in a household context.

A number of other ellipsoid bowls (types 4A and 4C, figs. 336-343) appear to have served similar purposes. These were also large (17-26 cm in diameter), with sooty exteriors and produced from the same stone type as types 1C and 28C. The only apparent difference is in the rim profile, which is a quite distinct thickened lip with a centred indentation. They also have geometrically decorated counterparts (types 4B and 4D). Quite a number of these bowls have multiple repair holes, sometimes with copper wire *in situ*.

Type 11A (fig. 344), an open ovaloid bowl, and type 23A (figs. 345-348), a closed ovaloid bowl, are slightly finer versions of types 4A and 4C. The protruding lip with a centred indentation (type 4) is less pronounced on these bowls, with the indentations appearing more like thin incisions. This bowl type is also found in a geometric variant (type 11B, fig. 309-312).

Type 23B (fig. 349) also has multiple incised indentations below the rim. It is a finely manufactured and polished small ellipsoid bowl with a thin incurving pointed lip which can be compared with multiple-grooved ceramic bowls, dated to period 3B (c. 1550 BC) on Failaka and period IIIa (c. 1550 BC) on Qala'at al-Bahrain (Højlund 1987: 79, figs.

301-304, 689, Højlund & Andersen 1994: 179, figs. 719-720).

A group of large ellipsoid closed bowls with flat bases were produced in soft (types 25A, 25A/42C, figs. 350-354) and hard stone (type 25B, fig. 355). One type 25A sherd is inscribed with an Amorite name (fig. 354). The orthography of the inscription provides only a general date in the 2nd millennium (Glassner 1984: 38, no. 29, fig. 7). Several of these bowls show cut marks and breaks resulting from reutilisation.

Based on a full vessel profile (fig. 356) it is possible to link several rim, body-sherd and base types together (types 20A, 50A, 51A, 68A, figs. 357-373). This finely produced bowl is characterised by a specific rim profile and characteristic concentric stepped ridges near the base. Two different types of base, ring base (types 51A, 51D, 54A, 54B, figs. 366-370, 374-377) and flat base (type 50A, figs. 361-365) are associated with the characteristic stepped ridged walls.

A rim sherd of type 20A (fig. 360) is inscribed with cuneiform script below the rim: '...the temple, ...lord of Dilmun (??), ...Inzak' and a flat base of type 50A (fig. 365) denotes '...Inzak of Akarum'. The exquisite workmanship of these bowls and their inscriptions indicate that they may have been used in cultic contexts in a similar way to the Figurative Failaka bowls.

The characteristic concentric stepped ridges are also present in the Figurative Failaka Style (e.g. type 50B, fig. 268), as is the characteristic rim (type 20B, fig. 216). The rim profile and overall shape of these bowls also appear in the Geometric Failaka Style (types 1B/48A, 20C/48A, figs. 288, 299).

There are a few parallels for the concentric stepped ridges near the base: A vessel fragment from Qala'at al-Bahrain has an identical ridged base combined with bunches of oblique parallel lines and a pierced lug handle, i.e. features that traditionally are associated with Wadi Suq vessels. It was found in a period IIIb1 context, c. 1400 BC (Højlund & Andersen 1997: 70, fig. 296). A second parallel is a small onyx vase found in a princess' tomb at Ebla dating from c. 1950-1600 BC (Bevan 2007: 111, 216, 220). Thirdly, a number of Iranian bronze vessels dating from the very end of the 3rd millennium BC to around the middle of the 2nd millennium BC have the same concentric stepped ridged near the base (Bellelli 2002).

A group of small ellipsoid bowls (type 19B, figs. 378-380) with indentation below the rim may be a minor variant of types 1C and 28C.

Bases of types 48A and 49A (figs. 381-393) are probably associated with some of the bowl types described above.

Jars

A number of undecorated jars form a group (type 35A, figs. 394-396) that cannot be associated with the traditional Wadi Suq jars. Some of these have indentations below the rims similar to those seen on several Plain Failaka Style bowls. This type of jar is also found in the Geometric Failaka Style (type 35B).

Vases

Two rim sherds may derive from the necks of vases (type 38, figs. 397-398).

Plates

Eight thick, shallow plates are either plain (types 18Aa, 18Aa/52A, 18B, 18B/52B) or inscribed with cuneiform script (types 18Ab, 18C) (figs. 399-406). Similar plates are known from the French and the recent Kuwaiti-Danish excavations at Tell F6 and from the Kuwaiti-Slovak excavation at Al-Khidr (Hilton *et al.* 2013).

This plate type has no exact parallels outside Failaka, but its shape and size shows some similarity to an altar plate from Ur, although the rim profile is slightly dissimilar.[3] This plate is dedicated to

Enmahgalanna, the high priestess of the moon god at Ur dating from around 2043 BC.

Type 18C (fig. 406) shows a certain similarity to a ceramic plate/bowl only found on the Barbar Temples, a variety of plate type B30 (Andersen & Højlund 2003: 328, fig. 480 (Temple IIb), figs. 569-570 (Temple III?). This piece is inscribed with cuneiform script on top of its rim.

The purpose of these plates is not entirely clear, but they appear to be related to temples and cultic rituals, based on their cuneiform inscriptions and a general similarity on the part of types 18A-B to much larger altars in the Dilmun civilisation (Andersen & Højlund 2003 figs. 61-64, 108-109, 162-166, 55 and 105-107) (Hilton *et al.* 2013: p. 420). One plate made from hard stone (Type 18Ab, fig. 406) bears an inscription possibly mentioning the *old temple*.

Box

One semi-finished box (type 40A/53A, fig. 407) has secondary carvings externally on its base. A similar box was found at Al-Khidr in a 2nd millennium BC context.

Body sherds

Two body sherds (type 69, figs. 408-409) are inscribed with cuneiform script and one of them (fig. 409) appears to derive from a bowl type similar to type 20A. This specific fragment is inscribed to Enki and the temple of Inzak and mentions a vessel, perhaps indicating that this bowl may have been donated or was involved in some cultic practices taking place within the Dilmun sphere (Glassner 2008: 187).

---

[3] Sincere thanks to Assistant Keeper Dr St John Simpson for allowing me examine this object exhibited in the British Museum (BM:118555).

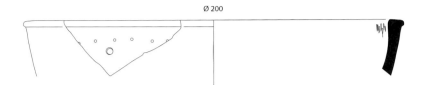

Fig. 324. Type 1C (KM3196/04).

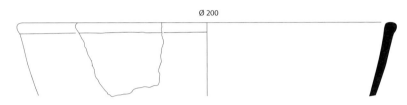

Fig. 325. Type 1C (KM6060/01).

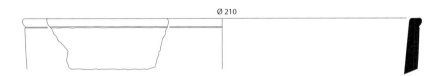

Fig. 326. Type 1C (KM6060/03).

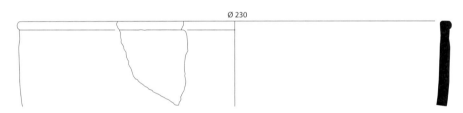

Fig. 327. Type 1C (KM6063/07).

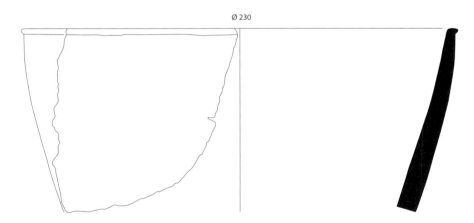

Fig. 328. Type 1C (KM6058/01).

Fig. 329. Type 1C (KM6064/04).

Ø 380

Fig. 330. Type 1C (KM6060/04).

Ø 240

Fig. 331. Type 1C (KM6058/02).

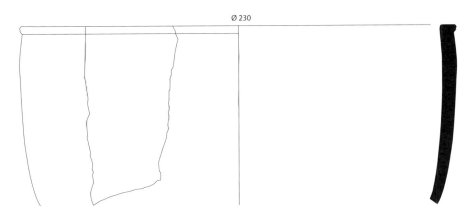

Fig. 332. Type 28C (KM6059/02).

Fig. 333. Type 28C (KM6063/08).

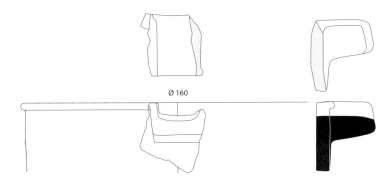

Fig. 334. Type 1D/60A (KM3136).

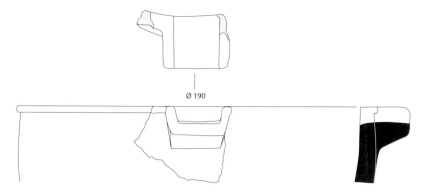

Fig. 335. Type 1D/60A (KM3135).

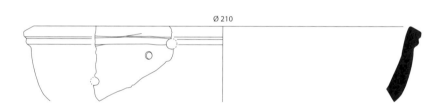

Fig. 336. Type 4A (KM3198/02).

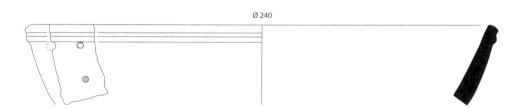

Fig. 337. Type 4A (KM3198/01).

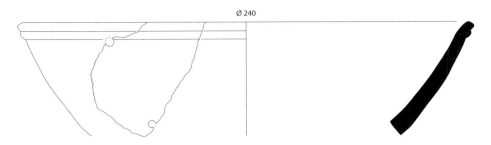

Fig. 338. Type 4A (KM6056/03).

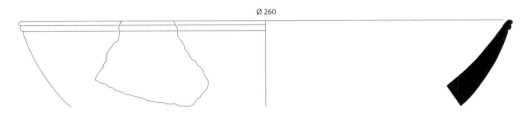

Fig. 339. Type 4A (KM6056/04).

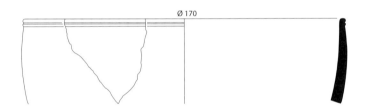

Fig. 340. Type 4C (KM6056/01).

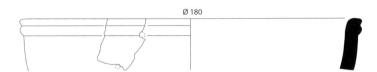

Fig. 341. Type 4C (KM6056/02).

Ø 240

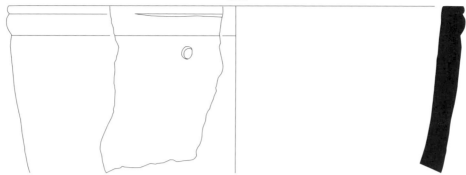

Fig. 342. Type 4C (KM3198/04).

Ø 260

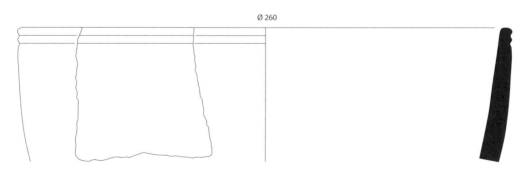

Fig. 343. Type 4C (KM6056/06).

Fig. 344. Type 11A (KM6055/03).

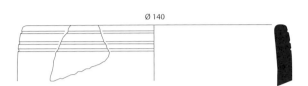

Fig. 345. Type 23A (KM6057/01).

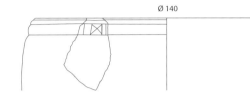

Fig. 346. Type 23A (KM6055/02).

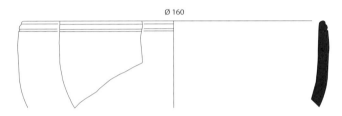

Fig. 347. Type 23A (KM6057/03).

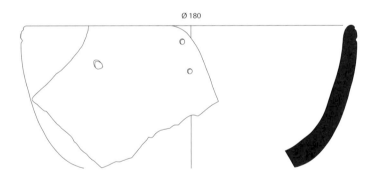

Fig. 348. Type 23A (KM3198/03).

Fig. 349. Type 23B (881.ASZ, BET, AJO).

Fig. 350. Type 25A/42C (881.ARA).

Fig. 351. Type 25A (KM6065/01).

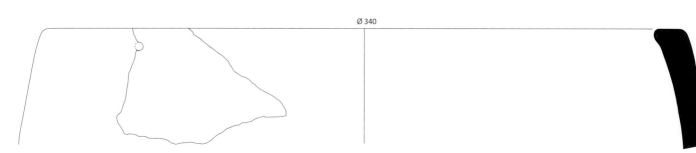

Fig. 352. Type 25A (KM6065/05).

Fig. 353. Type 25A (881.BPK).

Fig. 354. Type 25A (KM1296).

Fig. 355. Type 25B (881.ATR).

Fig. 356. Type 20A/50A-51A (881.BAU).

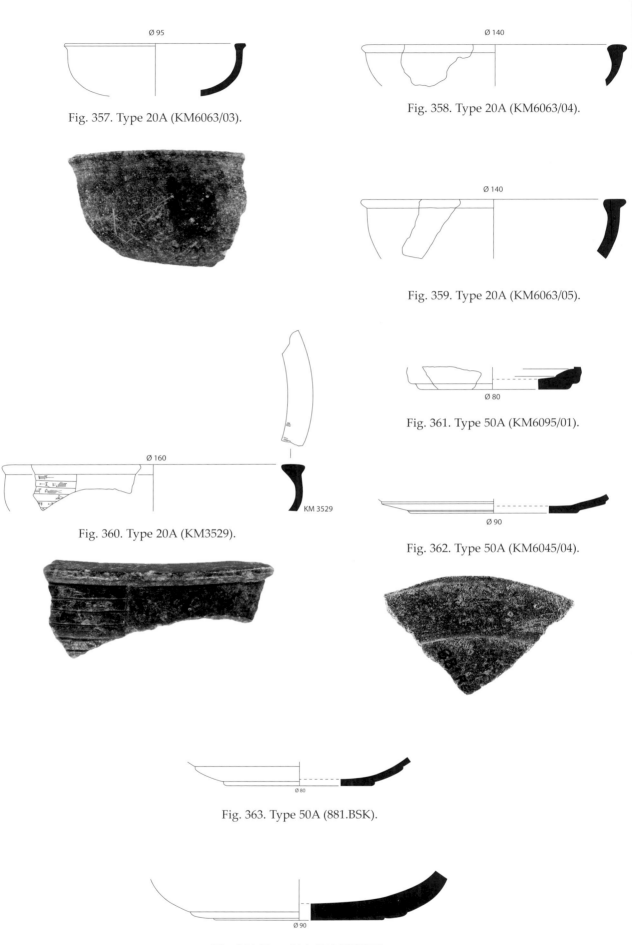

Ø 95

Fig. 357. Type 20A (KM6063/03).

Ø 140

Fig. 358. Type 20A (KM6063/04).

Ø 140

Fig. 359. Type 20A (KM6063/05).

Ø 80

Fig. 361. Type 50A (KM6095/01).

Ø 160

KM 3529

Fig. 360. Type 20A (KM3529).

Ø 90

Fig. 362. Type 50A (KM6045/04).

Ø 80

Fig. 363. Type 50A (881.BSK).

Ø 90

Fig. 364. Type 50A (881.BVX/02).

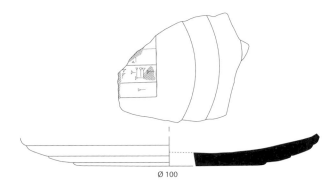

Fig. 365. Type 50A (KM1518).

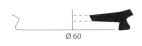

Fig. 366. Type 51A (881.BSN).

Fig. 367. Type 51A (KM6081/01).

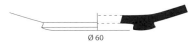

Fig. 368. Type 51A (KM6093/01).

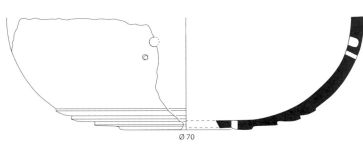

Fig. 370. Type 51A (KM6081/05).

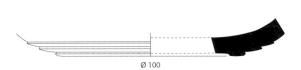

Fig. 369. Type 51A (KM6081/03).

Fig. 371. Type 68A (KM6045/03).

Fig. 372. Type 68A (KM6045/02).

149

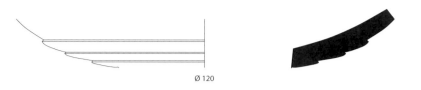

Fig. 373. Type 68A (KM6081/04).

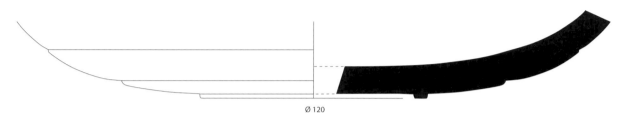

Fig. 374. Type 51D (KM6080).

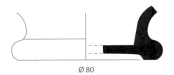

Fig. 375. Type 54A
(KM6093/02).

Ø 160

Fig. 376. Type 54B (KM6105/03).

Ø 200

Fig. 377. Type 54B (KM6105/02).

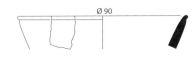

Ø 90

Fig. 378. Type 19B (KM1508).

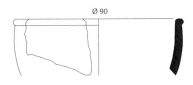

Ø 90

Fig. 379. Type 19B (KM6060/02).

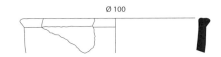

Ø 100

Fig. 380. Type 19B (KM6063/01).

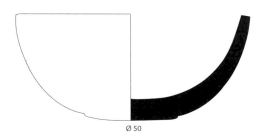

Ø 50

Fig. 381. Type 48A (KM66).

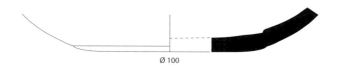

Fig. 382. Type 48A (KM6096/01).

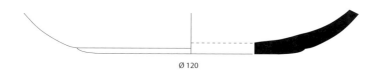

Fig. 383. Type 48A (KM6102/03).

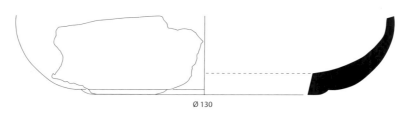

Fig. 384. Type 48A (KM6054/03).

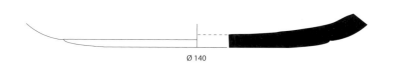

Fig. 385. Type 48A (KM6102/02).   Fig. 386. Type 48A (KM6095/03).

Fig. 387. Type 48A (KM6102/06).

Fig. 388. Type 48A (KM6102/04).

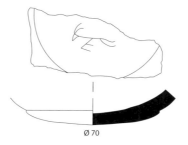

Fig. 389. Type 48A (KM3050).

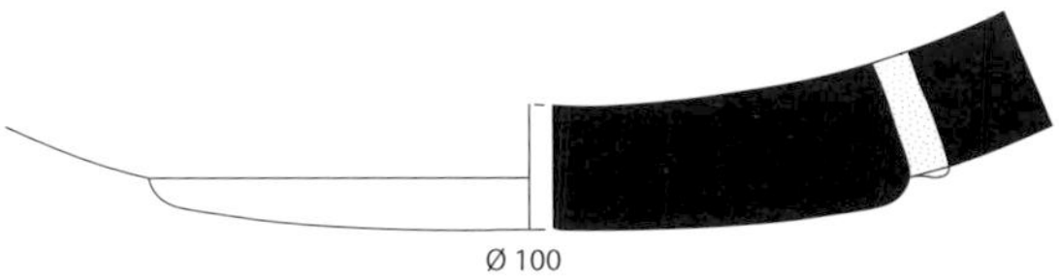

Ø 100

Fig. 390. Type 48A (KM6096/02).

Ø 130

Fig. 391. Type 48A (KM6095/04).

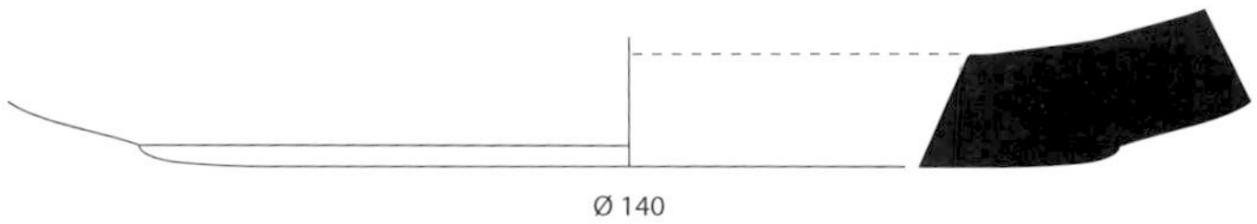

Ø 140

Fig. 392. Type 48A (KM6095/02).

Ø 110

Fig. 394. Type 35A (KM6042/07).

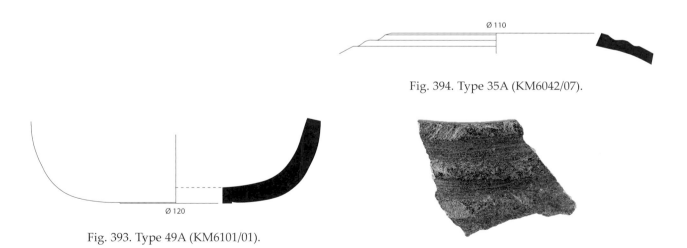

Ø 120

Fig. 393. Type 49A (KM6101/01).

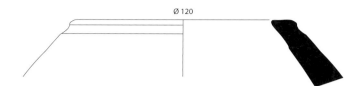

Fig. 395. Type 35A (KM6103/05).

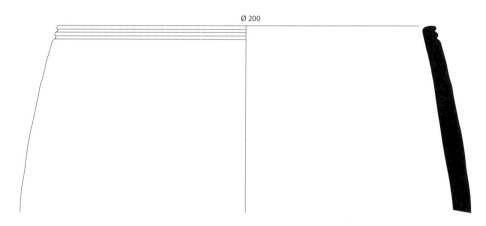

Fig. 396. Type 35A (881.BXD).

Fig. 397. Type 38 (KM6063/02).

Fig. 398. Type 38 (KM6046).

Fig. 399. Type 18Aa/52A (881.ZE).

Fig. 400. Type 18Aa/52A (KM6097/03).

Fig. 401. Type 18Aa/52A (F6.311).

Fig. 402. Type 18Ab (KM1642).

Fig. 403. Type 18B (881.BVX/01).

Fig. 404. Type 18B/52B (KM6098/02).

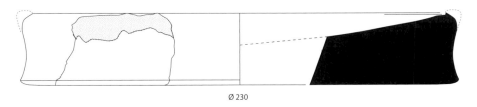

Fig. 405. Type 18B/52B (KM6098/01).

155

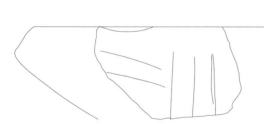

Fig. 406. Type 18C (KM1649).

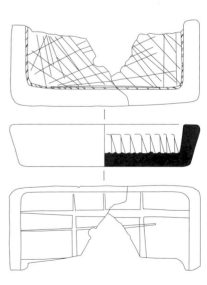

Fig. 407. Type 40A/53A (KM3151-3152).

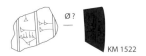

Fig. 408. Type 69 (KM1522).

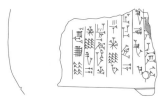

Fig. 409. Type 69 (KM3528).

3.9. Miscellaneous

A small group of 17 sherds could not be referred to any of the above defined styles. The group includes a number of bowls, bases and a lid and they have been divided between eight different types (figs. 410-426).

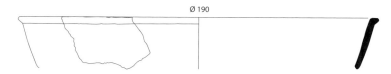

Fig. 410. Type 2A (KM6064/02).

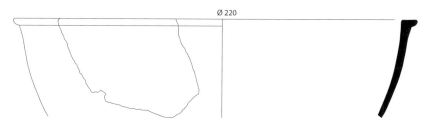

Fig. 411. Type 2A (KM6063/09).

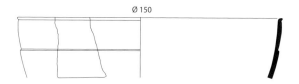

Fig. 412. Type 2B (KM6045/01).

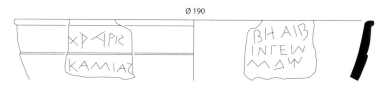

Fig. 413. Type 2B (KM1643).

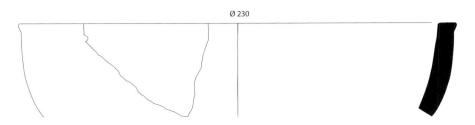

Fig. 414. Type 1A (KM6059/01).

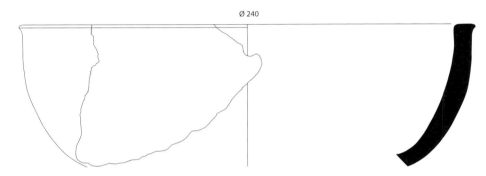

Fig. 415. Type 1A (KM6064/05).

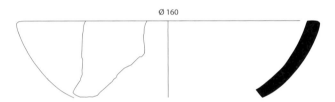

Fig. 416. Type 8A (KM6062/09).

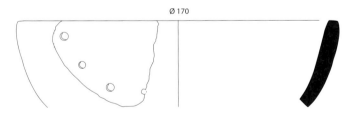

Fig. 417. Type 8A (KM3197/03).

Ø 170

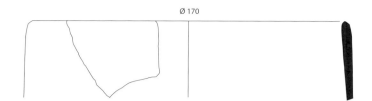

Fig. 418. Type 24A (KM6062/11).

Ø 170

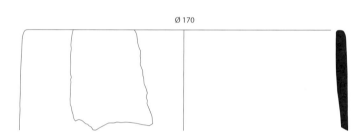

Fig. 419. Type 24A (KM6062/08).

Ø 136

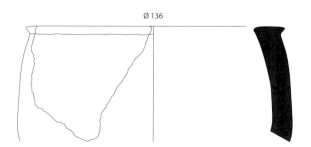

Fig. 420. Type 32B (KM6063/10).

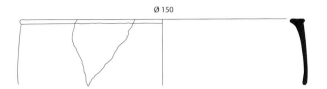

Fig. 421. Type 32B (KM6064/03).

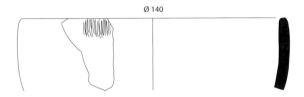

Fig. 422. Type 24B (KM6062/03).

Fig. 423. Type 24B (KM6062/04).

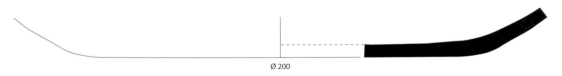

Fig. 424. Type 42D (KM6101/03).

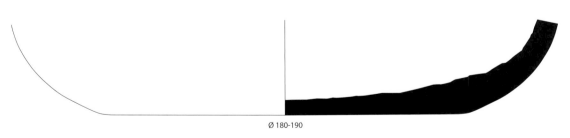

Fig. 425. Type 43C (KM6099).

Fig. 426. Type 62A (KM3125).

4. Reuse of stone vessels

There is ample evidence of reuse and reworking of broken soft stone vessels into a wide range of other objects. Of the diagnostic sherds in the Failaka assemblage 91 were intentionally cut with a sharp instrument and then broken (figs. 427-429).

59 of the diagnostic sherds from Tell F3 (24 %) were reused, from Tell F5 and Tell F6 the corresponding figures are 9/31 % and 10/16.4 % (fig. 450).

The transformation of vessel fragments into other objects can be followed from square or rounded *blanks* with roughly worked edges (fig. 430) to finished objects such as pendants and spindle whorls. The blanks are clearly derived from soft stone vessels, as the original decoration (fig. 431) is sometimes preserved or the former uses are evident (fig. 432). The average size of these blanks is 3 × 4 x 1.5 cm.

A number of artefacts cut from soft stone vessel sherds have been recorded: pendants (figs. 433-435), spindle whorls (figs. 436-437), and possible oil lamps (fig. 438).

The average size of *pendants* is 3 × 3.5 cm, ranging from c. 1 × 2.5 cm to c. 3 × 4.5 cm. They were predominantly made from stone types 3, 4 and 2. Holes for suspension were made in the medial upper part of the pendant, with the exception of some circular pendants where holes were made through the centre of the object. Several of the pendants show wear marks from suspension.

The pendants were shaped (circular, elliptical, ovoid, square or rectangular) (fig. 439) and thereafter polished and decorated, occasionally on top of original stone vessel decoration (figs. 440-441). Alternatively, the original decoration was retained and new decoration was added to the reverse (fig. 442). Occasionally only two sides were decorated, but usually it was applied to all six sides of the pendant. The decoration consists of short incisions making up simple geometric decoration, in a few cases elaborated with two humans with raised arms standing either on top of a raft or a decorated po-

dium (fig. 443), a boat (KM3162/06) or a branch (fig. 444).

Spindle whorls range in diameter from 2 to 6.8 cm and in height from 0.8 to 1.5 cm. In cross-section, they vary from flat discs to short circular and long ellipsoid convex cones. Original geometric decoration, including dot in single circles and horizontal and oblique lines, as seen in the Wadi Suq stone vessel repertoire, may still be preserved (fig. 445).

With reference to the above-mentioned rounded blanks made from broken stone vessels, it has been suggested that *stamp seals* were manufactured on Failaka (Ciarla 1985: 402, 1990: 476; Moorey 1994: 49; Howard-Carter 1989: 262; Crawford 1998). Since the dimensions of stamp seals are slightly smaller than the majority of the stone blanks excavated at Failaka, it is at least theoretically possible. Whether it is likely that the peak of Dilmun artistic production used old broken vessels as raw material is another matter.

A few sherds had been secondarily incised with graffiti of a caprid (fig. 446), a boat (fig. 296), a star (KM3183/02), a cross (KM3124/01), pseudo-writing (KM3046, KM3000), Greek letters (fig. 447) and, in three cases, a branch (fig. 448, KM6041, 3126/04).

Reuse of broken softstone vessels appears to have taken place throughout all periods in the settlement history of Tells F3 and F6, with a somewhat larger frequency in period 4A (fig. 451). In several cases there was an apparent disregard for cultic decorations such as processional scenes (fig. 270) and cuneiform dedications to the gods Enki and Inzak (fig. 69), suggesting that the symbolic value of these vessels was no longer of any significance for the people who were reshaping them, but the generally poor context and dating information of the material does not allow further discussions of this theme.

None of the 3rd Millennium Undecorated vessels made from the harder stone types 9 and 10 show any signs of being recut.

Fig. 427. Body sherd with repair hole and cutmark followed by breakage (KM3083).

Fig. 428. Body sherd with cutting followed by breakage (KM3168/01).

Fig. 429. Spout with cut mark followed by breakage (KM3133).

Fig. 430. Blank with roughly worked edges (KM3174/02).

Fig. 431. Blank made from a body sherd with Wadi Suq decoration (KM3160/08).

Fig. 432. Blank made from a body sherd with one face sooted (KM3160/07).

Fig. 433. Pendant made from stone vessel sherd (KM3171/03).

Fig. 434. Pendant carved from vessel with geometric decoration (KM3163/01).

Fig. 435. Pendant carved from vessel with geometric decoration (KM3163/02).

Fig. 436. Roughly fashioned spindel whorl (KM3156/08).

Fig. 437. Spindel whorl (KM3156/15).

Fig. 438. Possible oil lamp (881. ANR).

Fig. 440. Pendant (KM3122).

Fig. 441. Pendant (KM3159/01).

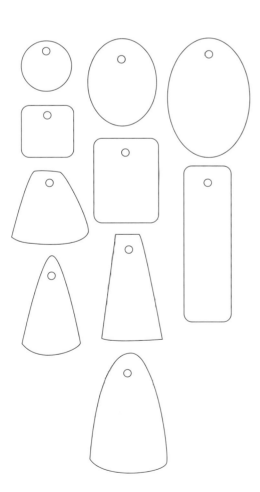

Fig. 439. Basic pendant shapes: circular, elliptical, ovoid, square and rectangular.

Fig. 442. Pendant carved from bowl in Figurative Failaka Style with rosette decoration (right) and secondary decoration (left) (KM3009).

Fig. 443. Pendant incised with
two humans in gesture of
worship (KM1636).

Fig. 446. Graffito of caprid (KM3050).

Fig. 444. Pendant decorated
with branch (KM3159/02).

Fig. 447. Inscription in Greek (KM1643).

Fig. 445. Spindle whorl with traces of Wadi Suq
decoration (KM3157/03).

Fig. 448. Graffito of branch
(KM3065).

166

5. Conclusion

As stated at the beginning of this study there are major problems associated with dating the stone vessels on Failaka on the basis of their archaeological context. The assemblage has therefore been classified typologically into a number of styles which have been dated either by comparison with similar material from neighbouring regions or with other elements of material culture on Failaka.

Eight different stone vessel styles were identified, of which three date from the mid to late 3rd millennium: the *Figurative Style*, the *Undecorated Style* and the *Umm an-Nar Style*. There are also two 2nd millennium styles: the *Wadi Suq Style* and the *Late Bronze Age Style*. In addition to these well-known styles, three new groups, dated to the mid 2nd millennium, were established: the *Figurative Failaka Style*, the *Geometric Failaka Style* and the *Plain Failaka Style*.

It now remains to examine whether there is a pattern in the distribution of these eight stone vessel styles in the various settlement phases of Tells F3, F5 and F6 and to ascertain whether any conclusions can be drawn from such patterns and from traces of use and reuse as to their function and to the significance of their occurrence on Failaka.

Of the 387 diagnostic fragments included in this study, 336 (or 86.6%) can be referred to either Tell F3, Tell F5 or Tell F6. The largest number recovered was from Tell F3 (63.6%, N: 246), followed by Tell F6 (15.8%, N: 61) and Tell F5 (7.5%, N: 29). The remaining 51 fragments (13.2%) derive from the 1958-1963 excavations of one of these three sites, though it is not possible to specify which one, and from later cleaning and restoration activities on the sites.

If the stone vessels from the three tells are compared *en masse* the most apparent difference is that the Late Bronze Age Style, the Figurative, the Geometric and the Plain Failaka Styles are relatively more common in Tell F3 than in Tell F6 (fig. 449). Almost all the stone vessel styles are represented in the material from Tell F5 and also, it may be added, from the French excavations of the temple in Tell F6 (Calvet & Pic 1986. David 1990), but the numbers are too small to be significant.

The percentage of diagnostic sherds with remains of soot or traces of heat exposure, repair holes and marks from reuse is very similar in the materials from Tells F3, F5 and F6 (fig. 450).

Going into more detail with respect to the dating of the stone vessel finds there is no relevant contextual information for the stone vessels from *Tell F5*. A number of 3rd-2nd millennium objects were found during the Danish and the later French excavations in the otherwise Hellenistic Tell F5; these included pottery (Hannestad 1983: 123, note 1), stamp seals and a number of stone vessel fragments. Kjærum mentions the possibility of a deep occupation layer dating to the 2nd millennium (Kjærum 1983: 8), whereas the French excavators describe these finds as random intrusions into the Hellenistic layers (Gachet & Salles 1986: 304).

Stone vessel sherds from *Tell F6* are few in number and the area excavated within and below the

Vessel style	Tell F3 (N)	Tell F5 (N)	Tell F6 (N)
3rd millennium Figurative Style	23	1	19
3rd millennium Undecorated Style	16	2	6
3rd millennium Umm an-Nar Style	16	3	5
2nd millennium Wadi Suq Style	40	4	14
2nd millennium Late Bronze Age Style	13	3	–
2nd millennium Figurative Failaka Style	45	6	4
2nd millennium Geometric Failaka Style	28	–	7
2nd millennium Plain Failaka Style	59	6	6
Miscellaneous	6	4	–
Total	246	29	61

Fig. 449. Frequency distribution of styles on Tell F3, Tell F5 and Tell F6.

	N	Soot and/or heat exposure	Repair holes	Reuse
Tell F3	246	45 / 18.3 %	27 / 11 %	59 / 24 %
Tell F5	29	5 / 17.2 %	2 / 6.9 %	9 / 31 %
Tell F6	61	11 / 18%	6 / 9.8%	10 / 16.4 %
Tells F3 / F5 / F6	54	6 / 11.3%	6 / 11.3%	11 / 20.8%

Fig. 450. Frequency of traces of use and reuse, and repair holes on diagnostic sherds from Tells F3, F5 and F6.

walls of the 'Palace' in 1958-1963 was so disturbed by stone plundering and other activities that the distribution of these few stone vessel sherds produces no meaningful pattern. Pottery was more plentiful, and pockets of undisturbed areas could be isolated on the basis of which the architectural phases of Tell F6 could be dated to Failaka periods 1-4A, or c. 2000-1400 BC (Højlund 1987).

From *Tell F3* more trench and level information is available for the stone vessel fragments and it is therefore possible to assign a number of stone sherds to specific layers within some kind of stratigraphy. It seems that Tell F3 was less disturbed by stone plundering than Tell F6, perhaps due to the larger sizes and greater amounts of building stone used in the 'Palace' of Tell F6 (Kjærum & Højlund 2013: 99-101).

A total of 134 stone vessel sherds could be related to layers at Tell F3 in which the accompanying pottery gives at least an indication of the date within the Failaka periods represented at Tell F3, i.e. periods 2-4B, or c. 1900-1300 BC.

Of this total, 14.2 % (N:19) of the stone vessels were found in contexts dating from period 2, 9.7 % (N:13) from period 3A, 8.2 % (N:11) from period 3A/3B, 8.2 % (N:11) from period 3B, 22.4 % (N:30) from period 4A, 13.4 % (N:18) from period 4A/4B and 8.2 % (N:11) from period 4B. It should be noted that this gives a date of the pottery found in the same level as the stone vessel fragment, but there is no certainty that the context is undisturbed. These datings should thus be treated with caution and can only indicate trends in the material.

It is, however, immediately apparent that a significant proportion of the Failaka stone vessel assemblage predates the establishment of settlement at Tells F3 and F6 around 2000-1900 BC, and that the remainder is contemporary with the sequence of settlement phases at Tells F3 and F6 stretching from c. 2000 to 1300 BC (fig. 2) (Højlund 1987. Kjærum & Højlund 2013).[4]

---

[4]   The recent discovery in 2009 of a Mesopotamian settlement in Tell F6 dating to the Ur III period has not changed these conclusions (Højlund 2010. Højlund & Abu-Laban in prep.).

5.1. Stone vessel styles predating the settlement of Tells F3 and F6

Stone vessels of the *3rd Millennium Figurative Style* occurred in layers dated to all periods at Tell F3. Two sherds were found in a period 2 layer, and eleven came from layers dating from periods 3A-4B.

Vessels belonging to the *Undecorated 3rd Millennium Style* likewise occurred in layers from all periods at Tell F3; four sherds were found in period 2 layers and eight pieces came from periods 3A-4B.

Of the Umm an-Nar Style fragments one came from period 2 and four from periods 3A-4B.

In summary, the fragments belonging to the 3rd Millennium Styles occur in Tell F3 throughout the Failaka period 2-4B sequence and they are not concentrated specifically in the oldest or any other period.

18 of all 99 diagnostic sherds from the 3rd millennium styles from Tell F3, F5 and F6 (18.2 %) show cut marks indicating that, after their primary function as containers, they were reused as raw material for the

	Period 1	Period 1 v	Period 2	Period 3A	Period 3A/3B	Period 3B	Period 4	Period 3A/4A	Period 4A	Period 4A/4B	Period 4B	Sieve, unsecure or no context
F3	–	–	4 / 17	3 / 10	3 / 8	0 / 11	2 / 10	3 / 10	11 / 18	2 / 5	2 / 9	26 / 62
F6	1 / 16	6 / 17	0 / 1	–	–	–	–	–	–	–	–	3 / 19

Fig. 451. Frequency of reused/non-reused diagnostic sherds that could be assigned to a specific layer in Tells F3 and F6.

production of a number of other items, e.g. spindle whorls, pendants and blanks (see chapter 4).

It seems very likely that the occurrence of vessels of the *3rd Millennium Figurative, Undecorated and Umm an-Nar Styles* at the tells on Failaka is unrelated to the primary functions of these vessels. As argued by Ciarla (1985, 1990), they were probably rather valued for the properties of their stone and their capacity to be reutilised and transformed into new objects. On the other hand, the possibility that vessels of Umm an-Nar Style were still in use in the earliest settlement of Tells F3 and F6 cannot be completely discounted, as similar material was actually present at Qala'at al-Bahrain in the contemporaneous period IIb (Højlund & Andersen 1994 figs. 1904, 1907, 1908, 1910 and 1911).

None of the *3rd Millennium Figurative* and *3rd Millennium Undecorated vessels* are sooty or show other signs of having being exposed to heat and they rarely display evidence of heavy wear. These stone vessels were probably not utilised in a domestic context (e.g. for cooking) during the period of their primary use, but were associated with other environments. This is also indicated by their primary disposal contexts in graves and temples in Iran, Mesopotamia and Tarut. It is not unlikely that the Failaka vessels were looted from such contexts, but whether these graves or temples were located on Failaka, somewhere on the coastline of Arabia like the island of Tarut or in Mesopotamia or Iran is unknown.

It has previously been suggested that the figuratively decorated vessels found in Tell F3 were votive vessels which had been placed in the small temple courtyard at Tell F3 (Howard-Carter 1989: 265), but only a few soft-stone sherds were found inside the temple enclosure (trenches N, Z, Æ, X, M and Q (Højlund 1987: fig. 1) and none of these belong to the *3rd Millennium Figurative Style.*

5.2. Stone vessel styles contemporary with settlement phases at Tells F3 and F6

Five different styles of stone vessels are contemporary with the settlement phases at Tell F3 and F6, the *Wadi Suq*, the *Late Bronze Age*, the *Figurative Failaka*, the *Geometric Failaka*, and the *Plain Failaka Styles*.

Wadi Suq Style vessels occur in all periods at Tell F3 (periods 2-4B), but the greatest concentration of sherds was found in layers dated to periods 2 (7) and 3A (5) with 2 from period 3A/4A, 2 from period 3B, 3 from period 4A and 2 from period 4A/4B.

This group is characterised by traces of soot, evidence of heat, residues and extensive wear marks and may have been used in a domestic context. Several Wadi Suq vessels have repair holes and *in situ* copper wire demonstrating that they were repaired when broken.

Since there is a certain agreement between the dating of the Wadi Suq Style vessels in Tell F3 with their dating on the Oman peninsula it is not unlikely that these vessels were actually imported and used as containers in the settlements of Tell F3 and F6.

Nevertheless, there is also clear evidence that the raw material of these vessels were reused. Of 70 diagnostic Wadi Suq Style sherds from Tells F3, F5 and F6 23 (32.8%) have secondary cut marks.

Eight sherds belonging to the *Late Bronze Age Style* were excavated at Tell F3, one sherd from a period 3A/3B context and 5 from period 4A/4B layers. They all show external wear marks, but less than the Wadi Suq material and, one sherd has traces of soot and discolouration arising from exposure to fire. Two sherds out of 16 (12.5%) from Tells F3 and F5 had marks from secondary recutting followed by smoothing of the edges.

Again the dating of the Late Bronze Age Style vessels in Tell F3 agrees fairly well with the dating of these vessels on the Oman peninsula, so maybe they were also imported and used in a domestic context in the settlements on Failaka.

The three remaining stone vessel styles, *Figurative, Geometric and Plain Failaka Styles*, are connected by certain morphological elements and by the use of the same stone types and they are therefore assumed to be contemporary.

At Tell F3 one *Figurative Failaka Style* sherd (Type 65C:KM3033) was found in a period 2/4B context. The remaining Figurative Failaka Style sherds were found in layers dating from period 3A (N: 1), period 3A/B (N: 3), period 3B (N: 4), period 4A (N: 8), period 4A/4B (N: 3) and period 4B (N: 2).

The same pattern is seen with respect to the *Geometric Failaka Style* with period 3A (N: 2), period 3A/4A (N: 2), period 3B (N: 2), period 4A (N: 4), period 4B (N: 1) and period 4A/4B (N: 1).

The *Plain Failaka Style* was predominantly found in contexts dated to period 4A-4B (11 sherds) and, to a lesser degree, period 2 (six sherds) and period 3A (three sherds).

Thus, though there is a certain tendency for the three Failaka styles to cluster in the later periods at Tell F3 there is no precise evidence for their date. As argued above the many close similarities between the Figurative Failaka Style and Style III of the Dilmun stamp seals point towards a dating to the mid second millennium BC, more specifically somewhere after Failaka period 3A and into period 3B, corresponding to Qala'at al-Bahrain late period II or early period IIIa; in Mesopotamia this would be the late Old Babylonian and early Kassite period.

The vessels of the Figurative Failaka Style lack soot, residues and extensive use/wear marks, and as their decoration depicts scenes of worship, deities and cuneiform inscriptions referring to cultic practices it seems very likely that they were utilised in rituals. 21 diagnostic sherds out of 61 (34.4 %) from Tells F3, F5 and F6 have secondary cuts incl. secondary smoothening on broken edges.

Both the Geometric and the Plain Failaka Styles show traces of heat/fire, wear marks and repair holes and may therefore have been used in a domestic context, e.g. for cooking. 9 out of 38 (23.7 %) Geometric Failaka Style sherds and 15 out of 81 (18.5 %) Plain Failaka Style sherds from Tells F3, F5 and F6 had marks of reutilization.

Whereas the 3rd Millennium Figurative Style vessels eventually came from Iran it seems clear that the Figurative Failaka Style vessels were produced and partook in ritual activities within a Dilmun sphere, cf. above p.106. Their cuneiform inscriptions mentioning temples, dedications and their imagery displaying religious processions suggest that these rituals were public rather than private.

No sherds of this style can, however, be related with certainty to the temple court yard in Tell F3 as suggested by Howard-Carter (1989: 265). A possible exception is the sherd inscribed 'temple of Inzak' (fig. 242) which was found in the northern part of Trench RM between c. 40 and c. 60 m and between level c. 8.00 and 9.00 m (Højlund 1987 figs. 1 and 6). This part of Trench RM covers c. 100 m², and one fifth of this area (c. 20 m²) is positioned within the temple enclosure. The levels correspond to the two upper floors of the enclosure.

From the temple in Tell F6 a few Figurative Failaka Style sherds were found, but the other stone vessel styles were just as prominent here, so even though it cannot be ruled out it is not compelling that the vessels originally were placed in this building.

The original context of the Figurative Failaka Style vessels is thus far from evident, and the possibility that their find contexts are due to secondary reuse rather than primary use should not be discounted.

The same problem is related to the Geometric and Plain Failaka Style vessels. They were probably originally used in domestic circumstances in the mid 2nd millennium settlements of Tells F3 and F6, but their final find contexts may be explained by their use as raw materials.

Even though the precise dating and context is uncertain the occurrence of the *Failaka Figurative Style* on Failaka in the mid 2nd millennium is intriguing. The late Old Babylonian-Early Kassite period is a time of increasing Mesopotamian influence in Dilmun, probably related to the decline of the lucrative Dilmun trade after 1800 BC (Højlund 1989, 2007, in press.). This growing Mesopotamian influence can be seen in the transition from individual to collective burials in Bahrain (Velde 1998. Højlund 2007: 135), and it is expressed in the style of the pottery, from the bowl rims in period "IIF" at Qala'at al-Bahrain (Højlund 2007: 13) over the so-called "Enigmatic pottery" of the post-IIc period found in Bahrain burials (Denton 1997: 182-184, 1999: 135, 145; Højlund 2007: 11-15, fig. 3) to the dominance of "Early Kassite" pottery in Mesopotamian tradition in Failaka period 3B and Qala'at al-Bahrain period IIIa (Højlund 1987: 121, 1989: 11, fig. 1).

During the same period, i.e. from the reign of Samsuiluna and for several hundred years the finds disappear from South Mesopotamia (Gasche 1989), and we are left completely in the dark. This explains why the local Gulf corpus of Style III stamp seals, the Figurative Failaka Style vessels, and the "Early Kassite" pottery on the one hand bears an undeniably Mesopotamian imprint (as well as local components), but on the other hand completely lacks specific Mesopotamian parallels. In this situation Denton can call Style III "distinctly un-Babylonian" and find the strongest affinities to Style III seals in the glyptic repertoires of Khuzistan and Anatolia (Denton 1997: 176).

That South Mesopotamia was not uninhabited in this period is amply shown by cuneiform tablets from the First Sealand Dynasty (Dalley 2009)[5], and rather than trying to explain Style III and the Figurative Failaka Style as entirely local phenomena (perhaps influenced by far-away places) it seems more profitable to view them as oriented towards the Sealand entity.

---

[5] Note that persons with both arms raised in a gesture of worship – the most popular motif in the Figurative Failaka Style – seem to be common in cylinder seal impressions on this Sealand collection of tablets, cf. MS 2200 – 29, 47, 264, 276, 308, 325, 367, 350A.

Bibliography

Amiet, P. 1966: *Elam*. Archer Editeur.

Al-Sindi, Kh. M. 1999: *Dilmun seals*. Ministry of Cabinet Affairs and Information, Bahrain.

Andersen, H.H. & Højlund, F. 2003: *The Barbar Temples*, vol. 1. JASP 48. Højbjerg.

Aruz, J. (ed.) 2003: *Art of the First Citites*. The Metropolitan Museum of Art. Yale University Press: New Haven & London.

Bellelli, G. M. 2002: *Vasi Iranici in Metallo dell'Età del Bronzo*. Prähistorische Bronzefunde, Abteilung II, 17. Band. Franz Steiner Verlag: Stuttgart.

Benediková, L. (ed.) 2010: *Al-Khidr 2004-2009, Primary Scientific Report on the Activities of the Kuwait-Slovak Archaeological Mission*. National Council for Culture, Arts & Letters, Kuwait City. Archeologicky ústav Slovenska akadémie vied, Nitra.

Bevan, A. 2007: *Stone Vessels and Values in the Bronze Age Mediterranean*. Cambridge University Press: Cambridge.

Bibby, T.G. 1970: *Looking for Dilmun*. Pelican Books Ltd. Ringwood, Victoria, Australia.

Burkholder, G. 1971: Steatite Carvings from Saudi Arabia. In: Porada, E. (ed.): Some Results of the Third International Conference on Asian Archaeology in Bahrain, March 1970: New Discoveries in the Persian/Arabian Gulf States and Relations with Artifacts from Countries of the Ancient Near East. *Artibus Asiae* 33:4, pp. 291-338.

Burkholder, G. 1984: *An Arabian Collection: Artifacts from the Eastern Provinces*. G.B. Publications. Boulder City.

Calvet, Y. 2005: Agarum, une île de la civilisation de Dilmoun. In: Callot, O. (ed.): *L'île de Failaka Archéologie du Koweït*. Éditions Somogy, Lyon.

Calvet, Y. & Pic, M. 1986: Un nouveau bâtiment de l'Age du Bronze sur le Tell F6. In: Calvet, Y. & Salles, J.-F. (eds.): *Failaka. Fouilles Françaises 1984-1985*. Travaux de la Maison de l'Orient 12. Lyon, pp. 13-87.

Calvet, Y. & Salles, J.-F. (eds.) 1986: *Failaka. Fouilles Françaises 1984-1985*. Travaux de la Maison de l'Orient 12. Lyon.

Casanova, M. 1991: *La vaisselle d'albatre de Mésopotamie, d'Iran et d'Asie centrale aux IIIe et IIe millénaires av. J.-C.* Èditions Recherche sur les Civilisations, Paris.

Casanova, M. 2003: Alabaster and Calcite Vessels. In: Andersen, H.H. & Højlund, F. 2003. *The Barbar Temples*, pp. 283-288.

Ciarla, R. 1979: The Manufacture of Alabaster Vessels at Shahr-I Sokhta and Mundigak in the 3rd Mill. BC. A Problem of Cultural Identity. In: Gnoli, G. & Rossi, A.V. (eds.): Iranica. Instituto Universitario Orientale Seminario di Studi Asiatic. Series Minor. X, pp. 319-335.

Ciarla, R. 1981: A preliminary Analysis of the Manufacture of Alabaster Vessels at Shar-i Sokhta and Mundigak in the 3rd Millennium BC. In: Härtel, Herbert, (ed.): *South Asian Archaeology 1979*. Dietrich Reimer Verlag Berlin, pp. 45-63.

Ciarla, R. 1985: Bronze-Age Crafts at Failaka: Some Preliminary Observations on Stone Vase Fragments. *East and West* 35, pp. 396-406.

Ciarla, R. 1990: Fragments of Stone Vessels as a Base Material. Two Case Studies: Failaka and Shahr-i Sohkta. In: Taddei, M. (ed.): *South Asian Archaeology* 1987, part 1. Istituto Italiano Per Il Medio Ed Estremo Oriente. Rome, pp. 475-491.

Cleuziou, S. 2003: Jiroft et Tarut sur la côte orientale de la Péninsule Arabique. In: *Dossiers d'Archeologie n° 287 oct. 2003* pp. 114-125.

Collon, D. 1987: *First Impressions. Cylinder Seals in the Ancient Near East*. British Museum Publications. London.

Crawford, H. 1998: *Dilmun and its Gulf neighbours*. United Kingdom: Cambridge University Press.

DA 2003 = *Dossiers d'Archeologie n°287 oct. 2003*: Jiroft, Fabuleuse Découverte en Iran.

Dalley, S. 2009: *Babylonian Tablets from the First Sealand Dynasty in the Schøyen Collection*. Cornell University Studies in Assyriology and Sumerology vol. 9. Maryland.

David, H. 1990: La Vaisselle en Chlorite de Failaka. In: Calvet, Y. & J. Gachet (eds.): *Failaka. Fouilles Françaises 1986-1988*. Travaux de la Maison de l'Orient 18. Maison de l'Orient. Lyon, pp. 141-146.

David, H. 1991: A First Petrographic Description of the Soft Stone Vessels from Shimal. In: Schippmann, K., Herling, A. & Salles, J.F. (eds.): *Golf-Archäologie, Mesopotamien, Iran, Kuwait, Bahrain, Vereinigte Arabische Emirate und Oman*. Internationale Archäologie 6. Dobiat, C. und Leidorf, K. (eds.). Maison de l'Orient Méditerranéen, Lyon.

David, H. 1996: Styles and Evolution: Soft stone vessels during the Bronze Age in the Oman Peninsula. *Proceedings of the Seminar for Arabian Studies* 26, pp. 31-46.

David, H. 2002: Soft Stone Mining Evidence in the Oman Peninsula and its relation to Mesopotamia. In: Cleuziou S., Tosi M. & Zarins J. (eds): *Essays on the Late Prehistory of the Arabian Peninsula*, IsIAO, Rome, pp. 317-335.

David, H. 2011: Les Vases en Chlorite. In: Cleuziou, S., Méry. S. & Vogt, B.: *Protohistoire de l'oasis d'al-Aïn (Émirate d'Abou Dhabi)*. Travaux de la Mission Archéologique Française en Abou Dhabi, vol.1. Les Sépultures de l'âge du Bronze. BAR. London, pp. 184-201.

David, H., Tegyey, M., Le Metour, J. & Wyns, R. 1990: Les vases en chlorite dans la peninsula d'Oman: un etude pétrographique appliquée à l'archaéologie. C.R. Acad.Sci.Paris, t.311, Série II, pp. 951-958.

David, H. & Phillips, C. 2008: A Unique Stone Vessel from a Third Millennium Tomb in Kalba. In: Olijdam, E. & Spoor, R.H.: *Intercultural Relations Between South and Southwest Asia. Studies in the Commemoration of E.C.L. During Caspers (1934-1995)*. BAR International Series 1826, pp. 118-123.

De Cardi, B. 1968: Excavations at Bampur, S.E. Iran: A Brief Report. *Iran* 6, pp. 135-155.

De Cardi, B. 1988: The Grave-goods from Shimal Tomb 6 in Ras al-Khaimah, U.A.E. In: Potts, D.T. (ed.): *Araby the Blest – Studies in Arabian Archaeology*. Museum Tuscelanum Press, pp. 45-72.

Delougaz, P. 1960: Architectural Representation on Steatite Vases. *Iraq* 22, pp. 90-95.

Denton, B.E. 1994: Pottery, cylinder seals, and stone vessels from the cemeteries of al-Hajjar, al-Maqsha and Hamad Town on Bahrain. *Arabian Archaeology and Epigraphy* 5, pp. 121-151.

Denton, B. E. 1997: Style III seals from Bahrain. *Arabian archaeology and epigraphy* 8, pp. 174-189.

Failaka 1966: *Archaeological Investigations in the Island of Failaka 1958-1964*. Ministry of Guidance and Information, Department of Antiquity & Museums, Kuwait Government Press.

Franke-Vogt, U. 1991: *The Settlement of Central-Shimal*. In: Schippmann, K., Herling. A, Salles J-F. (eds.): *Internationale Archäologie 6, Golf-Archäologie, Mesopotamien, Iran, Kuwait, Bahrain, Vereinigte Arabische Emirate und Oman*, pp. 179-204.

Gachet, J. & Salles, J-F. 1986: Chantier F5: rapport préliminaire 1985. In: Calvet, Y. & Salles, J.-F. (eds.): *Failaka. Fouilles Françaises 1984-1985*. Travaux de la Maison de l'Orient 12. Lyon, pp. 297-330.

Glassner, J.-J. 1984: Inscriptions cunéiformes de Failaka. In: Salles, J.-F. (ed.): *Failaka Fouilles Française 1983*. Traveaux de la Maison de l'Orient, Lyon, pp. 31-50.

Glassner, J.-J. 2008: Textes cunéiformes. In: Calvet, Y. & Pic, M. (eds.): *Failaka Fouilles Françaises 1984-1988. Matériel céramique du temple-tour et épigraphie*. Traveaux de la Maison de l'orient et de la Méditerranée, pp. 171-205.

Hakemi, A. 1997: *Shahdad, Archaeological Excavations of the Bronze Age Center in Iran*. IsMEO.

Hannestad, L. 1983: *The Hellenistic Pottery from Failaka* vol. 2:1. Ikaros. The Hellenistic Settlements. JASP 16:2, Højbjerg.

Harper, P.O. & Pittman, H. 2005: *Ancient Near East*. In: O'Neill, J.P. (ed.): The Metropolitan Museum of Art (New York, N.Y.), Egypt and the Ancient Near East. Yale University Press, pp. 90-159.

Hilton, A., Højlund, F., David-Cuny, H. & Eidem, J. 2013: Altar plates from second millennium BC Failaka, Kuwait. *Bibliotheca Orientalis* LXIX, pp. 411-419.

Hilton, A. in prep. Stone vessels. In: Højlund, F. & Abu-Laban, A.: *Tell F6 on Failaka Island. Kuwaiti-Danish Excavations 2008-2012*.

Howard-Carter, T. 1989: Voyages of Votive Vessels in the Gulf. In: Behrens, H., Loding, D., and Roth, M.T. (eds.): *DUMU-E$_2$-DUB-BA-A, Studies in Honor of Åke W. Sjöberg*. Occasional Publications of the Samuel Noah Kramer Fund, 11. Philadelphia, pp. 253-266.

Häser, J. 1990: Soft-stone vessels of the 2nd Millennium B.C. in the Gulf Region. *Proceedings of the Seminar for Arabian Studies* 20, pp. 43-54.

Häser, J. 1991: Soft-stone vessels from Shimal and Dhayah, Ras al-Khaimah. In: Schippmann, K., Herling, A. & Salles, J.-F. (eds.): *Golf-Archäologie, Mesopotamien, Iran, Kuwait, Bahrain, Vereinigte Arabische Emirate und Oman*. Internationale Archäologie 6. Universität Göttingen, Bundesrepublik Deutschland & Maison de l'Orient Méditerranéen, Lyon, France, pp. 221-232.

Højlund, F. 1987: *The Bronze Age Pottery*. Failaka/Dilmun. The Second Millennium Settlements, vol. 2. JASP 17:2. Højbjerg.

Højlund, F. 1989: Dilmun and the Sealand. *Northern Akkad Project Reports* 2 p. 9-14.

Højlund, F. 1995: Bitumen-coated basketry in Bahraini burials. *Arabian archaeology and epigraphy* 6:2, pp. 100-02.

Højlund, F. 2007: *The Burial Mounds of Bahrain. Social Complexity in Early Dilmun*. JASP 58. Højbjerg.

Højlund, F. 2010: *Between the temple and the "Palace" in Tell F6, Failaka, Kuwait: Two seasons of excavation by the Kuwait-Danish Mission 2008-2009*. Unpublished paper presented at the Seminar for Arabian Studies, London July 2010.

Højlund, F. in press: Transformations of the Dilmun state, c. 2050-1600 BC. *Twenty Years of Bahrain Archaeology (1986-2006)*. International Conference, December 9.-13. 2007.

Højlund, F. & Andersen, H. H. 1994: *Qala'at al-Bahrain. The Northern City Wall and the Islamic Fortress*, Vol.1. JASP XXX:1. Højbjerg.

Højlund, F. & Andersen, H. H. 1997: *Qala'at al-Bahrain. The Central Monumental Buildings*, Vol. 2. JASP XXX:2. Højbjerg.

Jacobsen, T. 1976: *The Treasures of Darkness – A History of Mesopotamian Religion*. Yale University Press: New Haven and London.

Jasim, S.A. 2006: The Archaeological sites of Jebel al-Buhais. In: Uerpmann, H-P., Uerpmann, M. & Jasim, S.A.: *Funeral Monuments and Human Remains from Jebel al-Buhais*, Vol. 1. Department of Culture and Information, Government of Sharjah, U.A.E. Institut für Ur- und Frühgeschichte und Archäologie des Mittelalters Universotät Türbingen, Germany. Kerns Verlag, Tübingen, pp. 13-68.

JASP: Jutland Archaeological Society Publications. Højbjerg.

Jeppesen, K. 1989: *The Sacred Enclosure in the Early Hellenistic Period* (Ikaros. The Hellenistic Settlements vol. 3). JASP 16:3. Højbjerg.

Killick, R. & Moon, J. 2005: *The Early Dilmun Settlement at Saar*. London-Bahrain Archaeological Expedition. Saar Excavation Report 3. Archaeology International Ltd, Ludlow, UK.

King, L. W. 1912: *Babylonian boundary-stones and memorial tablets in the British Museum*. London, British Museum.

Kjærum, P. 1980: Seals of the 'Dilmun type' from Failaka, Kuwait. *Proceedings of the Seminar for Arabian Studies* 10, pp. 45-54.

Kjærum, P. 1983: *The Stamp and Cylinder Seals. Plates and Catalogue Descriptions*. (Failaka/Dilmun. The Second Millennium Settlements 1:1). JASP 17:1.

Kjærum, P. 1994: Stamp-seals, seal-impressions and seal blanks. In: Højlund, F. and Andersen, H.H.: *Qala'at al-Bahrain. The Northern City Wall and the Islamic Fortress*, pp. 319-351.

Kjærum, P. 2003: Stamp Seals and Seal Impressions. In: Andersen, H.H. & Højlund, F. *The Barbar Temples*, pp. 289-305.

Kjærum, P. & Højlund, F. 2013: *The Bronze Age Architecture*. (Failaka/Dilmun. The Second Millennium Settlements 3). JASP XVII: 3. Højbjerg.

Kohl, P.L. 1975: Carved Chlorite Vessels: A trade in finished commodities in the mid-third Mill. BC. *Expedition* 18, 1, pp. 18-31.

Kohl, P.L. 1978: The Balance of Trade in Southwestern Asia in the Mid-Third Millennium BC. *Current Anthropology* 19:3, pp. 463-492.

Kohl, P.L. 1992: *Analyses of soft-stone vessels from Failaka, Kuwait*. Report in the archive of Moesgård Museum.

Kohl, P.L. 2001: Reflections on the Production of Chlorite at Tepe Yahya: 25 years later. In:

Lamberg-Karlovsky, C.C. & Potts, D.T.: *Excavation at Tepe Yahya, Iran, 1967-1975 – The Third Millennium*. American School of Prehistoric Research Bulletin 45. Peabody Museum of Archaeology and Ethnology. Harvard University, Cambridge, Massachusetts, pp. 209-230.

Kohl, P.L., Harbottle, G. & Sayre, E.V. 1979: Physical and Chemical Analyses of Soft Stone vessels from SW Asia. *Archeometry* 21, pp. 131-159.

Konishi, M.A. 1996: Legendary spring and the stepped wells of 2000 B.C., Bahrain – from the excavations at 'Ain Umm es-Sujur. *Lahore Museum Bulletin* vol. IX, no. 1.

Lamberg-Karlovsky, C.C. 1970: *Excavations at Tepe Yahya, Iran, 1967-1969*. Massachusetts: Cambridge.

Lamberg-Karlovsky, C.C. 1988: The Intercultural Style Carved Vessels. *Iranica Antiqua* 23, pp. 45-95.

Lombard, P. (ed) 1999: *Bahrain: The Civilisation of the Two Seas from Dilmun to Tylos*. Paris.

Madjidzadeh, Y. 2003: La découverte de Jiroft. In: *Dossiers d'Archeologie n°287 oct. 2003*, pp. 18-63.

Magee, P., Barber, D., Sobur, M. & Jasim, S. 2005: Sourcing Iron Age softstone artefacts in southeastern Arabia. *Arabian archaeology and epigraphy* 16, pp. 129-143.

Miroschedji, P. de 1973: Vases et objets en stéatite susiens du musée du Louvre. *Cahiers de la Délégation Archéologique Française en Iran* 3, pp. 9-80.

Moorey, P.R.S. 1994: *Ancient Mesopotamian Materials and Industries – the Archaeological Evidence.* Clarendon Press, Oxford.

Muscarella, O.W. 2005: Jiroft and "Jiroft-Aratta". A Review Article of Yosef Madjidzadeh, Jiroft: The Earliest Oriental Civilization. *Bullentin of the Asia Institute 15,* pp. 173-198.

Nashef, Kh. 1986: The Deities of Dilmun. *Bahrain through the Ages,* pp. 340-366.

Nijhowne, J. 1999: Politics, Religion and Cylinder Seals: A Study of Mesopotamian Symbolism in the Second Millennium B.C. *BAR International Series 772.*

Perrot, J. 2003: L'iconographie de Jiroft. In: *Dossiers d'Archeologie n° 287 oct. 2003,* pp. 97-113.

Pittman, H. 2003: La Culture du Halil Roud. In: *Dossiers d'Archeologie n° 287 oct. 2003,* pp. 78-87.

Porada, E. 1963: *Iran – Den Førislamiske Kunst.* Hassings Forlag. København.

Possehl, G.L. 2002: *The Indus Civilization: a contemporary perspective.* Oxford: Rowham & Littlefield Publishers, Inc.

Potts, D.T. 1991: *Further Excavations at Tell Abraq, The 1990 Season.* Munksgaard. Copenhagen.

Potts, D.T. 2003: A soft-stone genre from Southeastern Iran: 'zig-zag' bowls from Magan to Margiana. In: Potts, T., Roaf, M. & and Stein, D. (eds.): In *Culture Through Objects. Ancient Near Eastern Studies in Honour of P.R.S. Moorey,* pp. 77-93.

Potts, D.T. 2010: North-Eastern Arabia (circa 5000-2000 BC). In: Al-Ghabban et al. eds., *Roads of Arabia. Archaeology and History of the Kingdom of Saudi Arabia.* Paris pp. 172-183.

Potts, T.F. 1989: Foreign Stone Vessel of the Late Third Millennium B.C. from Southern Mesopotamia: Their Origins and Mechanisms of Exchange. *Iraq 51,* pp. 123-164.

Potts, T.F. 1993: Patterns of Trade in Third-Millennium BC Mesopotamia and Iran. *World Archaeology 24:3,* pp. 379-402.

Potts, T.F. 1994: *Mesopotamia and the East – An Archaeological and Historical Study of Foreign Relations ca. 3400-2000 BC.* Oxford: Oxford University Committee for Archaeology.

Reade, J. & Searight, A. 2001: Arabian softstone vessels from Iraq in the British Museum. *Arabian archaeology and epigraphy* 12, pp. 156-172.

Rice, P.M. 1987: *Pottery Analysis: A Sourcebook.* University of Chicago Press.

Rossignol-Strick, M. 2003: Climat et vegetation sur le plateau iranien à l'aube des temps historiques. In: *Dossiers d'Archeologie n° 287 oct. 2003,* pp. 4-18.

Salvatori, S & Tosi, M. 1997: Some Reflections on Shahdad and Its Place in the Bronze Age of Middle Asia. In: Hakemi, A. *Shahdad – Archaeological Excavations of a Bronze Age Center in Iran.* IsMeo-Rome, pp. 121-132.

Schneider, T.J. 2011: *An Introduction to Ancient Mesopotamian Religion.* William B. Eerdmans Publishing Company Grand Rapids: Michigan/Cambridge, United Kingdom.

Shepard, A.O. 1976: Ceramics for the Archaeologist. Carnegie Institution of Washington: Washington D.C.

Vallat, F. 2003: La Ziggurat. In: *Dossiers d'Archeologie (n°287 oct. 2003),* pp. 92-95.

Velde, C. 1998: The Dilmun Cemetery at Karanah 1 and the change of burial customs in late City II. In: Phillips. C.S., Potts, D.T. & Searight, S.: *Arabia and Its Neighbours: Essays on Prehistorical and Historical Developments.* Abiel II. Brepols, pp. 245-261.

Velde, C. 2003: Wadi Suq and Late Bronze Age in the Oman Peninsula. In: Potts, D., Naboodah, H.A., Hellyer, P. (eds.): *Proceedings of the First International Conference on the Archaeology of the U.A.E.* Trident press, pp. 102-113.

Vogt, B. and Franke-Vogt, U. (eds.) 1987: *Shimal 1985/1986. Excavations of the German Archaeological Mission in Ras Al-Khaimah, U.A.E. A Preliminary Report.* Berliner Beiträge zum Vordern Orient: Band 8. Dietrich Reimer Verlag. Berlin.

Vogt, B., Häser, J., Kästner, J-M, Schutkowski, H. & Velde, C. 1989: Preliminary Remarks on two recent excavated tombs in shimal, Ras al-Khaimah. In: Frifelt, K. & Sørensen. P. (eds.): *South Asian Archaeology 1985.* Scandinavian Intititute of Asian Studies Occasional Papers No. 4, pp. 62-73.

Woolley, C.L. 1934: *The Royal Cemetery.* Ur Excavations 2. Oxford.

Yasin al-Tikriti, W. 1985: The Archaeological Investigations on Ghanadha Island 1982-1984: Further Evidence for the Coastal Umm an-Nar culture. *Archaeology in the United Arab Emirates* 4, pp. 9-19.

Zarins, J. 1978: Typological Studies in Saudi Arabian Archaeology, Steatite Vessels in the Riyadh Museum. *ATLAL Journal of Saudi Arabian Archaeology 2,* pp. 65-93.

Ziolkowski, M.C. & Al-Sharqi, A.S. 2006: Dot-in-circle: An ethnoarchaeological approach to soft-stone vessel decoration. *Arabian archaeology and epigraphy* 17, pp. 152-162.

Appendix

FORM CODES

Rims
Rounded lip (1)
RO1, a: Everted sloping rim with outcurving rounded lip.
RO1, b: Everted sloping rim with indentation below rounded lip.
RO1, c: Vertical rim with indentation below rounded lip.
RO1, d: Vertical rim with rounded lip.
RO1, e: Everted sloping rim with rounded lip.
RC1, f: Incurving rim with rounded lip.
RC1, g: Inverted rim with rounded lip.
RC1, h: Incurving rim with indentation below rounded lip.
RC1, i: Inverted sloping rim with rounded lip.
RC1, j: Horizontal everted rim with rounded lip.
RC1, k: Slightly incurving rim with rounded lip.
RC1, l: Slightly insloping rim with indentation below rounded lip.
RC1, m: Slightly insloping rim with outcurving rounded lip.

Flattened lip (2)
RO2, a: Everted sloping rim with flattened lip.
RO2, b: Vertical rim with flattened lip.
RC2, c: Incurving rim with flattened lip.
RC2, d: Inverted rim with flatten lip.

Pointed Lip (3)
RO3, a and RC3, a: Vertical rim with pointed lip.
RO3, b: Everted sloping rim with pointed lip.
RC3, c: Incurving rim with pointed lip.

Thickened lip (4)
RO4, a: Vertical rim with external thickened lip.
RO4, b: Everted sloping rim with external thickened lip.
RO4, c: Everted sloping rim with external thickened lip with a centred indentation.
RO4, d: Vertical rim with external thickened lip with a centred indentation.
RO4, e: Vertical rim with internal thickened lip.

RC4, f: Incurving rim with external thickened lip.
RC4, g: Inverted sloping rim with external thickened lip.
RC4, h: Incurving rim with external thickened lip with a centred indentation.
RC4, i: Slightly incurving rim with external thickened rounded lip.

Bases
Flat base (1)
Ba1, a: Flat base with rounded base-edge.
Ba1, b: Flat base with semi-angular base-edge.
Ba1, c: Flat base with angular base-edge.

Round base (2)
Ba2, a: round base with rounded base-edge.

Disk base (3)
Ba3, a: disk base with rounded base-edge.
Ba3, b: disk base with angular base-edge.

Ring base (4)
Ba4, a: ring base with angular base-edge.
Ba4, b: ring base with rounded base-edge.

Stump base (5)
Ba5, a: tall stump base.
Ba5, b: short stump base.

Spouts
S1: Plain square spout.
S2: Geometric decorated square spout.
S3: Squarish spout with rounded corners.
S4: Trapezoid spout.
S5: Round spout.

Handles
H1: Rectangular lug-handle.
H2: Square lug-handle.
H3: Cylindrical handle.
H4: Square handle.
H5: Half-ellipsoid handle.

Lids
L1: Large circular lid with stemmed handles.

L2: Circular lid with stemmed knob-handle, flat bottom.
L3: Circular lid with stemmed knob-handle, concave bottom.
L4: Square box lid.

Boxes
Bx: All boxes are unique and were labelled Bx1-5.

Manufacture codes
1: Hand-carved i.e. without the use of mechanical aid like a grinding slot or a lathe. This stage relate exclusively to the shaping of the vessel not including decoration.
2: Chisel marks.
3: Blunt tool.
4: Grinding slot.
5: Lathe.
6: Surface polish done by abrasives.
7: Carved raised relief.
8: Incised decoration.

Use and reuse codes:
1: Wear marks. 1I: interior, 1E: exterior or 1EI: exterior and interior.
2: Soot.
3: Heat exposure.
4: Hole, either drilled or carved, including mending holes.
5: Copper wire in situ in mending hole.
6: Secondary cuts on surface or a clean transection.
7: Secondary cut and intentional breakage.
8: Secondary cut and polished/smoothen on damaged edges.
9: Polish on broken edges.
10: Small parallel thin incised lines ("scarification").
11: Secondary circular carvings.
12: Graffiti.
13: Residue.

Vessel type	Figure	KM.no.	DK.reg	Site	Trench	Dating	Style	Form	Size	Stone type	Decoration	Manu-facture	Use
1A	415	6064/05	1961.AFE	F5	–	–	Misc.	R.O.4, a	240	2	–	1,6	1,4
1A	414	6059/01	F5.62.AQY	F5	∎	–	Misc.	R.O.4, a	230	2	–	1,6	1,6
1B, 48A	288	3183/01-6069/01-6069/03	881.IY,881.JG	F3	RM	3A/4A	GFS	R.O.4, a, Ba.3, a	200	2	G1, G3, G10	1,6,8	1,2,3,4,5
1B	286	3173	881.BXD	F3	RM	–	GFS	R.O.4, a	150	2	G2, G3	1,6,8	1,3
1B	287	3190	–	F3	G	4A	GFS	R.O.4, a	130	2	G2, G6	1,6,8	1,3
1C	325	6060/01	1962.APN	F5	–	–	PFS	R.O.4, a	200	3	–	1,6	1
1C	329	6064/04	882.AD	–	–	–	PFS	R.O.4, a	280	4	–	1,6	1
1C	327	6063/07	881.AL	F3	–	–	PFS	R.O.4, a	230	4	–	1	1,2,3
1C	326	6060/03	881.CLY, BJQ	F3	AY	4	PFS	R.O.4, a	210	4	–	1	1,2
1C	328	6058/01	881.GJ	F3	RM	–	PFS	R.O.4, a	230	3	–	1,6	1,2,3,6
1C	330	6060/04	–	–	–	–	PFS	R.O.4, a	380	4	–	1	1,2
1C	331	6058/02	–	–	–	–	PFS	R.O.4, a	240	3	–	1,6	1
1C	324	3196/04	–	–	–	–	PFS	R.O.4, a	200	4	–	1	1,4
1D, 60A	334	3136	881.BFP	F3	AO	4A/4B	PFS	R.O.4, a, S.1	160	4	–	1,6	1
1D, 60A	335	3135	881.CHU, BFP	F3	AO	4A/4B	PFS	R.O.4, a, S.1	190	3	–	1,6	1
1E	289	6042/05	881.MT	F3	RM	Sieve	GFS	R.O.4, a	110	4	G3, G4	1,8	1
1E	293	6042/03	881.MT	F3	RM	Sieve	GFS	R.O.4, a	190	–	G3	1,8	1
1E	291	6042/02	881.SS	F3	–	–	GFS	R.O.4, a	100	4	G1, G3, G4	1,8	1
1E	290	6042/01	881.M	F3	–	–	GFS	R.O.4, a	90	4	G3, G4	1,8	1
1E	294	1516	–	F3	–	–	GFS	R.O.4, a	250	4	G3, G4	1,6,8	1I
1E	292	6042/04	–	–	–	–	GFS	R.O.4, a	150	4	G3, G4	1,8	1I
1F, 51E	255	3063, 8435	1129 949, A129-X454	F6	–	Sieve	FGFS	R.O.4, a, Ba.4, a	140	6	G1, G3, F20	1,6,7,8	1
1G	198	3108	881.BEZ	F3	–	–	LBAS	R.O.4, b	200	–	G2,G5,G8,G10	1,8	1
2A	410	6064/02	881.BBQ	F3	–	–	Misc.	R.O.4, b	190	4	–	1,6	1
2A	411	6063/09	–	–	–	–	Misc.	R.O.4, b	220	2	–	1	1,6
2B	413, 447	1643	1962.AKN	F5	–	–	Misc.	R.O.4, b	190	4	Greek inscription	1,5?,6	1,12
2B	412	6045/01	–	–	–	–	Misc.	R.O.4, b	150	4	–	1,5?,6	–
3	96	1737	1129 560	F6	D1	1 <	US	R.O.4, a	90	10	–	6	1
3, 55	97	1735	1961.AGÅ	F5	–	–	US	R.O.4, a, Ba.2, a	60	10	–	6	1

Vessel type	Figure	KM.no.	DK.reg	Site	Trench	Dating	Style	Form	Size	Stone type	Decoration	Manu-facture	Use
4A	339	6056/04	881.CDU, BBR	F3	AB	–	PFS	R.O.4, c	260	4	–	1,3	1
4A	338	6056/03	–	F3?	–	–	PFS	R.O.4, c	240	4	–	1,2,6	1,2,3,4,13
4A	336	3198/02	881.SS	F3	–	–	PFS	R.O.4, c	210	4	–	1	1,2,3,4
4A	337	3198/01	881.ÆS	F3	–	–	PFS	R.O.4, c	240	4	–	1,2,6	1,4,5
4B	304	3176/01	881.BH	F3	BB	–	GFS	R.O.4, c	210	4	G2, G3, G4	1,2,6,8	1E,3,6
4C	343	6056/06	881.CDU, BBR	F3	–	–	PFS	R.O.4, d	260	4	–	1,2,6	1
4C	341	6056/02	881.ÆS	F3	–	–	PFS	R.O.4, d	180	4	–	1,6	1,2,3,4
4C	340	6056/01	881.CHA, BFB	F3	AA	2	PFS	R.O.4, d	170	4	–	1,6	1
4C	342	3198/04	881.CHA, BFB	F3	AA	2	PFS	R.O.4, d	240	4	–	1	1,2,3,4
4D	306	6057/02	–	F3	AC	3B	GFS	R.O.4, d	190	4	G4	1,6,8	1,4
4D	308	3177/03	881.CFM, BDI	F3	AT	4	GFS	R.O.4, d	280	4	G2, G3, G4	1,8	1
4D	305	3189	–	F3	–	–	GFS	R.O.4, d	180	4	G2, G3, G4, G6	1,6,8	1
4D	307	3185/08	1129 949K	F6	–	Sieve	GFS	R.O.4, d	220	4	G1, G3, G10	1,6,8	1,7
5A	72	6062/10	881.QY	F3	–	–	US	R.O.1, a	170	1	–	1	1
5A	69	3196/05	881.BEY	F3	–	–	US	R.O.1, a	160	1	–	1,2,6	1,4
5A	71	6065/03	–	–	–	–	US	R.O.1, a	170	1	–	1	1
5A	73	–	881.ACJ	F3	E	2	US	R.O.1, a	170	1	–	1	1
5A	75	–	881.AHS	F3	–	4B	US	R.O.1, a	200	1	–	1	1
5A	76	–	881.ASS	F3	D	4A	US	R.O.1, a	210	1	–	1	1,6
5A	74	–	881.ALT	F3	C	3A/4A	US	R.O.1, a	180	1	–	1	1
5A	77	6064/01	–	–	–	–	US	R.O.1, a	300	1	–	1	1,4
5A	70	–	1129.443 HK	F6	–	–	US	R.O.1, a	60	1	–	1	1
5B	211	3199	881.BI	F3	BB	–	FFS	R.O.1, a	160	4	F12	1,7	1E,9
6A	300	3185/04	881.KI	F3	RM	3B	GFS	R.O.1, b	150	4	G2, G3, G4	1,8	1
6A	301	3185/03	881.QJ	F3	Y	4B	GFS	R.O.1, b	160	4	G1, G4	1,8	1
6B	302	1645	–	F6	Surface	–	GFS	R.O.1, b	250	11	C, G4	1,8,9	1
7A	212	3076	881.BEZ	F3	–	–	FFS	R.O.1, c	200	4	F12	1,6,7	1
7A	214	3045	–	–	–	–	FFS	R.O.1, c	240	4	F12, F16, F17	1,6,7	1,6

Vessel type	Figure	KM.no.	DK.reg	Site	Trench	Dating	Style	Form	Size	Stone type	Decoration	Manu-facture	Use
7A	213	1513	–	–	–	–	FFS	R.O.1, c	220	2	F12, F13, F17, F18, F20	1,6,7	1
7B, 60E	215	1517	1962.AKP	F5	–	–	FFS	R.O.1, b, S.5	160	–	C, F12, G11	1,6,7,9	1
8A	416	6062/09	881.FJ	F3	RM	4A	Misc.	R.O.2, a	160	4	–	1	1
8A	417	3197/03	–	F3	–	–	Misc.	R.O.2, a	170	–	–	1	1,4,8
8B	197	3172	–	F3	K	4A	LBAS	R.O.2, a	140	4	G2, G7, G8	1,6,8	1,4,5,13
9A	99	6062/14	1129 1008	F6	F1	1<	UANS	R.O.1, d	220	3	–	1	1,13
9A	98	3192/03	881.EM	F3	–	–	UANS	R.O.1, d	200	3	–	1	1
9B	133	3180/02	1962.AKR	F5	–	–	WS	R.O.1, d	230	3	G1, G3, G4	1,8	1,3,13
9B	131	3188	1129 1223	F6	F1	1	WS	R.O.1, d	160	2	G1, G3, G4	1,8	1
9B	127	6049/03	881.CEL, BCG	F3	AN	2	WS	R.O.1, d	150	4	G3, G4	1,6,8	1
9B	130	–	1129 736	F6	F2	1	WS	R.O.1, d	120	–	G1, G3, G4	1,6,8	1
9B	128	6048	–	–	–	–	WS	R.O.1, d	160	2	G3, G4	1,6,8	1,6
9B	132	3185/07	1129 249	F6	D2	1<	WS	R.O.1, d	190	4	G1, G3	1,6,8	1,6
9B	129	3185/06	–	F6?	–	–	WS	R.O.1, d	180	4	G2, G3	1,2,8	1,3
9C/60E	148	–	1129 732	F6	F2	1	WS	R.O.1, d, S.5	130	–	G1, G3, G4	1,2,8	1,3
10A	104	3182/08	881.VE	F3	AL	Sieve	UANS	R.O.1, e	200	3	G1, G3	1,8	1,2,3,9
10A, 41A	102	63	881.BUP ÅA	F3	AL	3B	UANS	R.O.1, d, Ba.2 a	130	3	G2, G3, G4	1,6,8	1
10A	103	–	881.AJB	F3	–	2	UANS	R.O.1, e	110	2	G2, G3	1,8	1
10A	105	8537	–	–	–	–	UANS	R.O.1, e	215	–	G2, G3	1,8	1
10B, 60E	107	3130	881.BJL	F3	–	–	UANS?	R.O.1, e, S.5	220	3	G1, G3	1,6,8	1
10C	126	3180/01	881.ALY	F3	–	–	WS	R.O.1, e	320	3	G1, G3, G4	1,6,8	1
10C	125	3176/02	881.YS	F3	–	–	WS	R.O.1, e	290	3	G1, G3, G4	1,2,8	1,3,6,13
10C	124	3183/02	–	–	–	–	WS	R.O.1, e	280	2	G1, G3, G4	1,6,8	1,9,12
11A	344	6055/03	–	–	–	–	PFS	R.O.1, e	220	4	–	1,6	1
11B	312	3194/01	881.FT	F3	RM	3A	GFS	R.O.3, a	190	4	G1, G3	1,6,8	1
11B	311	3193/01	881.SC	F3	RM	3A	GFS	R.O.3, a	180	4	G2, G3	1,6,8	1,4
11B	310	3193/02	–	–	–	–	GFS	R.O.1, e	190	2	G2, G3	1,6,8	1,4
11B	309	3181/02	–	–	–	–	GFS	R.O.1, e	190	4	G2, G3	1,8	1E,6

Vessel type	Figure	KM.no.	DK.reg	Site	Trench	Dating	Style	Form	Size	Stone type	Decoration	Manufacture	Use
11C	52	3081-3114	1129 900	F6	M2	Sieve	FS	R.O.1, e	340	4	F7	1,6,7	1,13
12A	141	3175	1129 949 E	F6	–	Sieve	WS	R.O.2, b	180	2	G1, G3	1,6,8	1
12A	143	3185/05	881.FU	F3	RM	–	WS	R.O.2, b	260	3	G1, G3	1,8	1,6,7
12A	142	3179/11	–	F3	RM	3A	WS	R.O.2, b	270	3	G1, G3	1,6,8	1,2,3
12B, 60C	152	3129, 6076/04	881.BST	F3	AD	3A/3B	WS	R.O.2, b, S.3	200	3	G2, G3, G4, G5, G11	1,6,8	1
12C, 61D	154	3141	881.OO	F3	RM	3A	WS	R.O.2, b, H.4	220	3	G1, G3, G5, G11	1,6,8	1,2,3,9
13A	134	3194/02	881.FB	F3	RM	3A	WS	R.O.3, a	230	3	G1, G3	1,6,8	1,2,3,4,5,6
13B, 60C	150	3128	881.HE	F3	RM	–	WS	R.O.3, a, S.3	200	4	G2, G3, G4, G11	1,6,8	1E,4,9
13B, 60E	149	–	881.BBU, ARF	F3	D	4A	WS	R.O.3a, S.5	150	4	G1,G3, G4, G5	1,2,3,6,8	1,10
13C	135	3193/03	881.CFP, BDL	F3	Y	2	WS?	R.O.3, a	360	2	G1, G3	1,2,6,8	1,2,3,4
13C	136	3184-3186	881.CDN, BBJ, I, BEQ	F3	AB/AT	4, 2	WS?	R.O.3, a	420	2	G1, G3, G5	1,2,6,8	1,6,9
15, 61E	316	6052	1129 1163	F6	F1	1<	GFS	R.O.1, e, H.5	210	4	G3, G4, G7	1,2,6,8	1,2,3,13
16, 47	51	422	881.BAU, VY	F3	AE/AD	Sieve/4A	FS	R.O.2, b, Ba.1, b	300	4	F1	1,6,7	1E
17A	29	3024	–	F3?	–	–	FS	R.O.4, a	110	1	F5	1,6,7	1
17A, 46	27	367	1129 1055	F6	N2	1	FS	R.O.4, a, Ba.1, b	90	1	F5	1,2,6,7	1E
17A, 46	28	3027-3028	881.GF, AGG	F3	RM/B	4A?/3A-3B	FS	R.O.4, a, Ba.1, b	100	1	F5	1,6,7	1E,7
17B	35	3097	1129 193	F6	A3	1<	FS	R.O.1, d	90	–	F9	1,6,7	1
17B, 44	33	3040	881.IO	F3	RM	4A	FS	R.O.1, d, Ba.1, a	90	1	F6, F15, F23	1,6,7	1E
17B	36	3007	881.ND	F3	RM	2<	FS	R.O.1, d	100	1	F1	1,6,7	1
17B	31	3004	881.BEZ	F3	–	–	FS	R.O.3, a	70	1	F6, F22	1,7	1,7
17B	32	3104	1129 912	F6	D2	1	FS	R.O.1, d	70	1	F6, F13	1,6,7	1
17B	37	3085	1129 1072	F6	M1	1<	FS	R.O.1, d	140	1	F7	1,7	1,6
17B	34	3086	1129 177	F6	A1	1<	FS	R.O.3, a	100	1	F7	1,7	1,6
18Aa, 52A	399	–	881.ZE	F3	A	3A	PFS	R.O.4, e, Ba.1, a	140	4	–	1	1,6
18Aa, 52A	401	–	1129 311 KJ	F6	C3	1<	PFS	R.O.4, e, Ba.1, a	250	–	–	1	1

Vessel type	Figure	KM.no.	DK.reg	Site	Trench	Dating	Style	Form	Size	Stone type	Decoration	Manu-facture	Use
18Aa, 52A	400	6097/03	881.CFZ, BDU	F3	Y	2	PFS	R.O.4, e, Ba.1, a	240	3	–	1	1,2,3
18Ab	402	1642	–	–	–	–	PFS	R.O.4, e	360	11	C	1,6,9	1
18B	403	–	881.BVX_01 AVD	F3	AL	4B	PFS	R.O.4, e	200	–	–	1,2	1
18B, 52B	405	6098/01	1129 1066	F6	–	–	PFS	R.O.4, e, Ba.1, a	210	2	–	1,6	1
18B, 52B	404	6098/02	1129 1006 AFP	F6	F1	1<	PFS	R.O.4, e, Ba.1, a	185	2	–	1,6	1,2,3
18C	406	1649	881.AYL	F3	–	–	PFS	R.O.2, a	420	4	C	1,6,9	1,9
19A	101	6061/02	881.NN	F3	RM	–	UANS	R.O.3, b	130	4	–	1,6	1
19A	100	6065/02	–	–	–	–	UANS	R.O.3, b	110	2	–	1,6	1
19B	379	6060/02	1962.APN	F5	–	–	PFS	R.O.1, c	90	4	–	1	1
19B	378	1508	1129 1092	F6	–	–	PFS	R.O.1, c	90	–	–	1,6	1
19B	380	6063/01	–	–	–	–	PFS	R.O.4, a	100	2	–	1	1
19C, 57	196	6054/02	–	F3?	–	–	LBAS?	R.O.1, e, Ba.1, a	100	3	–	1,6	1
19C	195	6062/06	881.QL	F3	–	–	LBAS?	R.O.1, d	70	4	–	1	1
20A	359	6063/05	881.QV	F3	RM	3A?	PFS	R.C.4, f	140	2	–	1	1
20A	358	6063/04	881.?	F3	–	–	PFS	R.C.4, f	140	2	–	1	1,4
20A, 50A/51A	356	–	881.BAU	F3	H	4A	PFS	R.C.4, f, Ba.3, a/ Ba.4,a	120	4	▪	1,5?,6	1,3
20A	357	6063/03	881.WK	F3	–	–	PFS	R.C.4, f	95	4	–	1,5?,6	1,6
20A	360	3529	–	–	–	–	PFS	R.C.4, f	160	4	C	1,6,9	1
20B	216	1520	1962.ALA	F5	–	–	FFS	R.C.4, f	280	4	C, F20	1,6,7,9	1,9
20C	297	–	881.AAJ	F3	F	Sieve	GFS	R.C.4, f	140	4	G1, G3	1,5?,8	1
20C	298	–	1129.BH.72	F6	A1	1<	GFS	R.C.4, f	230	4	G1, G3	1,8	1,2,10
20C, 48A	299	–	881.AQM,BEZ,ASE,AJH	F3	H	4A	GFS	R.C.4, f, Ba.3, a	210	4	G1, G3	1,8	1,2
21A	138	6061/01	1962.ANX	F5	–	–	WS?	R.C.1, f	200	4	–	1	1
21A	137	3196/01	–	–	–	–	WS?	R.C.1, f	120	3	–	1	1,4
21B	140	–	881.BNC	F3	–	–	WS	R.C.1, f	200	3	G1, G3, G4	1,8	1,2,3,4
21B	139	3192/01	881.XL	F3	–	–	WS	R.C.1, f	140	3	G1	1,8	1
21C, 41E, 60E	151	6053	881.QV	F3	–	–	WS?	R.C.1,f, Ba.1, a, S.5	160	3	–	1	1,9

181

Vessel type	Figure	KM.no.	DK.reg	Site	Trench	Dating	Style	Form	Size	Stone type	Decoration	Manu-facture	Use
22A	106	3178/06	1129 1171	F6	–	–	UANS?	R.C.1, k	160	4	G2, G3	1,6,8	1
22B	146	3178/03	881.MS	F3	RM	3A/3B	WS	R.C.1, k	180	3	G1, G3	1,8	1,3
22B	147	3177/01	881.OR	F3	RM	3A	WS	R.C.1, k	230	3	G1, G3	1,8	1,2,3
22B	145	3178/04	–	–	Sieve	–	WS	R.C.1, k	120	2	G1, G3	1,8	1
22B	144	–	1129 783	F6	M2	1 <	WS	R.C.1, k	95	–	G2, G3	1,8	1,6
22C/60C	153	3131	–	–	–	–	WS	R.C.1, k, S.3	150	3	G2, G4, G8, G11	1,6,8	1,3,6
23A	347	6057/03	881.CDU, BBQ	F3	–	2	PFS	R.C.1, k	160	2	–	1	1,6
23A	345	6057/01	881.AZ	F3	–	–	PFS	R.C.1, k	140	3	–	1	1,2,3
23A	348	3198/03	881.AVP	F3	–	–	PFS	R.C.1, k	180	3	–	1	1,2,3,4,9
23A	346	6055/02	1962.APN	F5	–	–	PFS	R.C.1, k	140	3	–	1	1
23B	349	–	881.ASZ,BET,AJO	F3	H/K	4A/3A-4A	PFS	R.C.3, c	125	–	–	1	1
24A	418	6062/11	–	–	–	–	Misc.	R.C.1, k	170	8	–	1	1
24A	419	6062/08	–	–	–	–	Misc.	R.C.1, k	170	8	–	1	1
24B	423	6062/04	881.RN	F3	–	–	Misc.	R.C.1, k	160	2	–	1	1
24B	422	6062/03	881.AEV	F3	–	–	Misc.	R.C.1, k	140	2	–	1	1
25A	352	6065/05	–	–	–	–	PFS	R.C.2, c	190	4	–	1	1,4
25A	351	6065/01	–	–	–	–	PFS	R.C.2, c	210	4	–	1	1
25A	353	–	881.BPK	F3	AB	Sieve	PFS	R.C.2, c	420	–	–	1	1
25A/42C	350	–	881.ARA	F3	G	3A	PFS	R.C.2, c, Ba.1, a	250	–	–	1,5?,6	1
25A	354	1296	1961	F3	–	–	PFS	R.C.2, c	360	3	C	1,6,9	1,6,11
25B	355	–	881.ATR	F3	K	Sieve	PFS	R.C.2, c	270	11	–	1	1
26	53	3023	881.BEZ, PD	F3	RM	? > 3B	FS	R.C.1, g	160	1	F3	1,6,7	1E,4,9
26	54	3200	–	–	–	–	FS	R.C.1, g	180	1	F4	1,6,7	1E,9
27/41D	218	3051-3082-1394	881.BQK,AB,US	F3, F5	B/AH	3A/3B	FFS	R.C.4, f, Ba.2, a	150	–	C, F10, F12, F13, F15, F18	1,6,7,9	1,3
27	217	3070	881.BES	F3	K	3A	FFS	R.C.4, f	140	–	F10, F12	1,6,7	1

Vessel type	Figure	KM.no.	DK.reg	Site	Trench	Dating	Style	Form	Size	Stone type	Decoration	Manu-facture	Use
28A	222	3059	881.YM	F3	F	Sieve	FFS	R.C.4, g	160	4	F14	1,7	1E
28A	221	3044	881.BUP ÅA	F3	AL	3B	FFS	R.C.4, g	130	4	F13, F14	1,7	1,9
28A	220	3020	881.BSJ	F3	AB/AF	Sieve	FFS	R.C.1, l	80	4	F17	1,7	1
28B	295	3174	881.ARK	F3	G	4A	GFS	R.C.4, g	190	2	G2, G6	1,6,8	1,6
28B	296	3113	881.AXC	F3	K/P/O	Sieve	GFS	R.C.4, g	230	4	G4, F19	1,2,6,8	1E,4,6,12
28C	333	6063/08	–	–	–	–	PFS	R.C.4, g	240	3	–	1,6	1
28C	332	6059/02	–	F5	–	–	PFS	R.O.4, g	230	3	–	1,6	1E,2,3
29	223	3008/03	881.APY	F3	H	4A	FFS	R.C.4, i	200	4	F12, F17, F21	1,6,7	1,6
29	223, 224	3008/02	881.BBC	F3	C	3A/4A	FFS	R.C.4, i	200	4	F12, F17, F21	1,6,7	1
29	223, 225	3008/01	881.BDK	F3	–	Sieve	FFS	R.C.4, i	160	4	F12, F17, F21	1,6,7	1
30	271	3057	881.BJL	F3	–	Sieve	FFS	R.C.4, h	100	4	F15	1,6,7	1,6,8
31A	79	6065/04	–	–	–	–	US	R.C.1, h	180	5	–	1	1
31A	78	3196/03	1129 949 FZ	F6	–	–	US	R.C.1, h	160	5	–	1	1,4
31B	80	1519	881.CFX, BDS	F3	Y	2	US	R.C.1, h	120	1	–	1,2,6	1
32A	109	6042/10	1129 999	F6	–	–	UANS	R.C.1, g	–	4	G3	1,8	1,6
32A	111	6041	1961.AEN	F5	–	–	UANS	R.C.1, g	250	3	G3	1,6,8	1,12
32A	110	6042/06	881.BOU	F3	AE/AD	3A/3B	UANS	R.C.4, f	120	3	G3	1,8	1,2
32A	108	6039	881.AXI	F3	AN	4	UANS	R.C.3, a	160	4	G3	1,8	1,4,5
32B	421	6064/03	–	F3?	–	–	Misc.	R.C.4, f	150	4	–	1,6	1
32B	420	6063/10	–	–	–	–	Misc.	R.C.4, f	135	2	–	1,6	1
33Aa	116	6042/08	881.BJL	F3	–	–	UANS	R.C.1, i	58	2	G3	1,8	1
33Aa	117	6042/09	–	F3	–	–	UANS	R.C.1, i	110	4	G3	1,8	1
33Aa	114	3181/01	881.NN	F3	RM	3A/4A	UANS	R.C.1, i	–	3	G2, G3	1,8	1
33Aa	115	3181/03	881.CAR, AYP	F3	AN	4	UANS	R.C.1, i	100	3	G2, G3	1,8	1,2,3
33Ab	173	3178/05	1129 153	F6	Skakt 1 N	1 <	WS	R.C.1, i	85	2	G1	1,8	1,6
33Ab	178	6040	881.CEN, BCI	F3	AN	2	WS	R.C.1, i	150	4	G3, G4	1,8	1,4,6

Vessel type	Figure	KM.no.	DK.reg	Site	Trench	Dating	Style	Form	Size	Stone type	Decoration	Manufacture	Use
33Ab	174	3185/02	881.AZP	F3	RM	-	WS	R.C.1, i	100	3	G1, G3	1,8	1,6,10
33Ab	177	3177/04	881.BSV	F3	AE	3A	WS	R.C.1, i	80	2	G2, G3	1,8	1E
33Ab	176	3177/02	-	-	-	-	WS	R.C.1, i	75	2	G1, G3	1,6,8	1E,3,6
33B	179	3192/02	881.CEN, BCI	F3	AN	2	WS	R.C.1, i	340	3	G1, G3	1,8	1
33C, 43A	168	65	881.BUP ÅA	F3	AL	3B	WS	R.C.1, i, Ba.1, c	72	4	G3, G4	1,2,3,6,8	1E,2,3,10
33D	200	6043/02	1962.ALZ	F5	-	-	LBAS	R.C.1, i	160	7	G3, G4	1,8	1
33D	201	6043/01-6047/02	1962.ALX, APN	F5	-	-	LBAS	R.C.1, i	120	7	G3, G4	1,8	1
33E, 41C,61A	162	3123	1962.AQY	F5	-	-	WS	R.C.1, i, Ba.2, a, H.1	52	4	G2, G3, G4	1,2,3,6,8	1,6
33E, 43A, 61A	163	59	881.ÅS	F3	-	-	WS	R.C.1, i, Ba.1, c, H.1	48	-	G1, G3, G4	1,2,3,6,8	1E,10
33E, 61A	180	-	881.BCX	F3	O	Sieve	WS	R.C.1, 1, H.1	70	-	G2,G3	1,2,8	1
33F	202	1635	-	F3	Surface	-	LBAS	R.C.1, g	120	3	G2, G6, G8	1,8	1
33G	203	-	881.ZV	F3	I	4B	LBAS	R.C.3, a	70	4	G3, G6	1,2	1
34A	270	3048-3068-3069	881.NN,AXT	F3	RM/D	3A/4A	FFS	R.C.1, i	100	4	F13, F18	1,6,7	1,7
34B	68	3001-3005	881.BEZ, ARF, AOX, AOA	F3	D/H	3A/4A	FS (ZZ)	R.C.1, i	130	2	F11, G3, G4	1,6,7,8	1,12
35A	394	6042/07	881.MT	F3	RM	Sieve	PFS	R.C.2, d	110	4	-	1,6	1
35A	395	6103/05	881.MT	F3	RM	Sieve	PFS	R.C.2, d	120	4	-	1	1
35A	396	-	881.BXD	F3	RM	-	PFS	R.C.2, d	200	2	-	1	1
35B	321	-	881.BFF	F3	-	-	GFS	R.C.1, m	70	4	G4	1,8	1,2
35B	318	-	881.BNX	F3	AE-AD	3A/4A	GFS	R.C.1, m	130	4	G4	1,8	1
35B	319	-	881.BAR	F3	-	-	GFS	R.C.1, m	110	4	G1,G3	1,8	1
35B	320	-	1129 711	F6	D2	2	GFS	R.C.2, d	140	3	G4	1,8	1
36	112	-	1129 638	F6	D2	1	UANS	R.C.1, c	90	-	G2, G3	1,6,7	1E
37	55	3003	1129 1077	F6	N1/M1	Sieve	FS	R.O.1, a	140	1	F5, F11	1,7	1
38	398	6046	1129 752	F6	F2	1	PFS	R.C.1, l	70	4	-	1	1
38	397	6063/02	-	-	-	-	PFS	R.C.1, l	45	2	-	1	1

Vessel type	Figure	KM.no.	DK.reg	Site	Trench	Dating	Style	Form	Size	Stone type	Decoration	Manu-facture	Use
39A	84	1732/02	881.SS	F3	RM	Sieve	US	R.C.1, i	180	9	–	1,6	1
39B	85	1733	1129 1024a	F6	–	–	US	R.O.4, a	130	9	–	1,6	1
39C	86	1727	881.KA	F3	RM	3B?	US	R.C.1, j	165	9	–	1,6	1
40A, 53A	407	3151-3152	–	F5	–	–	PFS	Bx.1	–	4	–	1,2	1,2,3,4,7
40B, 53B	272	3062	1129 216	F6	B2	1 <	FFS	Bx.2	–	–	F17, F19	1,7	1
40C	122	3178/01-3178/02	1129 1053	F6	M1	–	UANS?	Bx.5	–	1	G1	1,6,8	1,4
41A	119	6100/03	1962.AKE	F5	–	–	UANS	Ba.2 a	180	–	–	1	1,9
41A	118	6100/02	1962.ANM	F5	–	–	UANS	Ba.2 a	120	2	–	1	1,2,3,9
41A	120	6101/02	–	F3?	–	–	UANS	Ba.2 a	100	2	–	1	1,2,3,9
41B	169	6091/07	1129 1199	F6	M1	1	WS	Ba.2, a	90	2	G4	1,8	1
41B	172	6092/03	–	F3?	–	–	WS	Ba.2, a	120	2	G3, G4	1,8	1
41B	170	6094	881.BDG	F3	–	–	WS	Ba.2, a	145	4	G3	1,2,8	1
41B	171	6091/01	–	–	–	–	WS	Ba.2, a	100	3	G5	1,8	1
41C, 61A	164	6090	–	–	–	–	WS	Ba.2, a, H.1	140	2	G3, G4	1,2,6,8	1
41D	219	3052	–	–	–	–	FFS	Ba.1, a	160	2	F12, F16	1,6,7	1,3,6
41F	210	–	881.AHU	F3	B/M	3A/3B	LBAS	Ba.2, a	60	3	G1, G3, G4	1,8	1
42A	182	6091/06	881.AG	F3?	–	–	WS	Ba.1, a	180	2	G3, G4	1,6,8	1
42A	181	6068/01	1129 1116	F6	–	–	WS	Ba.1, a	120	2	G2, G3, G4	1,8	1,3,4
42B	264	3060	881.BYM, AWO	F3	AN	4	FFS	Ba.1, a	160	–	F14	1,6,7	1
42B	256-263	3030-3031-3032-3099-372-8338	1129 1104, 1101, 559 DY, X147-A30	F6	D1/F1/A	1 </1	FFS	Ba.1, a	80	4	F11,F12,F13,F17, F18,F20	1,2,3,6,7	1,4
42D	424	6101/03	–	–	–	–	Misc.	Ba.2, a	200	4	–	1	1,2,3,13
43A	188	6101/04	881.CCX, BAU	F3	AQ	> 4	WS	Ba.1, c	180	2	–	1	1,2,3,13
43A	187	6091/05	–	–	–	–	WS	Ba.1, c	120	2	G4	1,6,8	1
43A	186	6091/04	–	–	–	–	WS	Ba.1, c	80	3	G3, G4	1,8	1
43A	184	6091/03	881.BL	F3	–	–	WS	Ba.1, c	90	2	G3, G4	1,8	1
43A	185	6091/02	–	–	–	–	WS	Ba.1, c	130	2	G4	1,8	1
43A	183	–	881.AEI	F3	Q	–	WS	Ba.1, c	140	3	G4	1,8	1,2,8,13

Vessel type	Figure	KM.no.	DK.reg	Site	Trench	Dating	Style	Form	Size	Stone type	Decoration	Manu-facture	Use
43B	113	-	881.ASN	F3	C-D,G-H,K-L	-	UANS	Ba.1, c	110	2	G2,G3	1,8	1
43C	265	3098	881.BYM, AWO	F3	AN	4	FFS	Ba.1, c	360	4	F1,F13	1,6,7	1E
43D	425	6099	-	-	-	-	Misc.	Ba.1, a	180-190	4	–	1,2,3,6	1
44	33	3043	881.AIC, AUC	F3	F	3A/3B	FS	Ba.1, a	90	1	F6, F15	1,6,7	1E,6
45	56	3006	1129 1200	F6	M1/N1	1<?	FS	Ba.1, a	90	1	F8	1,7	1E
46	30	3019	881.HP	F3	RM	3A	FS	Ba.1, b	160	1	F2	1,6,7	1
48A	389, 446	3050	881.AKQ	F3	D	4A	PFS	Ba.3, a	70	3	F13	1	1,12
48A	381	66	-	F3	-	-	PFS	Ba.3, a	50	4	–	1,6	1,3,7
48A	383	6102/03	881.BJL	F3	-	-	PFS	Ba.3, a	120	4	–	1,6	1E
48A	385	6102/02	1962.APN	F5	-	-	PFS	Ba.3, a	100	2	–	1,6	1E
48A	391	6095/04	881.AWE	F3	-	-	PFS	Ba.3, a	130	2	–	1,6	1,2,3,6
48A	386	6095/03	881.QB	F3	-	-	PFS	Ba.3, a	120	2	–	1,6	1
48A	387	6102/06	881.RN	F3	AF	4B	PFS	Ba.3, a	120	4	–	1,6	1,6
48A	390	6096/02	-	F3	R	2	PFS	Ba.3, a	100	2	–	1,6	1E,2,3,4,5
48A	384	6054/03	881.CKZ, BIQ	F3	AY	4	PFS	Ba.3, a	130	4	–	1,5?,6	1,6
48A	388	6102/04	881.RN	F3	-	-	PFS	Ba.3, a	140	3	–	1	1E
48A	382	6096/01	-	-	-	-	PFS	Ba.3, a	100	2	–	1,6	1E,3
48A	392	6095/02	-	-	-	-	PFS	Ba.3, a	140	4	–	1,6	1E,11
48B	313	6102/05	-	F3?	-	-	GFS	Ba.3, a	200	2	G4	1,6,8	1
48C	223, 228	3101	881.AKT	F3	D	4A	FFS	Ba.3, a	180	4	F17	1,6	1,6,7,8
48C	267	1515	881.BAR	F3	K-P-O	Sieve	FFS	Ba.3, a	80	–	F13, F16	1,6,7	1
49A	393	6101/01	881.BS	F3	-	-	PFS	Ba.3, b	60	3	–	1	1,6,9
49B	314	6082/03	881.CHQ, BFK	F3	Surface	-	GFS	Ba.3, b	70	4	G4	1,8	1
49B	315	3154	-	F3?	-	-	GFS	Ba.3, b	75	4	G3, G4	1,6,8	1,6,7

Vessel type	Figure	KM.no.	DK.reg	Site	Trench	Dating	Style	Form	Size	Stone type	Decoration	Manu-facture	Use
50A	365	1518	881.ADK	F3	E	2	PFS	Ba.3, a	100	4	C	1,6,9	1
50A	361	6095/01	881.CBY, AZV	F3	AP	4	PFS	Ba.3, a	80	–	–	1,6	1
50A	362	6045/04	881.RG	F3	RM	3A/4A	PFS	Ba.3, a	90	4	–	1,6,7	1
50A	363	–	881.BSK	F3	AB/AF	Sieve	PFS	Ba.3, a	80	4	–	1,6	1
50A	364	–	881.BVX_02	F3	AL	4B	PFS	Ba.3, a	90	–	–	1	1
50B	268	3058	881.AXH	F3	O	4A	FFS	Ba.3, a	40	2	F14	1	1,6
51A	367	6081/01	1129 1119	F6	–	–	PFS	Ba.4, a	50	3	–	1,6	1
51A	368	6093/01	881.CCP, AZY	F3	AO	4A/4B	PFS	Ba.4, a	60	4	–	1,6	1,4,5
51A	370	6081/05	881.BZR, AXP	F3	AA/AY	4	PFS	Ba.4, a	70	4	–	1	1,4
51A	369	6081/03	881.RG	F3	RM	–	PFS	Ba.4, a	100	4	–	1,6	1,2
51A	366	–	881.BSN	F3	AD	3A/4A	PFS	Ba.4, a	60	4	–	1,6	1
51B	266	6051-6081/02	881.XP	F3	F	3A/3B	FFS	Ba.4, a	20	1	F12	1,6,7	1,8
51C	269	425	881.ÅB, XO	F3	AL	3B	FFS	Ba.4, a	70	4	F12, F14, F17	1,2,7	1E
51D	374	6080	881.VC	F3	AB	4B	PFS	Ba.4, a	120	4	–	1,6	1,3
53C	81	3155	–	F6	M2	1<?	US	Bx.3	c. 60×60	4	–	1,2,6	1,2,3,4
53C	82	–	881.BUK	F3	AL	2	US	Bx.3	c. 45×50	4	–	1,6	1,3
53D	60	3115	1129 783	F6	M2	1<	FS	Bx.4	c. 80×80	1	F10	1,6,7	1,4,7,9
54A	375	6093/02	881.QK	F3	X	3B/4B	PFS	Ba.4, b	80	4	–	1,5,6	1E,6
54B	376	6105/03	–	F3?	–	–	PFS	Ba.4, b	160	2	–	1	1
54B	377	6105/02	–	F3?	–	–	PFS	Ba.4, b	200	2	–	1,6	1
56	199	1478	881.AQT, APZ, BEZ	F3	K	4A	LBAS	Ba.3, b	180	2	G2, G3, G5, G6	1,6,8	1E
58A	87	1731	1129 1243	F6	–	–	US	Ba.1, a	75	9	–	1,4	1
58B	95	1729/03	–	–	–	–	US	Ba.5, a	60	9	–	1	1
58C	89	1730	881.CKY, BIP	F3	AH	3A/3B	US	Ba.5, b	60	9	–	1	1

Vessel type	Figure	KM.no.	DK.reg	Site	Trench	Dating	Style	Form	Size	Stone type	Decoration	Manu-facture	Use
60B	123	3134	-	F3	AE	3A	UANS?	S.2	-	4	G1	1,6,8	1
60D	155	3132	881.BSA	F3	AC	3B	WS	S.4	180	4	G3, G11	1,8	1,6,13
60E	157	1662	1129 1115	F6	D1/E1	1<	WS	S.5	-	4	G11	1,8	1,4
60E	158, 429	3133	881.AQJ	F3	K	4A	WS	S.5	-	4	G11	1,6,8	1,2,3,4,6
60E	156	3139	1962.ALN	F5	-	-	WS	S.5	-	-	-	1,6	1,7
61A	160	3143	-	F3?	-	-	WS	H.1	-	2	G1, G3, G10	1,8	1
61A	166	3142	881.RN	F3	RM	4A-4B	WS	H.1	-	2	G3, G5	1,8	1,9
61A	161	3140	881.BRM	F3	Ø	2	WS	H.1	-	-	G1, G3, G4	1,6,8	1
61A	165	-	881.AQH	F3	K	4A	WS	H.1	-	3	G4, G6	1,8	1
61B	167	1493	-	F3?	-	-	WS	H.2	-	2	-	1,6	1,8
61C	322	3145	1129 1047	F6	N2	1	GFS	H.3	-	5	G4	1,8	1,3,6
61C	323	6105/01	-	F3?	-	-	GFS	H.3	-	3	G4	1,6,8	1,2,3
61D	159	3148/02	881.SS	F3	RM	Sieve	WS?	H.4	220	4	G1	1,8	1
61E	317	3149	1129 124	F6	A2	1<	GFS	H.5	-	4	G4	1,6,8	1
62A	426	3125	1962.ANL	F5	-	-	Misc.	L.1	110	3	G1, G3	1,8,10	1,10
62B	191	3126/02	1129 284	F6	Skakt 1 N	1<	WS	L.2	65	3	G2	1,6,8	1
62B	189	3124/01	-	-	-	-	WS	L.2	14	4	G1	1,8	1,12
62B	190	3124/02	1129 1145	F6	F6	1	WS	L.2	42	4	G1, G3	1,8	1
62B	193	3124/03	-	F6	N1	1	WS	L.2	50	3	G1, G5	1,8	1
62B	192	3126/03	881.CFP, BDL	F3	Y	2	WS	L.2	110	2	G2	1,6,8	1
62B	194	3126/04	881.BQJ	F3	AH	4?	WS	L.3	60	4	G2	1,6,8	1,12
62C	121	3126/01	-	F3	AH	3B/4	UANS	L.3	100	-	G2	1,6,8	1
62D	60	3150	-	F3	Surface	-	FS	L.4	-	1	F10	1,6,7	1E
62E	83	-	881.ZR	F3	J	4B	US	L.5	c. 70-80	4	-	1,2,10	1
63A	38	3093/02-3022-3107	1129 750, 1220, 1962 APN	F6, F5	F2, M1, -	1/1 /-	FS	Bo	200	1	F2	1,6,7	1
63A	50	3105	1129 912a	F6	D2	1	FS	Bo	220	1	F2	1,6,7	1
63A	47	3014	1129 378	F6	D1	1<	FS	Bo	220	1	F2	1,6,7	1
63A	43	3013	1129 1193	F6	F1	1	FS	Bo	200	1	F2	1,6,7	1
63A	39	3012	1129 1200	F6	M1	1	FS	Bo	200	1	F2	1,6,7	1

Vessel type	Figure	KM.no.	DK.reg	Site	Trench	Dating	Style	Form	Size	Stone type	Decoration	Manu-facture	Use
63A	46	3011	1129.WR 322	F6	C3	–	FS	Bo	200	1	F2	1,7	1
63A	40	3074	881.AXM	F3	D	3A/4A	FS	Bo	160	1	F2	1,6,7	1,4,9
63A	44	3073	881.LI	F3	RM	Sieve	FS	Bo	100	1	F2	1,6,7	1
63A	48, 448	3065	881.ATB	F3	H	4A	FS	Bo	120	1	F2	1,6,7	1,8,9,12
63A	41	3018	881.KY	F3	–	–	FS	Bo	120	5	F2	1,7	1
63A	45	3100/01	881.APE	F3	H	4A	FS	Bo	200	1	F2	1,6,7	1
63A	49	3010	–	–	–	–	FS	Bo	140	1	F2	1,6,7	1
63A	42	3100/02	881.BYI, AWK	F3	AM	4B	FS	Bo	110	1	F2	1,7	1
63B	61	3111	1129 918	F6	D1/D2	1	FS	Bo	140	1	F8	1,7	1
63B	59	3002	881.MB, 1129 177	F3/F6	RM/A1	3B/ 1 <	FS	Bo	110	5	F8, F11	1,7	1I
63C	63	3025	881.HV	F3	RM	4A	FS	Bo	180	1	F5	1,6,7	1
63C	62	3026	–	–	–	–	FS	Bo	80	1	F5	1,7	1
63D	64	3042	881.QB, KH	F3	RM	2	FS	Bo	220	1	F6, F23	1,6,7	1
63D	57	3041	1129 980	F6	F1	1 <	FS	Bo	80	1	F6	1,7	1
63E	65	3072	881.BBG	F3	D	> 4A	FS	Bo	60	1	F7	1,7	1
63F	58	3112	881.YX	F3	F	3A/3B	FS	Bo	80	1	F13, F20	1,7	1,9
64A	66	3017	881.BAV	F3	I	2	FS	Bo	120	5	F10, F11	1,7	1
64B	67	–	822	F6	–	–	FS (ZZ)	Bo	70	1	F11	1,7	1,8
65A	229	3095	881.BVH ÅR	F3	AL	4B	FFS	Bo	110	4	F12	1,7	1E,6
65B	232	3055	881.AQK	F3	H	4A	FFS	Bo	100	4	F12, F13	1,6,7	1
65B	231	3054	881.BBC, AQM	F3	C	3A/4A	FFS	Bo	100	4	F13	1,6,7	1,7,8
65B	235	3049	881.BTS, ØK	F3	AE	Sieve	FFS	Bo	160	–	F12, F13	7	1
65B	233	3035	881.BBA	F3	K	3A/4A	FFS	Bo	100	4	F17, F20	1,6,7	1
65B	234	3021	–	–	–	–	FFS	Bo	150	–	F12, F14, F16, F17	1,6,7	1
65B	230	–	881.ALN, ABQ	F3	D	4A	FFS	Bo	–	–	F12, F14, F21	1,7	1
65C	239	3064	881.AVM	F3	AH	3B	FFS	Bo	320	2	F12, F13, F17, F22	1,6,7	1,3
65C	238	3033	881.BPF	F3	AF	2/4B	FFS	Bo	240	2	F12, F17	1,6,7	1,6
65C	240	3000	881.CHS, BFM	F3	AO	4A/4B	FFS	Bo	–	2	F12, F13, F16, F17. F23	1,6,7	1,12,13
65C	241	1514	881.AQL	F3	H	4A	FFS	Bo	360	2	F12, F13, F16. F17	1,6,7	1,9,11,13
65C	237	3118	1129 949p	F6	Sieve	–	FFS	Bo	–	4	F12, F17	1,7	1

Vessel type	Figure	KM.no.	DK.reg	Site	Trench	Dating	Style	Form	Size	Stone type	Decoration	Manu-facture	Use
65C	236	3053	–	–	–	–	FFS	Bo	160	–	F12, F13, F18	1,6,7	1
66A	223, 224	371	1962.ALK	F5	–	–	FFS	Bo	160	4	F17, F21	1,6,7	1,6
66A	223, 227	3036	881.AZP	F3	D	Sieve	FFS	Bo	–	4	F17	1,6,7	1
66A	223, 226	3075	881.ASF	F3	H	4A	FFS	Bo	160	4	F17	1,6,7	1,6
66A	223	3038/03	881.SZ	F3	RM	Surface	FFS	Bo	160	4	F17	1,7	1
66A	223	3038/02	881.BEZ	F3	–	–	FFS	Bo	160	–	F17	1,7	1
66A	223	3038/01	881.BEQ	F3	–	Sieve	FFS	Bo	140	4	F17	1,7	1
66A	223	3091	881.BBZ	F3	H	4A	FFS	Bo	160	4	F17	1,7	1
66A	223, 225	3037	–	–	–	–	FFS	Bo	200	4	F17	1,6,7	1,7
66B	242	–	138/881.HU	F3	RM	3B/4B	FFS	Bo	–	–	C, F13, F17	1,7,9	–
66B	243	–	881.ABE	F3	J	4B	FFS	Bo	–	–	F13, F17, F20	1,7	–
67A	244	3106	881.AZN	F3	D	Sieve	FFS	Bo	100	4	F18	1,6,7	1,9
67A	246	3102	881.AOV	F3	G	4A	FFS	Bo	160	–	F17, F18	1,6,7	1
67A	245	3029	881.BHP	F3	AP	3B	FFS	Bo	–	4	F18	1,6,7	1,3
67A	247	3015	881.VC	F3	B	3A/3B	FFS	Bo	160	–	F16, F18	1,6,7	1
67A	248	3103	–	F5	–	–	FFS	Bo	–	–	F13,F18	1,7	1
67B	252	3046	1962.KZ	F5	–	–	FFS	Bo	160	4	F13	1,6,7	1,8,12
67B	251	3066	881.TG	F3	RM	Surface	FFS	Bo	–	4	F13	1,7	1
67B	249	1637	881.BTS	F3	AE	Sieve	FFS	Bo	120	–	F13	1,6,7	1
67B	250	–	881.R	F3	–	–	FFS	Bo	140	4	F16	1,7	1,6
67C	253	3084	881.BIA	F3	–	–	FFS	Bo	160	4	F1	1,6,7	1
67C	254	3056	881.X	F3	BB	–	FFS	Bo	220	4	F1	1,7	1
68A	373	6081/04	–	F3?	–	–	PFS	Bo	120	2	–	1,6	1,2,13
68A	372	6045/02	–	F3	AO	4A/B	PFS	Bo	100	4	–	1,6	1,4,8
68A	371	6045/03	881.NN	F3	RM	4A	PFS	Bo	80	4	–	1,6	1,8
68B	303	6071	881.AKR	F3	C	4A	GFS	Bo	100	3	G1	1,8	1

Vessel type	Figure	KM.no.	DK.reg	Site	Trench	Dating	Style	Form	Size	Stone type	Decoration	Manu-facture	Use
69	408	1522	881.BUO ØÅ	F3	AE	Sieve	PFS	Bo	–	3	C	1,9	1
69	409	3528	–	–	–	–	PFS	Bo	200	4	C	1,6,9	1,4,6
70	205	6047/03	–	F5	sieve	–	LBAS	Bo	130	4	G1, G9	1,8	1,6,8
70	209	6077/01	881.BYB	F3	AM	Sieve	LBAS	Bo	80	4	G1, G5	1,6,8	1E
70	208	6077/03	881.SS	F3	RM	Sieve	LBAS	Bo	80	4	G1, G3, G4	1,6,8	1
70	204	6077/02	881.AWD	F3	RM	4A	LBAS	Bo	180	4	G1, G3, G4	1,6,8	1
70	207	6074/01	881.F	F3	B	–	LBAS	Bo	180	3	G1, G3, G9	1,6,8	1,2,3
70	206	6074/02	881.JN	F3	RM	4A	LBAS	Bo	280	2	G1, G3, G5	1,6,8	1,8
71A	91	1736	1962.AMX	F5	–	–	US	Bo	130	9	–	1,4	1
71A	93	1729/01	881.XF	F3	–	–	US	Bo	100	9	–	1	1
71A	94	1732/01	881.SS	F3	AE/AD	3A/3B	US	Bo	100	9	–	1,6	1
71A	92	1728	881.BZK, AXI	F3	AN	4	US	Bo	130	9	C	1,6,9	1E
71A	90	1726	881.BKG	F3	Y	2	US	Bo	240	9	–	1,4,6	1
71B	88	1729/02	–	–	–	–	US	Bo	140	9	–	1	1

Jutland Archaeological Society Publications on Near Eastern Archaeology

Atlas of the Stone Age Cultures of Qatar
Holger Kapel, 86 s. English and Arabic. 48 plates. 1967.   92,00

Preliminary Survey in East Arabia 1968
T.G. Bibby, 67 p. 1973.   60,00

The Maussolleion at Halikarnassos 1
Reports of the Danish Archaeological Expedition to Bodrum
The Sacrificial Deposit
Kristian Jeppesen, Flemming Højlund & Kim Aaris-Sørensen, 110 p. 1981.   140,00

The Maussolleion at Halikarnassos 2
Reports of the Danish Archaeological Expedition to Bodrum
The Written Sources and their Archaeological Background
Kristian Jeppesen & Anthony Luttrell, 220 p. 1986.   240,00

The Maussolleion at Halikarnassos 3
Reports of the Danish Archaeological Expedition to Bodrum
The Maussolleion Terrace and Accessory Structures 1-2
Poul Pedersen, Vol. 1: Text and appendices. 208 p. Vol. 2: Cataloque. 134 p. 1991.   320,00

The Maussolleion at Halikarnassos 4
Reports of the Danish Archaeological Expedition to Bodrum
The Quadrangle
Kristian Jeppesen, 182 p. 16 plates. 2000.   240,00

The Maussolleion at Halikarnassos 5
Reports of the Danish Archaeological Expedition to Bodrum
The Superstructure
Kristian Jeppesen, 265 p. 2002   240,00

The Maussolleion at Halikarnassos 6
Subterranean and pre-Maussollan structures on the site of the
Maussolleion
Jan Zahle & Kjeld Kjeldsen, 250 p. 2004.   280,00

The Maussolleion at Halikarnassos 7
Reports of the Danish Archaeological Expedition to Bodrum
The Pottery
Leif Erik Vaag, Winnie Nørskov & John Lund, 243 p. 85 plates. 2002   280,00

Failaka/Ikaros
Danish Archaeological Investigations on Failaka, Kuwait
The Hellenistic Settlements 1
The Terracotta Figurines
Hans Erik Mathiesen, 94 p. 1982.   115,00

Failaka/Ikaros
Danish Archaeological Investigations on Failaka, Kuwait
The Hellenistic Settlements 2
The Hellenistic Pottery from Failaka 1-2
Lise Hannestad, Vol. 1: Text. 140 p. Vol. 2: Cataloque and Plates. 128 p. 1983.   183,00

Failaka/Ikaros
Danish Archaeological Investigations on Failaka, Kuwait
The Hellenistic Settlements 3
The Sacred Enclosure in the Early Hellenistic Period
Kristian Jeppesen, 125 p. 1989.   185,00

Failaka/Dilmun
Danish Archaeological Investigations on Failaka, Kuwait
The Second Millennium Settlements 1
The Stamp and the Cylinder Seals
Poul Kjærum, Catalogue. 171 p. 79 plates. 1983.   150,00

Danish Archaeological Investigations on Failaka, Kuwait
The Second Millennium Settlements 2
The Bronze Age Pottery
Flemming Højlund, 197 p. 1987.   200,00

Danish Archaeological Investigations on Failaka, Kuwait
The Second Millennium Settlements 3
The Bronze Age Architecture
Poul Kjærum & Flemming Højlund, 162 p. 2013   250, 00

The Natufian Encampment at Beidha
Late Pleistocene Adaption in the Southern Levant
Brian F. Byrd, 126 p. 1989.   143,00

The Island of Umm an-Nar 1
Third Millennium Graves
Karen Frifelt, 188 p. 1991.   180,00

The Island of Umm an-Nar 2
Third Millennium Settlement
Karen Frifelt, 260 p. 1995.   230,00

Qala'at al-Bahrain 1
The Northern City Wall and the Islamic Fortress
Flemming Højlund & H. Hellmuth Andersen, 511 p. 1994.   360,00

Qala'at al-Bahrain 2
The Central Monumental Buildings
Flemming Højlund & H. Hellmuth Andersen, 288 p. 1997.   280,00

Excavations at Tepe Guran in Luristan
The Bronze Age and Iron Periods
Henrik Thrane, 225 p. 2001.   240,00

Islamic Remains in Bahrain
Karen Frifelt, 207 p. 2001.   280,00

The Barbar Temples 1-2
H. Hellmuth Andersen & Flemming Højlund, 380 p. 2003   400,00

The Burial Mounds of Bahrain
Social complexity in Early Dilmun
Flemming Højlund, 178 p. 2007   280,00

All prices are exclusive of VAT and postage. Distributed by
Aarhus University Press, Langelandsgade 177, DK-8200 Aarhus N. www.unipress.dk
Members of Jutland Archaeological Society get a discount of 30% on all orders sent directly to
Jutland Archaeological Society, Moesgaard, DK-8270 Højbjerg.